Poverty, Disadvantage, and the Promise of Enterprise

Poverty, Disadvantage, and the Promise of Enterprise

A Capabilities Perspective

Michael H. Morris
Susana C. Santos

LEXINGTON BOOKS
Lanham • Boulder • New York • London

Published by Lexington Books
An imprint of The Rowman & Littlefield Publishing Group, Inc.
4501 Forbes Boulevard, Suite 200, Lanham, Maryland 20706
www.rowman.com

86-90 Paul Street, London EC2A 4NE, United Kingdom

British Library Cataloguing in Publication Information Available

Library of Congress Cataloging-in-Publication Data

Names: Morris, Michael H., author. | Santos, Susana C., author.
Title: Poverty, disadvantage, and the promise of enterprise : a capabilities perspective / Michael H. Morris, Susana C. Santos.
Description: Lanham : Lexington Books, [2024] | Includes bibliographical references and index. | Summary: "This book explores entrepreneurship as both a pathway out of poverty and a vehicle for enhancing personal well-being"—Provided by publisher.
Identifiers: LCCN 2024015006 (print) | LCCN 2024015007 (ebook) | ISBN 9781666933802 (cloth) | ISBN 9781666933819 (epub)
Subjects: LCSH: Entrepreneurship. | Poverty. | Capabilities approach (Social sciences)
Classification: LCC HB615 .M67 2024 (print) | LCC HB615 (ebook) | DDC 338/.04—dc23/eng/20240419
LC record available at https://lccn.loc.gov/2024015006
LC ebook record available at https://lccn.loc.gov/2024015007

Contents

Preface

Poverty rates across the globe remain unacceptably high, in spite of trillions of dollars of spending by governments, non-governmental organizations, and nonprofit entities. Arguably, the single biggest contributor to poverty reduction over the past thirty-five years has been robust economic growth in particular countries, such as that experienced in China and India in the late 20th and early 21st century. Beyond this, we do not appear to have an especially effective toolkit for moving people out of poverty. Most of the spending that occurs provides people with a lifeline that simply enables them to survive, or introduces them to basic job skills but not to fulfilling jobs that result in a better life.

This book is about the promise of entrepreneurship as a means of poverty alleviation. Hence, instead of creating jobs for the poor, those in poverty create jobs for themselves. However, we believe that helping those in poverty conditions start more businesses is not the major challenge—they actually start millions of ventures every year. The difficulty lies in their ability to build a financially sustainable business that can change their economic circumstances. This ability, more often than not, is tied to contextual factors that are not under the control of the low-income entrepreneur. As we will explore in the chapters ahead, unlocking the potential of entrepreneurship lies in the ability of researchers, policymakers, scholars, economic development professionals, and participants in community entrepreneurial ecosystems to address those contextual factors. It is these stakeholders who are the targeted audience for this volume.

The beginning point lies in fundamentally changing how people think about and approach entrepreneurship. This is our focus in Part I of the book. Instead of being preoccupied with the ability of new ventures to generate financial returns, growth, or innovation, we emphasize their ability to contribute to human development. The promise of entrepreneurship lies in its ability to improve the overall well-being of people, particularly those in poverty conditions. As such, we adopt an integral human development lens to explore how venture creation can contribute to intellectual, social, economic, cultural, political, and spiritual well-being. Our approach builds upon two complementary theoretical foundations. The first of these, disadvantage theory, concerns how disadvantages rooted in the poverty experience have a dual impact, serving to both motivate and hold back an individual when attempting to launch a business. These dual forces help explain why those in poverty conditions frequently create marginal enterprises that do not significantly improve their well-being. This then leads us to capabilities theory, which provides insights into the ways that poverty-related disadvantages undermine the development of critical capabilities that contribute to desirable human outcomes.

In Part II of the book, we take a deeper dive into the specific ways in which the multi-dimensional nature of poverty influences the process of developing a business. Four key factors come into play, which we label the liabilities of poorness. Individuals are impacted to different degrees by these factors, but in combination they significantly raise the barriers an entrepreneur must overcome. They limit the opportunities the entrepreneur is able to recognize and the kinds of ventures he or she is able to create. Importantly, they can undermine the ability to develop an entrepreneurial mindset and have implications for the elements of this mindset that matter most when launching a venture.

Overcoming the fragile nature of businesses created by the poor is the focus of Part III. We first introduce the concept of the commodity trap to capture the problematic nature of these businesses. It is this trap that both reflects the limited capabilities and hinders ongoing capability development on the part of these entrepreneurs. We highlight keys for escaping its debilitating effects. Attention is also devoted to the paradoxical effects of the fear of both failure and success on the growth and development of these businesses. Finally, given the higher levels of religiosity and belief in a higher power among those in poverty circumstances, we explore the role of faith in motivating and guiding the entrepreneurial journey.

We then turn to developing a roadmap for assisting low-income entrepreneurs in building the capabilities that can produce sustainable enterprises. Part IV begins with the introduction of a process model for working with these entrepreneurs. Noting the limitations of conventional approaches to entrepreneurship when it comes to those in poverty conditions, we advocate instead for a stepwise logic. The journey to a sustainable business is broken down into eighty activity steps, where progress in completing particular steps enables the accomplishment of subsequent steps. Using this process model and stepwise logic, we explore a sample intervention program that can be implemented at the community level.

The proposed methodology can be facilitated by directly addressing personal, social, and environmental factors that limit the ability of poverty entrepreneurs to convert resources into desired outcomes. Two key players in this regard are local entrepreneurial ecosystems and the public sector. The general failure of ecosystems to address the needs of these entrepreneurs is examined, and recommendations are made for creating a much more community-driven approach. Finally, the parallel role of supportive government policies and programs is discussed, including the introduction of a policy toolkit, with priority placed on policies that enhance local ecosystem development.

Given the tendency by many observers to downplay or marginalize the ventures of the poor, this book offers what may seem like a radical alternative. We argue for the critical importance to society of these businesses, while advocating for more informed investment in helping them become sustainable. By focusing on the human dimension, entrepreneurship can represent a vehicle for empowerment and transformation of the disenfranchised. When approached properly, it can become a means for developing dignity, self-worth, identity, human capital, a sense of achievement, a voice, and an ability to give back. We hope the ideas and insights shared in these pages serve as a useful guide for those committed to realizing this potential.

Michael H. Morris and Susana C. Santos

PART I

Entrepreneurship as Human Empowerment

Chapter One

The Promise of Entrepreneurship

An IHD Perspective

Is entrepreneurship a solution to poverty? Can starting a business make a difference in the lives of those who live in a world of scarcity and disadvantage? The answer is "it depends." What it depends upon is the subject of the chapters to come. However, before we delve into this question, we first establish a foundation in terms of both poverty and entrepreneurship, and how each relates to the other. While it has historically been largely ignored, the poverty and entrepreneurship interface has begun to receive significant interest from scholars (Amorós & Cristi, 2011; Banerjee & Duflo, 2007; Bruton et al., 2013; Morris, Santos, & Neumeyer, 2020; Sutter et al., 2019). Although our understanding remains limited, a number of important insights have emerged, and the purpose of this book is to share this emerging knowledge base.

In this opening chapter, we first establish a foundation in terms of what we mean by poverty. We consider both a developed and a developing country context. Poverty is about disadvantage, which begins with a lack of money, but is much more than this. In differing degrees, the poor experience scarcity when it comes to financial, social, human, experiential, intellectual, cultural, political, and cultural capital. They can suffer insecurity in all its forms, including that related to food, housing, employment, health, and safety, which can translate into more fundamental emotional and psychological insecurity. Those in poverty can perceive that they have no access and no voice. As we shall further explore, poverty is multi-dimensional, where the dimensions affect and are affected by one another.

We also lay a foundation in terms of how to think about entrepreneurship. This term has been used quite broadly, and applied to a wide variety of phenomena (e.g., social entrepreneurship, corporate entrepreneurship, green entrepreneurship, public sector entrepreneurship), but for our purposes, it is concerned with conceptualizing and launching a business. It involves a process, although one that can be messy, chaotic, and emergent. It is experienced in different ways by each person who pursues the entrepreneurial journey. Further, while typically approached in terms of income and wealth generation, entrepreneurship has a number of potential outcomes that can have important implications for the poor.

Our approach centers on the individual who, starting from a position of disadvantage, attempts to navigate the steps or stages involved in the creation of a sustainable enterprise. Here, sustainability refers to a business that can consistently generate enough profit to improve the entrepreneur's economic circumstances. This individualized approach finds the ill-prepared and under-resourced founder struggling mightily to interpret and make sense of novel phenomena, address uncertainty and ambiguity, think and act strategically, and develop the capabilities needed to build a profitable venture. Yet, our interest is more holistic. Beyond economic returns, we explore the potential for the venture creation experience to enhance the overall well-being of the low-income entrepreneur. We introduce an integral human development (IHD) perspective, where the implications of entrepreneurship for multiple dimensions of life quality are considered.

HOW IS POVERTY DEFINED?

Poverty can be defined in absolute or relative terms. Of these, the most popular conceptualization emphasizes absolute poverty, which refers to families or individuals not making enough money to meet their basic needs in such areas as food, clothing, and shelter. For instance, the U.S. government claims that a family of four that earns less than $29,960 per year, or an individual making less than $14,891 is living in poverty. Alternatively, in Ethiopia, the poverty line is ten times lower than this. Such numbers do not consider where in a country the family lives or its particular circumstances. Basic needs can vary depending upon a wide range of considerations, such as serious health challenges, mental well-being, or the need to care for people outside the household. Further, it can cost the poor more to address some of their basic needs than it might cost someone who is economically well-off, and poverty conditions can impose their own hidden costs.

As opposed to what is necessary to address basic needs, relative poverty shifts the focus to how an individual's economic situation compares to the way most people in society live. Hence, someone is poor if they do not have the income to maintain the average standard of living in a society. For example, in Britain a household is designated as poor if its residents do not earn at least 60% of the median household income. Approached in relative terms, poverty is always present and is a moving target as income levels improve.

This focus on income levels in both approaches is simplistic and misses much, particularly given the multi-dimensional nature of poverty (see Chapter 2). In an attempt to overcome these limitations, the United Nations has proposed the Human Poverty Index, an index that considers not only the percentage of the population living below the poverty line (in this case, 50% of the median household disposable income) but also how long people live (the probability at birth of not living past age 60) and knowledge levels, as reflected in the percentage of adults lacking functional literacy skills. Using this index, a number of nations (e.g., Ireland, Italy, Spain, Great Britain, the United States, and Australia) actually demonstrate more significant poverty challenges than conventional measures would suggest.

There are also fundamental differences between what has been labeled generational versus situational poverty. The former concerns individuals who belong to families experiencing poverty for at least two generations. The latter is where personal developments (e.g., a divorce, experiencing serious health problems, losing one's job, going through bankruptcy, or some other life crisis) push one into poverty. The individual finds themselves in a severely constrained financial position, struggling to meet basic needs. With situational poverty, individuals may cycle into and out of poverty conditions over time, while generational poverty tends to persist. Of these two, then, generational poverty is the more vexing challenge. The Pew Charitable Trusts (2013) found that 70% of those born into low-income families will never move into the middle class. Separately, of those in poverty at a given point in time within the U.S., about one-fourth will still be in poverty three years later (US Census Bureau, 2011). Further, the longer one is in poverty, the lower the likelihood of exiting. Sustained exposure to poverty can have a more profound effect on an individual's beliefs, perceptions, cognitive processing, and outlook (Dean, Schilbach, & Schofield, 2017). Payne, DeVol, and Smith (2001) find that the chronically or situationally poor can develop their own culture, hidden rules, and belief systems.

Based just on income-based measures, which understate the numbers, poverty is a serious problem in both developed and developing economies. Poverty rates range from well over 50% in some developing countries (e.g., South Sudan–82%, the Democratic Republic of the Congo–64%, and Guatemala–59%) to over 10% in most developed countries (e.g., Spain–20%, Japan–15%, the United States–13.8%) (OECD, 2022; World Bank, 2021). Overall, 22% of the world's population lives in poverty (less than $3.20 a day) and 10% live in extreme poverty (less than $1.90 a day) (World Health Organization, 2021). For every 1,000 children born, 39 will die before they turn five years old (UNICEF, 2021). One-third of the urban population across the globe lives in a slum (United Nations, 2021). Further, in most countries, poverty rates are higher for minority groups, women, and children (Wilson, 2019).

DO EXISTING SUPPORT PROGRAMS ACTUALLY ALLEVIATE POVERTY?

Many people, organizations, and institutions across the globe are dedicated to reducing or eliminating poverty. Each year, millions of hours and trillions of dollars are devoted to this cause. The impact of these efforts on the poor and the pathway out of poverty is less clear and rather controversial. Some would claim initiatives to fight poverty are quite effective (Ben-Shalom, Moffitt, & Scholz, 2011; Si, Ahlstrom, Wei, & Cullen, 2021; Sumner & Tiwari, 2011), while others would argue that the progress resulting from such initiatives is much less or even negative (e.g., Tanner, 2022; Ravallion, 2007; Wade, 2020).

Much has been made of the estimated reductions in poverty rates in the thirty years leading up to the COVID-19 global pandemic. The evidence suggests significant progress was made in poverty alleviation around the world (Ravallion, 2020; World Bank, 2020), with the pandemic and other world crises undoing some of that progress (Miguel & Moborak, 2022; World Bank, 2022b). However, two countries (China and India) were disproportionately responsible for much of this reduction, with a number of other countries actually seeing poverty levels increase. During this time period, both nations experienced rapid economic growth, which was driven by an explosion in entrepreneurial activity (Kharas & Dooley, 2022). So, here we have the classic argument regarding poverty reduction: by doing the things necessary to stimulate mainstream economic development, the poor will benefit. In a sense, then, the adage "a rising tide lifts all boats" would seem to apply. Such development can produce more and better paying jobs, enhanced goods and services, increased tax revenues, and a greater social safety net for the poor. Unfortunately, the reality is that even a robust economy leaves behind many people. Further, it tends to widen the income gap between the haves and have nots.

This brings us to the role of governments in directly assisting the poor. In the United States alone, over $1 trillion is spent annually on poverty-related programs. Spending per person is over $13,000 at the federal level, with total spending more than tripling since 1980 on a per person basis (Chetty & Hendren, 2015). Many more trillions are spent by governments around the world. This money supports a wide variety of different approaches and solutions, depending on the country in question. Examples include:

- Income subsidies

- Tax credits
- Educational programs and subsidies
- Food and nutritional assistance
- Healthcare services
- Childcare services
- Housing subsidies and low-cost housing
- Assistance with utilities and transportation
- Assistance to those with disabilities

Arguably, government spending on jobs-related initiatives is at the center of direct efforts by the government to actually move people out of poverty—better equipping them for jobs that are more attractive, helping them find such jobs, and incentivizing them to pursue these jobs (e.g., Abner et al., 2015). The success of these programs has been mixed, at best. The evidence here indicates that, while these programs can increase skill levels and modestly improve employment rates and earnings, at least in the short term, their long-term impact on poverty reduction is limited (Bratti et al., 2018; Holzer, 2014; 2017; Kluve et al., 2019). Shortcomings are often traced to the lack of enough hours available for the poor to dedicate to skills development, programs that are not integrative (e.g., are not holistic, do not mix classroom training with practical experience, or hard skills with soft skills, or are not tied to job referrals), lack of program flexibility to reflect the unique needs of the poor, lack of training quality, and the failure to focus on more relevant or emerging skills, or to reflect rapid changes to skill requirements (Cronen et al., 2021; Ferenstein, 2019; J-PAL, 2023).

Another source of assistance comes from churches, community organizations, foundations, and local non-profits. Relying on both public and private sources of funding and pools of volunteers, these parties provide those in poverty with everything from literacy training, temporary housing and daily meals to free legal services, shelters for victims of domestic violence, and winter coats and shoes. Such programs generally focus on one or a few specific needs, although efforts are sometimes made to coordinate efforts across different programs in a given locality or region.

The combined effect of all of these efforts is that those in poverty are receiving more support than has historically been the case. While inefficiencies can exist, and programs vary in their relative impact, these efforts are critical. These various forms of support represent a critical lifeline that enables the poor to survive, contributing to their most basic needs in such areas as food, housing, and medical assistance. For the most part, the poor would be much worse off without this lifeline, and so the miseries surrounding the poverty experience are slightly lessened. However, it does not appear that existing support efforts are moving large numbers of people out of poverty. In effect, the different parties are treating poverty without eliminating it. The implication is that alternative solutions are needed.

A variety of proposals have been made in terms of innovative approaches to poverty alleviation. Examples include different approaches to providing a guaranteed basic income for all citizens of a country (ILO, 2014; Coady et al., 2021), requiring that employers pay a minimum wage that ensures an ability to afford basic necessities (Johnson et al., 2019; Luce, 2014), or enabling the poor to attend college or receive comprehensive health care for free (Dynarski et al., 2018; Grignon, Perronnin, & Lavis, 2008). Another pathway involves investing in applications of technologies that address particular needs of the poor. Toward this end, novel technological solutions can facilitate educational access, banking access, food production, building good quality but low-cost houses or computers, producing and transporting clean water, or managing waste, among other applications (Smillie, 2019; Toyama, 2010).

A very different solution to poverty involves entrepreneurship. By starting a business of their own, might an individual be able to generate enough income to significantly improve their economic circumstances? The answer to this question, as the coming chapters will make clear, is that "it depends." For the most part, when people in poverty develop ventures of their own, these businesses provide a source of income, but not enough money to move the individual out of poverty. There are certainly instances where the business does not produce sufficient income to survive, or where the business can actually make the individual worse off from a financial standpoint. Yet, many low-income people have escaped poverty based on the creation of a successful enterprise, and the potential exists for many more to do so. To better understand this potential, let us consider the relevance of venture creation for a person in poverty.

ENTREPRENEURSHIP AS A SOLUTION TO POVERTY

Starting a business is something virtually anyone can do. There is no evidence to support the idea that people are born to be entrepreneurs, or that there is some sort of entrepreneurship gene. The reality is that entrepreneurship is inherently democratic. One's age, gender, race, ethnicity, creed, sexual orientation, or disability status does not matter. Neither should one's poverty status somehow disqualify a person from starting something. Success at venture creation is also not tied to a specific set of personality traits. It does depend, however, on the development of particular capabilities which low-income individuals often lack, as will be discussed in Chapter 2, and throughout this volume. As we shall see, development of these capabilities is the key for entrepreneurship to serve as a pathway out of poverty.

Yet another misconception regarding entrepreneurship is that it takes a lot of money to start a business, which would seem to eliminate this as an option for the poor. The reality is that most new businesses in developed economies are started with less than $5,000, and with significantly less in developing countries (Caramela, 2023; González & Cepeda, 2015). Moreover, where the low-income entrepreneur learns how to utilize the resources of others through sharing, bartering, collaborating, and other creative leveraging techniques, to use resources in unconventional ways, and to see the potential value in things that others do not see as resources, it becomes possible to accomplish more with less. Further, an advantage of the twenty-first century and the technological revolution is that it is easier than ever to start a venture, and to do so with very little in the way of one's own resources. While the degree of penetration of such technologies varies considerably among the poor in different contexts, the possibilities, even in some of the most undeveloped economies, are expanding.

An additional misconception concerns the belief that a very large proportion of new ventures fail. While wild claims are thrown out suggesting failure rates of over 90%, the actual rates are closer to 50% (which is still quite high). Not only are the rates lower than some claim, they vary by industry or type of business. They go down significantly if the entrepreneur can achieve certain thresholds in terms of sales and numbers of employees by a certain time interval (e.g., after two years or four years). It has also been argued that low-income and disadvantaged entrepreneurs fail at a higher rate than entrepreneurs who are better off financially (e.g., Kiggundu, 2002; Si et al., 2021). Yet, actual data on the failure and success rates of poverty entrepreneurs is limited or non-existent in most countries. Anecdotal evidence suggests the poor can be quite resilient and keep an enterprise going for a prolonged period despite ongoing ups and downs (Morris, Soleimanof, & Tucker, 2023). When they do fail, these ventures often lack much in the way of equipment or other capital investments, suggesting the downside risk of entrepreneurship may be lower. For these entrepreneurs, the cost of failure may be more non-financial than financial.

This discussion implies that the poor are able to start businesses with severely limited resources and keep those businesses from failing. People from disadvantaged conditions actually launch millions of businesses each year. However, we believe that a relatively small proportion of these businesses generate enough profit to meaningfully improve the economic circumstances of the entrepreneur and his/her family. A fundamental thesis of this book is that this proportion can be significantly increased.

Even so, attempting to build a sustainable business, one that consistently produces enough profit to not only support the entrepreneur, but improve their economic situation, might seem like an arduous undertaking that is beyond the reach of someone in poverty. Yet, it could be argued that this is actually a very natural path. Rather than being unemployed or underemployed in a relatively low-paying job with little room for development or advancement, and with no job security, pursuing the possibilities that surround venture creation might seem quite promising. It has been argued (see Chapter 3) that people either start businesses based on sheer necessity (they lack more attractive options) or based on recognition of an emerging opportunity, with the poor assumed to be necessity-driven entrepreneurs. This assumption suggests that they are starting businesses because they have to and will quickly abandon these enterprises if a good job comes along. We question this popular assumption, and believe that entrepreneurship offers a number of potential benefits to the disadvantaged individual beyond a much-needed source of income. These benefits derive from the underlying nature of the venture creation experience, a subject to which we now turn.

THE VENTURE CREATION PROCESS AND FORMATION OF AN ENTREPRENEUR

Many perspectives exist regarding entrepreneurship and its underlying nature. However, at its most simple level, entrepreneurship is about recognizing an opportunity and then launching and developing a new business to capitalize on that opportunity. An entrepreneur takes responsibility for assembling resources, overcoming obstacles, and implementing something new. As we will demonstrate in Chapter 3, these new ventures can take a number of different forms. Some are quite innovative, and others are less so. Some seek rapid growth and others start small and stay small. No two businesses are alike. More importantly, every entrepreneur has a unique journey.

Scholars in the discipline of entrepreneurship have come to understand entrepreneurship as a process. By this we mean the successful creation of a venture involves a set of stages. A typical conceptualization of this process finds the founder moving from opportunity recognition, to the development of a business concept and model, identification of needed resources, acquisition of those resources, implementation of a business, stabilization and growth, and eventually some sort of exit. It is not a linear process, as the entrepreneur is encountering roadblocks, having to revisit earlier steps, making mistakes and adapting. Learning from trial and error is the norm and adjustments are ongoing.

For the individual trying to start something, it is a messy process. Filled with ups and downs, it can be chaotic, ambiguous, and uncertain. Perhaps the most descriptive property of the entrepreneurial process concerns its *emergent* nature. With a successful enterprise, what one starts out to create is rarely what actually gets created. Things emerge as the entrepreneur encounters obstacles and setbacks, experiments, learns, and adapts. As a result, the products or services that generate the most profit, the target audiences producing the most revenue, the approaches to production and distribution that work the best, among many other aspects of the enterprise, are not what the entrepreneur initially envisioned or planned for. In practice, the nature of the opportunity, the design of the business, and the individual (as an entrepreneur) are all emerging.

These properties of venture creation suggest the idiosyncratic nature of the journey undertaken by a person in poverty circumstances. The entrepreneur is encountering an ongoing stream of novel and often unexpected events which can vary in terms of their volume, velocity, and volatility (Morris, Pryor, & Schindehutte, 2012). Examples of such events can include everything from making a big sale and hiring a first employee to being turned down for loans by multiple institutions, experiencing a break-in or theft, and encountering a major quality problem that compromises business performance. The entrepreneur processes these events, attempting to make sense of, and assign meaning to, each of them as they occur. He or she has cognitive, emotional, and even physiological responses to them. How these events are processed affects the way in which decisions are made. Poverty conditions affect the lens through which one interprets these ongoing developments. In Chapters 2 and 5, we will take a deeper dive into these conditions and their implications when starting a business.

One conclusion from an understanding of this process and the individual's personal journey is that the venture experience forms the individual into an entrepreneur. This is an important perspective, as it suggests people do not start off as entrepreneurs but are shaped into entrepreneurs based on the events they encounter, how these events are processed and responded to, the learning that takes place, the manner in which they adapt, and their sense of agency. Accordingly, every journey is unique and every entrepreneur is unique.

ENTREPRENEURSHIP RECONCEPTUALIZED

How does navigating this uncertain, messy, and emergent process impact the individual as a venture is developed? As we shall see in Chapter 2, poverty compromises individual freedoms. It can hinder the development of key capabilities that enable a range of life outcomes. Without the requisite capabilities, the creation of a venture might represent a source of constant frustration and contribute to a sense of failure. However, venture creation can also represent a platform for capability development. Consider the potential changes that occur as the individual engages with products, customers, suppliers, production, bookkeeping, and related aspects of a new venture. The entrepreneur is learning by doing as he or she attempts different approaches, makes mistakes, encounters obstacles, observes others, gets feedback, and adapts. This dynamic leads us to think differently about entrepreneurship. Beyond the launch of a business, or creation of an income stream, entrepreneurship can be conceptualized in terms of empowerment and transformation (see Figure 1.1).

The empowering potential of entrepreneurship is tied to the liberating and dignity-enhancing notion that a person in poverty is able to create their own job, their own income, and their own future. They are not dependent on the beneficence of government agencies or uncontrollable actions of an employer. In addition, overcoming obstacles and mastering unfamiliar tasks

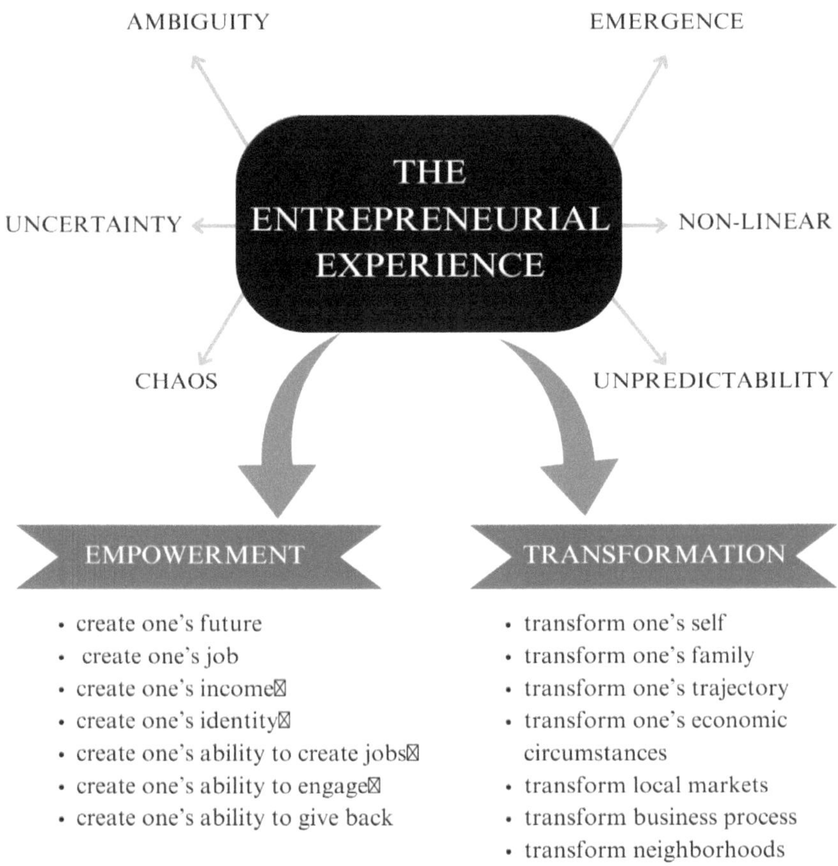

Figure 1.1. The Entrepreneurial Experience as a Vehicle for Empowerment and Transformation.
Created by Authors

is a source of enhanced self-efficacy and self-confidence in terms of what one is capable of. As the venture is an extension of the individual, and vice versa, the experience leads to the emergence of an identity as an entrepreneur, a woman entrepreneur, a Black entrepreneur, or some related aspect of how one sees themselves. Achieving some modicum of success enables the entrepreneur to hire others who come from similar circumstances. It can make it possible to engage more meaningfully in the community, and enhance the extent to which the individual has a voice. It can allow the entrepreneur to become a role model for others in adverse conditions.

When it comes to transformation, entrepreneurship is about taking actions that produce change. The individual is being transformed into an entrepreneur—a value creator. He or she is developing new skills and capabilities. The income being generated, as well as exposure to and involvement with the business, can lead to the transformation of the entrepreneur's family. A local market is being affected as it responds to a new source of value, and a competitive context is being altered by the presence of a new business. The entrepreneur may introduce new or novel business practices, serving as another source of change. When these businesses start to succeed, they can also have a positive impact on local neighborhoods, and a positive influence on others who might aspire to start something.

While the amount of empowerment and transformation will vary considerably across entrepreneurs and ventures, these two concepts go hand-in-hand. The more empowered the individual becomes, the more change they are potentially able to effect. At the same time, as the entrepreneur and venture produce change, this contributes to the sense of empowerment of the individual.

INTEGRAL HUMAN DEVELOPMENT AND ENTREPRENEURSHIP

Approached in terms of empowerment and transformation, it is worth considering how the venture creation experience affects personal welfare. Most discussions of entrepreneurship in the context of poverty focus on income generation for people who lack money. This is a very narrow and limiting perspective. The concept of integral human development (IHD) represents a useful perspective for approaching entrepreneurship more holistically. It emphasizes a sense of wholeness of the person. Normatively, IHD is concerned with a *state* of personal well-being in the context of just and peaceful relationships and a thriving personal environment—and the *process* of getting there. It prioritizes the ability of every individual to participate in the fullness of life.

IHD stresses diversity when it comes to livelihood strategies available to households and ways to reduce their vulnerability. Entrepreneurship is one such livelihood strategy, and one that arguably offers potential for the development of the whole self. At its heart is the development of capabilities that enable personal freedom, and so it is consistent with the work of Nobel Laureate Amartya Sen (1999) and his capabilities theory. It goes beyond economic well-being to consider the individual's social, cultural, political, and spiritual well-being. It allows for every individual to make a contribution to different facets of society. Goulet (2006) explains, "societies are more human, or more developed, not when men and women 'have more' but when they are enabled to 'be more.'"

Entrepreneurship is a vehicle for enabling an individual to 'be more.' Because the creation of a venture is about agency, personal effort, ownership of outcomes, learning by doing, deciding on courses of action and ways to adapt based on limited information, and approaching the business as an extension of oneself, it represents a vehicle for self-development and self-enhancement. Table 1.1 summarizes how, on the one hand, poverty conditions can significantly constrain the development of the individual and their ability to engage with and contribute to dimensions of integral human development, while, on the other hand, how entrepreneurship can contribute to such development.

While people living in poverty can certainly achieve a full life and a strong sense of personal well-being, for many individuals the experience can represent an assault on human dignity. It can lead to the erosion of basic

Table 1.1. Effects of Poverty and Entrepreneurship on Dimensions of IHD

IHD Component	*Poverty Impact*	*Entrepreneurship Benefit*
economic/ financial	*inadequate income, no wealth, unemployment, underemployment, no safety net, fragility*	*potential for income generation, wealth accumulation, control over one's economic well-being*
social	*social isolation; limits to social network and social engagement; discrimination*	*enhanced networks & social engagement and ability to socially contribute*
cultural	*deprivation in terms of the ability to benefit from community's cultural assets*	*ability to give back to one's community, leverage cultural assets, contribute to cultural richness*
political	*powerlessness; less of a voice; under-representation in issues impacting the poor*	*development of one's voice, access to platforms and means to channel one's voice*
spiritual	*lack of cognitive and emotional space to engage in deep thinking, nurture spiritual development*	*ability to find deeper meaning as one achieves more economic control, develops identity, expands network*

rights such as access to food, healthcare, adequate housing, education, and personal safety. Dignity is compromised when one is unable to adequately care for themselves and their family. Further, the poor can be treated as inferior in worth by those who are materially well-off. They can find themselves excluded from everyday aspects of life. The frequent result is economic insecurity and fragility, social isolation and limited social engagement, an inability to benefit from a community's cultural assets, powerlessness and lack of a voice, and limited space to engage in reflection and nurture spiritual development.

The experience of venture creation can counter the manner in which poverty undermines integral human development. Beyond the potential to take control of one's economic circumstances and generate wealth through business ownership, and the ongoing development of a range of capabilities, achievements in building a venture can result in strong positive affect, enhancing the individual's emotional well-being. Further, building a successful enterprise leads to significant expansion of one's social network and new ways of engaging with its members. A diversity of individuals and organizations far removed from the individual's poverty origins can become part of this network. In addition, the entrepreneur is in a considerably enhanced position to contribute to and benefit from the community and its cultural richness. Whether through hiring, provision of products and services, building of facilities, payment of taxes, service on community boards or councils, personal contributions, or other mechanisms, the business owner is making the community a better place. Moreover, he or she is in a stronger position to speak out and be listened to, meaningfully engage in public forums, and impact the advancement of issues and causes that matter to the individual. Finally, the venture experience can enable the entrepreneur to move beyond the preoccupation with immediate survival needs and simply getting through the week or month. He or she is able to adopt a broader perspective on life, meaning, and purpose. The individual is also able to develop a multi-faceted identity tied to being an entrepreneur, business owner, personal achiever, employer, winner, role model, community leader, among other aspects of their self-concept. The result can be an ability to find deeper meaning in life, develop a stronger sense of purpose, base one's actions on a more developed set of personal values and beliefs, and realize a richer spiritual awareness.

Does all of this actually happen? Our research findings (Morris, Soleimanof, & Tucker, 2023) suggest that it can occur, but often does so to only a limited degree. The more severe the personal challenges deriving from poverty conditions, the more the individual tends to create a more marginal or problematic venture. Further, the more marginal the venture, the lower the entrepreneur's perceived well-being. As a result, the ability of entrepreneurship to have such a positive impact is highly dependent on contextual factors that enable the creation of an economically sustainable enterprise. Family support, mentors, institutions (educational, governmental, financial, etc.), local infrastructure, community entrepreneurial ecosystems, and a range of other factors come into play as the low-income or disadvantaged person attempts to navigate the venture creation process.

At the same time, various aspects of entrepreneurship can actually take away from human development. A few examples of the possible downside of the venture creation experience include:

- high levels of stress, pressure, tension, anxiety and a sense of being overwhelmed;
- time demands of the business that can take away from family or personal time;
- frustration at being rejected or treated as unimportant by key resource providers and other stakeholders, or at being unable to develop certain capabilities;
- anger from others if the entrepreneur reinvests profits in the business (family, friends, extended network) instead of sharing financial returns with them;
- burnout, fatigue, substance abuse, sleeplessness, health problems;
- losing what little the entrepreneur has because it is all invested in a non-performing venture;
- reduced self-efficacy and depression if the venture does not succeed;
- undermining friendships and relationships by pushing them to support the business; and
- an ongoing debt burden and blacklisting resulting from unpaid financial obligations.

These and other negative aspects of the experience are very real and quite common. They are especially likely to adversely affect the entrepreneur who is unable to build a successful venture. However, success is certainly not a guarantee that the outcome will be enhanced personal well-being. The implication is that countervailing forces are at work as a new business emerges. Again, the interplay between the entrepreneur and a number of contextual factors is instrumental in determining the extent to which the net effect will be enhanced sense of well-being. We shall further investigate these factors in the chapters to come.

CONCLUSION: WHERE WE ARE GOING FROM HERE

Poverty is a complex challenge where those who must endure its debilitating effects are too often viewed as victims to be rescued (e.g., through government or social interventions). The priority in these interventions appears to be addressing vital unmet needs (food, clothing, housing, healthcare, education, etc.) and helping the poor get jobs. Less consideration has been given to enabling the poor to create their own pathway out of poverty through venture creation. This book focuses on how entrepreneurship can become a vehicle for overcoming disadvantage and enhancing the lives of those in poverty.

In this opening chapter, we have introduced entrepreneurship as a manageable process that anyone can pursue, regardless of their economic situation or the resources they have at their disposal. Yet, as Chapters 2, 5, and 6 will make clear, poverty creates additional burdens beyond those confronted by other entrepreneurs. These burdens suggest the poverty experience can significantly impact the entrepreneur's capabilities, perceptions, beliefs, and decision-making approaches, indicating that the poverty entrepreneur has unique needs. If these needs are not addressed, the poverty experience can limit the opportunities these entrepreneurs are able to recognize (Chapter 6), and negatively impact the nature of the ventures they tend to create (Chapters 3, 4, and 8). It can influence how success is defined and approached (Chapter 9), and the importance of spiritual faith in processing events and making decisions (Chapter 10).

More than financial resources, the ability to navigate what is a non-linear, unpredictable, and emergent process is dependent upon the nurturing of an entrepreneurial mindset. This mindset must be conceptualized in a different way to reflect the poverty context (see Chapter 7). Success is also dependent upon novel intervention approaches and support mechanisms (Chapter 11) and supportive institutional environments (Chapters 12 and 13), all of which must be tailored to reflect the poverty context and its associated burdens. The real challenge does not center on encouraging the poor to simply start businesses, but instead, on helping them capitalize on new business opportunities in ways that can meaningfully change their economic plight.

Yet, entrepreneurship represents more than a source of income to those who suffer from economic scarcity. It is a source of empowerment and transformation that can address other forms of scarcity in the lives of the poor. It can help restore dignity and contribute to overall well-being. Approaching the development of the individual more holistically, we have argued for the potential of venture creation to positively affect all of the dimensions of integral human development. Before exploring how this potential can be realized, we first turn to establishing a theoretical foundation for this work at the poverty and entrepreneurship interface.

REFERENCES

Abner, L., Butler, S., Danziger, S., Doar, R., Ellwood, D. T., Gueron, J. M., Haidt, J., Haskins, R., Hymowitz, K., Mead, L., Mincy, R., Reeves, R. V., Strain, M. R., & Waldfogel, J. (2015). *Opportunity, responsibility, and security: A consensus plan for reducing poverty and restoring the American dream*. American Enterprise Institute for Public Policy and The Brookings Institution, accessed June 6, 2018, at https://www.brookings.edu/wp-content/uploads/2016/07/full-report.pdf

Amorós, J. E., & Cristi, O. (2011). Poverty and entrepreneurship in developing countries. In M. Minniti (Ed.), *Dynamics of entrepreneurship* (pp. 209–230). Oxford: Oxford University Press.

Banerjee, A. V., & Duflo, E. (2007). The economic lives of the poor. *Journal of Economic Perspectives, 21*(1), 141–167.

Ben-Shalom, Y., Moffitt, R. A., & Scholz, J. K. (2011). *An assessment of the effectiveness of anti-poverty programs in the United States* (No. w17042). National Bureau of Economic Research.

Bratti, M., Ghirelli, C., Havari, E., Santangelo, G., Leikucs, J., & Strautmanis, N. (2018). *Vocational training and labour market outcomes. Evidence from Youth Guarantee in Latvia* (No. 11870). IZA Discussion Paper.

Bruton, G. D., Ketchen Jr., D. J., & Ireland, R. D. (2013). Entrepreneurship as a solution to poverty. *Journal of Business Venturing, 28*(6), 683–689.

Caramela, S. (2023). Startup costs: How much cash will you need? Business News Daily. https://www.businessnewsdaily.com/5-small-business-start-up-costs-options.html

Chetty, R., & Hendren, N. (2015). The impacts of neighborhoods on intergenerational mobility: Childhood exposure effects and county-level estimates. *NBER Working Paper No. 23001.*

Coady, M. D., Jahan, S., Shang, B., & Matsumoto, R. (2021). *Guaranteed minimum income schemes in Europe: Landscape and design*. International Monetary Fund.

Cronen, S., Salinger, T., Dalsimer, A., & Ahlstrand, A. (2021). *Providing pathways out of poverty and into careers: The case for intergrated education and workforce training for underserved adults*. Arlington, VA: American Institutes for Research.

Dean, E. B., Schilbach, F., & Schofield, H. (2017). Poverty and cognitive function. In *The economics of poverty traps* (pp. 57–118). University of Chicago Press.

Dynarski, S., Libassi, C. J., Michelmore, K., & Owen, S. (2018). *Closing the gap: The effect of a targeted, tuition-free promise on college choices of high-achieving, low-income students* (No. w25349). National Bureau of Economic Research.

Ferenstein, G. (2019). Jobs training programs are rarely flexible enough to succeed, Commentary. Brookings Institute. https://www.brookings.edu/articles/jobs-training-programs-are-rarely-flexible-enough-to-succeed/

González, E. R., & Cepeda, L. E. T. (2015). Determinants of the cost of starting a business in Mexico. *The North American Journal of Economics and Finance, 34,* 430–449.

Goulet, D. (2006) *Development ethics: A guide to theory and practice.* London: Zed Books.

Grignon, M., Perronnin, M., & Lavis, J. N. (2008). Does free complementary health insurance help the poor to access health care? Evidence from France. *Health Economics, 17*(2), 203–219.

Holzer, H. J. (2017). The role of skills and jobs in transforming communities. *Cityscape, 19*(1), 171–190.

Holzer, H. J. (2014). Are job training programs a good way to fight poverty. Democracy Journal. https://democracyjournal.org/arguments/are-job-training-programs-a-good-way-to-fight-poverty/

ILO (2014). World social protection report 2014/2015, building economic recovery, inclusive development and social justice. Geneva: International Labor Organization.

Johnson, M., Koukiadaki, A., & Grimshaw, D. (2019). The living wage in the UK: Testing the limits of soft regulation? *Transfer: European Review of Labour and Research, 25*(3), 319–333.

J-PAL (2023). Vocational and skills training programs to improve labor market outcomes. Adbul Latif Jameel Poverty Action Lab, Cambridge, MA: Massachusetts Institute of Technology.

Kharas, H., & Dooley, M. (2022). The evolution of global poverty, 1990–2030. Working Paper #166, Washington, DC: Brookings Institution.

Kiggundu, M. N. (2002). Entrepreneurs and entrepreneurship in Africa: What is known and what needs to be done. *Journal of Developmental Entrepreneurship, 7*(3), 239.

Kluve, J., Puerto, S., Robalino, D., Romero, J. M., Rother, F., Stöterau, J., . . . & Witte, M. (2019). Do youth employment programs improve labor market outcomes? A quantitative review. *World Development, 114,* 237–253.

Luce S. (2014). Living wages, minimum wages, and low-wage workers. In *What works for workers? Public policies and innovative strategies for low-wage workers*, ed. S. Luce, J. Luff, J .A. McCartin, R. Milkman, pp. 215–244. New York: Russell Sage Found.

Miguel, E., & Mobarak, A. M. (2022). The economics of the COVID-19 pandemic in poor countries. *Annual Review of Economics, 14,* 253–285.

Morris, M. H., Pryor, C. G., & Schindehutte, S. (2012). *Entrepreneurship as experience: How events create ventures and ventures create entrepreneurs.* Northhampton, MA: Edward Elgar Publishing.

Morris, M. H., Santos, S. C., & Neumeyer, X. (2020). Entrepreneurship as a solution to poverty in developed economies. *Business Horizons*, *63*(3), 377–390.

Morris, M. H., Soleimanof, S., & Tucker, R. (2023). Drivers of fragility in the ventures of poverty entrepreneurs. *Small Business Economics, 61*(1), 305–323.

OECD (2022). Organization for economic cooperation and development. https://data.oecd.org/inequality/poverty-rate.htm

Payne, R. K., DeVol, P., & Smith, T. D. (2001). *Bridges out of poverty: Strategies for professionals*. Highlands, TX: Aha! Process, Inc.

Pew Charitable Trusts (2013). Faces of economic mobility. September 17, accessed June 6, 2018, at http://www.pewtrusts.org/en/multimedia/data-visualizations/2013/faces-of-economic-mobility

Pew Charitable Trusts (2016). Neighborhood poverty and household financial security. Acessed June 6, 2018, at http://www.pewtrusts.org/~/media/assets/2016/01/chartbook--neighborhood-poverty-and-household-financial-security_v3.pdf

Ravallion, M. (2007). Evaluating anti-poverty programs. *Handbook of development economics*, *4,* 3787–3846.

Ravallion, M. (2020). On measuring global poverty. *Annual Review of Economics, 12,* 167–188.

Sen, A. (1999). *Development as freedom*. New York: Alfred A. Knopf.

Si, S., Ahlstrom, D., Wei, J., & Cullen, J. (2021). Introduction. In *Business, entrepreneurship and innovation toward poverty reduction* (pp. 1–20). Oxfordshire, UK: Routledge.

Si, S., Ahlstrom, D., Wei, J., & Cullen, J. (2021). Introduction: Business, entrepreneurship and innovation toward poverty reduction. In *Business, entrepreneurship and innovation toward poverty reduction* (pp. 1–20). Routledge.

Sumner, A., & Tiwari, M. (2011). Global poverty reduction to 2015 and beyond. *Global Policy*, *2*(2), 138–151.

Smillie, I. (2019). *Mastering the machine: Poverty, aid and technology*. Routledge.

Sutter, C., Bruton, G. D., & Chen, J. (2019). Entrepreneurship as a solution to extreme poverty: A review and future research directions. *Journal of Business Venturing, 34*(1), 197–214.

Tanner, M. (2022). Poverty and welfare. *CATO handbook for policymakers*. Washington, DC: CATO Institute.

Toyama, K. (2010). Can technology end poverty. *Boston Review, 36*(5), 12–29.

UNICEF (2021). *Levels and trends in child mortality.* United Nations Inter-Agency Group for Child Mortality Estimation. New York: United Nations Children's Fund.

United Nations (2021). Sustainable cities and communities—Make cities and human settlements inclusive, safe, resilient and sustainable. New York: United Nations. https://unstats.un.org/UNSDWebsite/.

US Census Bureau (2011, March 6). Census Bureau survey shows poverty is primarily a temporary condition. *Newsroom*. Washington, DC: US Census Bureau, accessed June 6, 2018, at https://www.census.gov/newsroom/releases/archives/poverty/cb11-49.html

US Census Bureau (2016). *Annual social and economic supplement of the current population survey*. Washington, DC: US Census Bureau.

Wade, R. H. (2020). Is globalization reducing poverty and inequality? In *Neoliberalism, globalization, and inequalities* (pp. 143–176). Routledge.

Wilson, W. J. (2019). When work disappears: New implications for race and urban poverty in the global economy. In *Celebrating 40 years of ethnic and racial studies* (pp. 220–240). Routledge.

World Bank (2017). *Monitoring global poverty: Report of the commission on global poverty*. Washington, DC: World Bank.

World Bank (2020). Informal economy database. worldbank.org/en/research/brief/informal-economy-database.

World Bank (2021). www.worldbank.org/en/research/brief/informal-economy-database

World Bank (2022a). Understanding poverty. https://www.worldbank.org/en/understanding-poverty

World Bank (2022b). Poverty and shared prosperity 2022: Correcting course. Washington, DC: World Bank, https://openknowledge.worldbank.org/entities/publication/a33782e6-415e-5699-a9a8-4a50dc4ae3bc

World Health Organization (2021). Population Below the international poverty line. https://www.who.int/data/gho/indicator-metadata-registry/imr-details/4744

Chapter Two

Disadvantage, Capabilities, and Entrepreneurship

Poverty can often represent a stigma that gets attached to an individual, as if it is their fault, or something is wrong with them (Reutter et al., 2009; Waxman, 1983). Such a stigma leads to social exclusion, lack of access, and underestimation of potential, among other costs borne by the individual. Poverty is not a characteristic of a person, or an affliction. Rather, it characterizes the circumstances in which a person finds themselves and must struggle to escape. So, the real need is to better understand those circumstances, what causes them, and how they impact how an individual thinks, interprets events, makes decisions, and behaves.

Poverty circumstances have major implications for the entrepreneurial process. The reality is that people in poverty often create marginal ventures that do not change their economic situation. Because these ventures lack efficiency, create few jobs, produce little intellectual property, and often fail, people tend to discount them. They are seen as "losers," not worthy of resource investments or attention from those interested in economic development (Shane, 2009).

In this chapter, we explore poverty circumstances and their implications for venture creation through two theoretical lenses, one from economics and the other from sociology. We believe these two theories are especially valuable in providing a foundation for understanding the poverty and entrepreneurship interface. The first of these is disadvantage theory (Light, 1979), which can help us understand the dual impacts of disadvantages created by poverty and how they affect motivations and behaviors when attempting to develop a business. The second theoretical perspective is capabilities theory (Sen, 1999), which is related to our focus on integral human development in Chapter 1. It provides a framework for explaining how a person's well-being can be enhanced through entrepreneurship. Capabilities enable an individual to do and be the things that they value. Poverty is a condition that deprives people of capabilities and limits their wherewithal to develop capabilities.

The combination of these two theoretical perspectives enables us to develop a model that integrates the disadvantage of poverty, the entrepreneurial process, the central role of capabilities, and the enhanced functionings or achievements that venture creation can make possible for the poor. This model provides a springboard that guides the development of the chapters to come.

THE COMPLEX MOSAIC OF POVERTY

People may tend to over-simplify the notion of poverty. This is not surprising, as poverty is typically defined in economic terms (i.e., earning less than a certain amount of income per day, month, or year). Scarcity of economic resources implies that a person struggles to address basic physiological or survival needs (e.g., food, shelter, warmth, clothing) and safety and security needs (e.g., health, employment, physical and emotional safety) (Maslow, 1954). However, the struggles of the poor can be far more profound. Understanding these struggles requires a more holistic view of poverty.

Poverty is an experience, and the nature of this experience (and how it is processed by the individual) is unique to each person. It is an experience that transcends a lack of income or wealth, and can be characterized by a complex web of interacting conditions. Let us highlight a number of these conditions. The poor suffer more food insecurity and less healthy diets (Bhattacharya, Currie, & Haider, 2004), higher crime rates and physical insecurity (Pare & Felson, 2014), more chronic medical conditions, and higher levels of childhood mortality (Van Agt, Stronks, & Mackenbach, 2000). They encounter fewer and less attractive job opportunities and demonstrate higher unemployment rates as well as underemployment in low-paying, labor-intensive jobs with no benefits and little room for advancement (Morris, Santos, & Neumeyer, 2018). Their housing conditions are frequently sub-standard and the threat of eviction is common (Morland et al., 2002). They often lack dependable transportation alternatives, including both personal and public forms of transit (Wachs, 2010). They attend lower quality schools and demonstrate above-average school drop-out rates (Orfield & Lee, 2005). Teenage childbearing and single parenthood are both common (Maldonado & Nieuwenhuis, 2015) as are high stress levels and constant fatigue (Banerjee & Duflo, 2011). They tend to be segregated from much of society (Abramson, Tobin, & VanderGoot, 1995), with limited social networks (Matthews & Besemer, 2015). They are more severely impacted by catastrophic events such as a major recession or the COVID-19 pandemic, and take far longer to recover (Rönkkö, Rutherford, & Sen, 2022; Wiwad et al., 2021).

The complex nature of poverty is the result of the myriad ways in which these conditions can interact with and reinforce one another. Consider how a lower quality education, limited social networks and lack of dependable transportation (each of which can affect the others) can lead to fewer and less attractive job opportunities; or, how higher unemployment rates, being a high school dropout, physical insecurity, and teenage childbearing can contribute to high stress levels; or, how food insecurity, a poor diet, and substandard housing can contribute to chronic health problems and shorter lifespans. Again, every person experiences poverty in their own idiosyncratic way, and is affected by a unique combination of these conditions. These combinations can limit options and force particular choices. They can undermine the individual's dignity and sense of worth, and make a person more vulnerable to setbacks, adverse developments, and missed opportunities.

How do these conditions and their complex interactions come into play when a person is thinking about starting a business? Some of these factors can actually motivate an individual to launch a venture. Lack of income, limited job opportunities, jobs with no upward mobility, and single parenthood can all serve as motives to launch a venture, either as a means of supplementing one's income or primary source of one's livelihood. Yet, all of these conditions can represent major obstacles when attempting to address basic tasks surrounding the development of an enterprise, as illustrated in Figure 2.1. Such tasks can include registering a business, obtaining necessary licenses, finding premises or a place to operate, obtaining equipment, procuring raw materials or ingredients, writing a business plan, creating a bookkeeping system, penetrating a market, ensuring product quality and consistency, addressing customer complaints, managing logistics, and a whole host of other critical activities in the early stages of a venture. More fundamentally, they limit the ability of the entrepreneur to obtain and interpret relevant information, access key people and resources, respond to unanticipated developments, and engage in planning and strategic thinking. The end result is that the complex mosaic of poverty impacts whether a business is started, what forms it takes, and how well it is able to perform (Alvarez & Barney, 2013; Sheehy-Skeffington & Rea, 2017).

What becomes apparent is that simply having more money with which to start a business is not enough to ensure the poverty entrepreneur can be successful. These other conditions typically remain in place, such that any number of them can continue to work against the ability of the entrepreneur to succeed. We will revisit the ways in which these conditions directly impact the starting of a business in Chapter 5. First, however, let us further explore the nature of disadvantage.

Figure 2.1. How the Complex Poverty Experience Affects the Ability to Build a Business.
Created by Authors

THE DUALITY OF DISADVANTAGE

Poverty entrepreneurs frequently start from a position of disadvantage when they launch a business. The multi-dimensional nature of poverty can produce severe resource constraints, while also limiting the kinds of opportunities available and how they are approached (Alvarez & Barney, 2014; Morris, 2020). Given the nature and severity of these challenges, disadvantage theory (Boyd, 2000; Light, 1979) represents a valuable framework for advancing our understanding of the poverty and entrepreneurship interface.

Disadvantage theory is concerned with how experiences of economic and social exclusion, labor market disadvantage, and discrimination impact the actions of afflicted individuals. It argues that these disadvantages can provide both motivations for and barriers to pursuing actions that can change one's circumstances (Light & Rosenstein, 1995). Applied to entrepreneurship, these dual effects have been used to explain the prevalence of venture creation activity among women, immigrants, and minorities (Boyd, 2000; Horton & DeJong, 1991). Ivan Light (1979), who pioneered this theory, has used it to explain how over-urbanization resulting from having rural residents in developing countries flock to cities, where they cannot find work, leads them to start businesses. Poverty, as a key indicator of economic exclusion, is an underlying characteristic of many of the groups examined in disadvantage studies (e.g., Boyd, 2000; Butler, 1991; Herring, 2004).

On the one hand, disadvantage can serve to enhance the attractiveness of entrepreneurship, particularly where the disadvantage has resulted in unemployment, under-employment, or employment at relatively low wages. It can foster the motivation needed to transcend one's circumstances, escape the status quo, and realize the fruits of one's labor (Krishna, 2004). The individual strives to not become a victim of poverty, and seeks to provide better opportunities for their family and future generations (Nakara, Messeghem, & Ramaroson, 2021). On the other hand, disadvantages associated with poverty can serve as an inhibitor when it comes to pursuing entrepreneurship, or they can push the individual into the informal sector (see Chapter 4). Poverty-induced disadvantages such as inadequate resources, insufficient capabilities, limited access to opportunities, and diminished self-perceptions of one's potential and place in society can undermine the willingness to create a business (Payne et al., 2012; Wilson, 2012).

Boyd (2000) suggests that there is a proportionate relationship between how much labor market disadvantage a particular group experiences and the level and nature of entrepreneurial activity demonstrated by that group, suggesting that the most disadvantaged groups are always the most entrepreneurial. Light and Rosenstein (1995) argue that regardless of the aggregate level of entrepreneurial activity its members demonstrate, as the amount of disadvantage being experienced by a given group increases over time, that group is likely to engage in more entrepreneurial activity.

Perhaps more important than the motive to start a business is the role played by disadvantage in explaining *how* entrepreneurship is pursued. It is likely to influence the kinds of opportunities the entrepreneur is able to recognize (see Chapter 6), the type of business started, how decisions are made, the ability to plan and think strategically, the skills and capabilities the entrepreneur brings to the venture, and the abilities to learn from experiences and adapt as the venture unfolds. As a result, disadvantaged entrepreneurs are more likely to create survivalist or very marginal types of enterprises (Adebayo & Nassar, 2014; Smith-Hunter & Boyd, 2004).

Others (e.g., Davis, 2002; Herring, 2004; Silverman, 2011) provide evidence suggesting that disadvantages resulting from social exclusion and discrimination lead individuals to focus on niche market opportunities that do not extend beyond their immediate neighborhoods and network connections. Instead of penetrating mainstream markets having greater profit potential, they are pushed into narrower (but more accepting) markets with limited potential. Butler (1991) refers to this as the "economic detour" variant of disadvantage theory.

In a related vein, Morris et al. (2018) have demonstrated how the disadvantages of poverty cause the poor to launch "commodity" ventures that lack differentiation, must compete on price, are labor-intensive with high unit costs, earn small margins, lack technology and sophisticated equipment, purchase in small quantities, and have very limited capacity (see Chapter 8). Such businesses are both vulnerable and fragile, and typically fail to move people out of poverty (Morris et al., 2022).

Conversely, certain aspects of disadvantage might actually contribute to the success of a venture. For instance, when immersed in poverty on a day-by-day basis, an individual can become acclimated to certain ways of thinking and acting in order to protect themselves and survive (Garmezy, 1991). An example is resiliency, or the ability to positively adapt in the presence of significant adversity and recover from difficult developments (Masten & Reed, 2002). Scholars contend that the poor are often quite resilient—able to survive despite the lack of resources, limited opportunity, and regular setbacks (Bene et al., 2014). They demonstrate a capacity to rebound from adversity, misfortune, and trauma (Walsh, 1998). Research findings suggest that some people can adapt to poverty and deprivation by learning to suppress particular wants, hopes, and aspirations (Clark, Fennell, & Hulme, 2017; Nussbaum & Sen, 1993). Yet, this suppression can also foster more clearly defined goals and, as a consequence, the resilience and drive required to achieve these goals. Beyond this, surviving in poverty can find the individual engaged in short-term opportunism (Griskevicius et al., 2013). Such opportunism can influence one to be more alert to readily accessible resources around them, particularly ones that can be leveraged to address poverty conditions. Scarcity forces those in poverty to be more creative in order to survive extremely lean conditions (McCubbin et al., 1997). In what is sometimes described as hustling (Fisher et al., 2020), they can learn to make unorthodox use of resources from their surroundings in order to get by. More generally, poverty conditions can compel frugality and bricolage on the part of the poor (Muradian, 2019). Finally, poverty can induce a drive for success. John and Poisner (2016) provide a series of case examples of people who took advantage of the fact that they had nothing, were hungry for success, retained focus, and had to scrape and scramble to make any progress.

They argue that these individuals demonstrated a greater need to succeed and tended to be more personally and emotionally invested.

In sum, the dualism involved with disadvantage theory introduces an important dynamic that may help us better understand the performance challenges experienced by low-income entrepreneurs. These dual forces are operating at the same time and against one another. As disadvantage motivates and inhibits the individual, the net effect can be the incentive to create a new venture, but one that is marginalized, with constrained potential (Morris et al., 2022). Disadvantage is simultaneously working for and against progress. It creates a kind of dialectic, where the drive to rise above poverty is in opposition to the way one thinks, makes decisions, and finds ways to survive. Paradoxically, we may find that an individual simultaneously demonstates: big dreams with a limited opportunity horizon (see Chapter 6); a desire to change their circumstances with a short-term orientation, an inability to focus, and an atomistic approach to decision-making (see Chapter 5); and a desire to avoid failure while also demonstrating a fear of success (see Chapter 9).

THE DEVELOPMENT OF CAPABILITIES

Our second source of theoretical underpinning comes from the capabilities theory of Amartya Sen, the Nobel laureate in economics, which focuses on human well-being. Also called the capabilities framework, it is based on two core assumptions: (a) the freedom to achieve personal well-being is of primary moral importance to the human race; and (b) achieving well-being is tied to the ability of people to do and be what they value. Freedom to achieve is determined by what a person is able to do and be, and hence the sort of life someone is able to lead. The gauge of whether a person has a quality life is tied to their ability to perform the functions that are instrumental to having a good life. In this manner, the theory places the central focus on *functionings* and *capabilities*.

In essence, a functioning refers to an achievement, and a capability is the ability to achieve (Sen, 1987). Consider personal mobility, or the ability to get around, an example used by Sen. Functionings related to personal mobility might include walking, riding a bike, driving a scooter or car, riding a bus, or taking an Uber ride. A person's well-being is defined through the functionings that they value. Capabilities concern which of these functionings the individual is able to select or achieve. They are defined as the doings and beings individuals can achieve if they choose. As such, a person's set of capabilities can be considered personal freedoms, as they affect the range of options an individual has in deciding the kind of life they want to live.

While the roles of income, material well-being and resources controlled are often stressed in gauging personal welfare, the emphasis with the capabilities approach is on what people are able to do with those resources in terms of producing outcomes, and how much in the way of resources the person requires to be able to produce a given outcome. People differ in their abilities to convert the same resources into functionings. Commodity requirements can differ, for instance, if a person has a disability, or alternatively, depending on the culture or society in which they reside (e.g., a society that subjugates women or discriminates against an ethnic group). As a result, the means or resources one has access to are less meaningful unless they are able to convert them into outcomes.

The capabilities approach has been applied in a number of different contexts, such as health economics, housing, gender equality, and labor market studies. In the field of education, Saito (2003) argues for the usefulness of the approach in helping us understand how educational institutions can enable future freedoms for the students being served by building their lifetime capabilities in relevant domains (or types of functionings). The challenge concerns the functionings that are valued, who should determine those functionings (teachers, parents, school boards, etc.), and the process of influencing human capabilities (and the associated intrinsic and instrumental values) through education. By creating a new capability set for the student, education makes a child autonomous, allowing her or him to make choices (i.e., having the freedom to choose) in their life. However, Saito (2003) also stresses the role of education in teaching values that govern the exercise of capabilities, including the values they place on a given capability and various outcomes that capabilities are used to achieve.

When applied to entrepreneurship, we seek to understand the potential of venture creation to enhance quality of life. The capabilities approach provides an entirely different lens when considering how to support and assist disadvantaged entrepreneurs, and yet one that is especially useful. It takes the spotlight off income growth as the guiding principle in deciding how to assist poverty entrepreneurs. It is not that income growth is not important. Rather, capabilities development represents a much more relevant factor in determining outcomes or achievements. It moves us away from a "pick the winners" mentality, such that we ignore or under-invest effort in what are judged to be more marginal or less promising ventures, and highlights the potential in all ventures launched by the poor. More fundamentally, it moves the focus from developing the venture to the development of the capabilities of the disadvantaged entrepreneur.

Using this lens, the purpose of entrepreneurship is to develop capabilities, and this is especially the case with the poor. For its part, profit is not the purpose of a new business, it is a guidepost that indicates if the correct decisions are being made. Further, businesses need profits to sustain themselves and grow. The purpose of a new business is to create value in the marketplace. However, creating value and earning profits are both dependent upon capabilities. Moreover, capabilities also make possible a number of other functionings or outcomes that can contribute to human flourishing.

When we speak of entrepreneurship as empowerment, we are referring to the opportunities for the creation of a business to enhance a person's ability to generate key functionings, outcomes, or achievements. The venture becomes a vehicle for developing capabilities. It is a means to personal development rather than an end. This perspective is consistent with the strong emphasis within entrepreneurship education and training on competency development (Morris et al., 2013). However, the existing literature tends to emphasize the competencies necessary to successfully create a venture, not the venture as a vessel for competency development.

In this regard, we have to distinguish the capabilities that the venture creation process can enable. Capabilities theory does not specify the relative importance of different functionings and capabilities. It emphasizes functionings that the individual personally values, and the various capabilities that can result in those functionings. In the context of venture creation, individuals are likely to differ in terms of relative importance of a given functioning or achievement. For instance, the ability to contribute to my community by creating jobs for others who experience poverty or disadvantage will be more important to one entrepreneur than another. Further, the extent to which an individual recognizes the potential functionings that can result from the venture creation process, or the relative importance of various capabilities for enabling particular functionings, will vary. As a case in point, many poverty entrepreneurs struggle with financial literacy, and may not value the importance of keeping precise financial records, developing a functioning bookkeeping system, and using the outputs to inform decision-making. Hence, the associated capabilities that enable effective financial management are not valued and may actually be resisted. Further, certain functionings and associated capabilites can be instrumental in achieving what we might think of as "higher-order" functionings. Thus, effective financial management can enable the ability to create a profitable enterprise, which can contribute to a sense of self-worth and a greater ability to contribute to one's community. Moreover, the individual may not set out to improve their sense of worthiness, and yet the fact that the venture creation process enabled the sense of worthiness can become critical in determining the net effect of venture creation on a person's quality of life. The failure of a disadvantaged entrepreneur to recognize or appreciate the importance of a given functioning or capability for producing desired venture outcomes highlights an important role for support organizations within the entrepreneurial ecosystem. The same is true in terms of the ability of the entrepreneur to understand the functionings that it may be possible for a given venture to enable.

As we suggested in Chapter 1, venture creation has the potential to produce a number of personal outcomes or functionings. In addition to income generation and wealth creation, the entrepreneurial experience can enable self-efficacy, identity development, and a sense of pride and purpose based on one's ability to create customer value, employ people, and pay taxes. It can give the disenfranchised a voice. As a means of human capital development, it enables freedom of choice. This potentiality is what makes the capabilities approach especially valuable.

The importance of a capability for achieving an outcome will vary depending upon the nature of the business being created (e.g., a hair salon versus a construction company or dress-making business). Individuals will also differ significantly in terms of the capabilities they have, the capabilities they need to be successful with a venture, and what it will require for them to develop those capabilities. Importantly, there is a temporal dimension to all of this, as potential functionings and relevant capabilities evolve as a venture moves from pre-start-up to launch and early adaptation to stabilization to growth. People will also display significant differences in what they value, and because of the freedom of choice principle, it becomes difficult to specify a universally important set of functionings or capabilities as they relate to entrepreneurship.

Yet, when we consider the poverty entrepreneur, a paramount concern is the need to distinguish the capabilities necessary to launch a business from those that can emerge through the venture experience (once a business is launched). It is this distinction that brings us back to the problems of disadvantage and how they impact the attitudes, perceptions, and behaviors of a person in poverty circumstances.

FROM DISADVANTAGE TO CAPABILITIES TO HOLISTIC WELL-BEING

It is the combination of disadvantage theory and capabilities theory that provides the underpinnings for the arguments and conclusions throughout this book. From the perspective of disadvantage theory, the complex mix of factors that constitute the poverty experience has both a motivating and inhibiting influence on the individual trying to create a business. If we consider the motivation to start a business, we have seen how disadvantage can discourage the individual to the point that they do not pursue entrepreneurship. Much of this can be explained in terms of capabilities. If creating a business that helps me pay the bills, or makes me better off, is a desirable functioning, then its attractiveness is tied to my sense that I have the capabilities to generate funding, attract customers, make sales, produce a quality product, manage cash flow, handle logistics, and accomplish of a number of other tasks. If the drive to improve my situation is sufficient to overcome my perception of inadequate capabilities, then I must confront the challenges created by the disadvantaged-induced lack of capabilities. As we shall see in Chapter 5, these are profound challenges. They affect my ability to process informational inputs, plan and think strategically, maintain focus on the business and where it is going, and operate without any margin for significant error.

Once a decision has been made to start a business, the emergent nature of the entrepreneurial journey finds the entrepreneur in need of critical capabilities to get a venture going, and poverty-related disadvantages can make this problematic. That is, these disadvantages work against taking the kinds of actions that would make the venture financially sustainable. Lack of basic capabilities complicates the capacity to develop higher-order capabilities. Instead, the entrepreneur may find they are creating a survivalist venture that produces low margins and volumes and keeps the entrepreneur in poverty (see Chapters 2 and 8). This represents a critical juncture in the venture creation process of the poverty entrepreneur, as the early decisions of the entrepreneur create a path-dependent trajectory. The establishment of a more marginal, survival venture starts one on a constrained path that is very difficult to redirect. The duality of disadvantage is at work, where disadvantage may push a person to start the venture, but undermines the ability to build a venture that can change their personal circumstances or enhance their well-being. Critical capabilities are missing, and the ability to overcome these shortcomings is hindered by literacy gaps, a short-term mindset, lack of resources, and other vestiges of the complex mosaic of poverty.

Stated differently, the poor have unique needs when it comes to capabilities, and may require more and different resources to develop a particular capability. When first launching a business, we would argue the priority must be placed on capabilities that overcome poverty liabilities (see Chapter 5 for a more detailed discussion of these liabilities). For example, where support systems can help nascent poverty entrepreneurs develop critical literacies, an enhanced ability to plan, a more strategic orientation, and the ability to leverage the resources of others, the result is likely to be a more viable business.

However, if one can get the venture to a point where revenues are generated on a somewhat consistent basis, and profits are generated, even if they are relatively marginal, then we begin to see how new capabilities can be developed from the venture experience itself. The entrepreneur is, to varying degrees, learning (from real time experiences) how to sell, manage cash flow, organize production and logistics, oversee procurement and inventory levels, address customer service, and a host of other capabilities. These capabilities can be enhanced as the venture moves from being an operating entity to becoming profitable and having a sustainable business model. Capabilities can also contribute to this progression. At the same time, the ongoing development of capabilities is affected positively and negatively by the liabilities associated with disadvantage. This duality, and the ability to compensate for or overcome these liabilities, is the key to determining the extent to which entrepreneurship can enhance different dimensions of the entrepreneur's quality of life.

This discussion suggests that the relevant functionings and capabilities change depending on the stage of venture development. It also suggests that disadvantage can significantly undermine the potential of the venture creation experience to contribute to enhanced quality of life through capability development. Even as poverty can contribute to resiliency and creative solutions for addressing resource shortages, these positive elements may only serve to keep a marginal venture going rather than enabling its potential for growth and development. Absent a well-conceptualized intervention or support system, this potential is likely to be negatively associated with the degree of disadvantage experienced by the entrepreneur. Unfortunately, entrepreneurial ecosystems are not generally designed with this kind of staged and capability-oriented approach in mind. That is, to the extent that they even prioritize the needs of poverty entrepreneurs, ecosystems are not structured to address disadvantages—particularly in ways that allow the entrepreneur to develop the relevant capabilities to get a viable venture launched and then enable the entrepreneur to enhance capabilities based on their ongoing venture experiences. We will further explore the kinds of changes needed in institutional environments, entrepreneurial ecosystems, and public policies in Chapters 12 and 13.

Figure 2.2 represents an attempt to capture these arguments. Here, a temporal model is adopted that consists of three parts, reflecting the decision by the disadvantaged entrepreneur to pursue entrepreneurship, the creation of some type of venture, and the ability of the venture creation experience to produce outcomes that have implications for well-being or life quality. While other contextual considerations may come into play, three key factors are especially paramount in the decision to pursue entrepreneurship. The first of these are liabilities that derive from the poverty experience, such as literacy gaps, a scarcity mindset, significant non-business distractions, and lack of resources. The second driver is the perceived capabilities the entrepreneur believes he or she has. Finally, the decision is influenced by the value the individual places on different venture-related functionings, such as income generation, autonomy, or the ability to give back to one's community. Having decided to launch a business, we then turn to the nature of the venture that is being created. To what extent will it be a marginal, survival venture, or

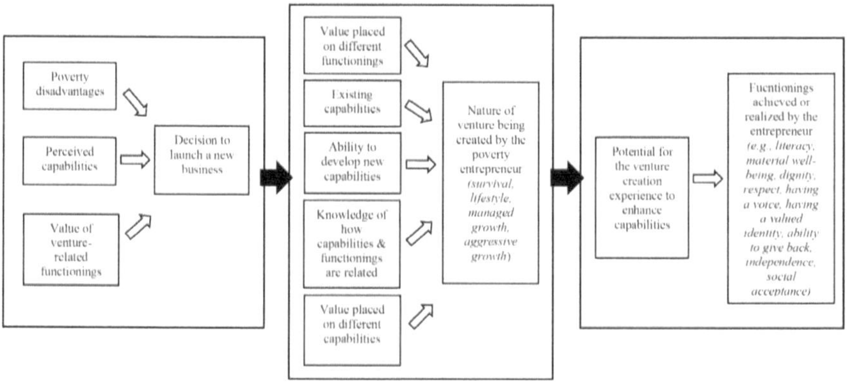

Figure 2.2. Model Integrating Disadvantage, Capabilities, and the Entrepreneurial Process.
Created by Authors

one that generates a modicum of income, or one that steadily expands, or one that produces explosive growth? Here we identify five key determinants. Capabilities theory would suggest the importance to the disadvantaged entrepreneur of (a) different functionings or achievements, (b) knowledge of the kinds of capabilities necessary to obtain those functionings, (c) the value the entrepreneur places on developing particular capabilities, and (d) the capabilities the entrepreneur currently has. Disadvantage also plays a key role here, as it affects the ability of the entrepreneur to develop any new capabilities. The final part of the model addresses how, through the venture creation experience, the entrepreneur is able to develop or enhance their capabilities. Enhanced capabilities or freedoms enable the entrepreneur to realize valued functionalities, such as material well-being, human dignity and respect, or an ability to contribute to one's community. Arguably, the type of venture being created has a direct influence on this. As we shall see in Chapter 3, those in poverty overwhelmingly create survival and lifestyle types of ventures. These types of ventures can significantly limit the capability development process, particularly for a disadvantaged entrepreneur.

Given the central role of the nature of the business being created by the poverty entrepreneur, it is important to determine the kinds of functionings that can be obtained when launching a marginal venture versus one that produces more significant profits and growth. It would seem that valuable functionings can be achieved without creating a growth-oriented or scalable enterprise. These kinds of ventures can certainly produce material well-being and other functionings that money makes possible. Yet, it would seem achieving such functionings as personal dignity, social connectivity, and development of a meaningful identity, among others, are quite possible based on the experience of building more modest ventures.

Based on this model, the challenge is not simply one of overcoming disadvantages through capability development, but also helping the entrepreneur to understand the importance of different functionings or achievements and the priorities that must be placed on particular capabilities that can lead to these functionings. For example, if poverty conditions result in significant gaps in financial literacy, attempts to enhance the associated financial management capabilities needed to develop a sustainable venture will be less productive if the entrepreneur does not develop an appreciation for such capabilities. However, the value they place on the functionings that these capabilities facilitate is just as important. These functionings can transcend the ability to generate profits—they can include additional outcomes related to human development and quality of life. Stated differently, the entrepreneur may not understand the potential of venture creation to affect a range of outcomes that make their lives better. As a result, their objectives and expectations regarding what they want from the venture are constrained.

Finally, individual agency and personal choice represent the fuel that drives the creation of a venture, but also drives the development of particular capabilities. Poverty can hinder both the sense of agency and the kinds of choices being made. Hence, it is not simply about the goals and functionings that the individual values, or their understanding of the relevance of different capabilities. Of central importance is the agency they exert in mastering and deploying particular capabilities. Further, individuals make trade-off decisions as they develop a business, and these directly influence the kinds of functionings they are able to obtain. As an example, the entrepreneur who endures high levels of stress in order to build a more financially successful enterprise, and allocates less time to family and personal needs relative to that devoted to the needs of the business, may develop the kinds of capabilities that produce more material well-being or a greater ability to give back. However, they may suffer in terms of the well-being that derives from good physical health and rich family relationships.

CONCLUSION

This chapter has introduced two key theories that provide a conceptual foundation for our understanding of entrepreneurship and poverty, and how entrepreneurship can serve as a vehicle for achieving a better life. These theories lead us to place the development of the individual over the potential for financial returns as the guiding principle when considering how entrepreneurship can be a solution to poverty. They require that we move away from a "pick the winners" mentality when it comes to supporting and investing in the ventures of the poor, and instead focus on capabilities and functionings. They highlight how the experience of venture development represents a stage or platform for the development of capabilities that disadvantaged individuals would otherwise struggle to acquire, or perceive as not attainable. Poverty conditions can be a critical determinant of the capabilities that receive priority. They can also influence the kinds of functionings that the disadvantaged entrepreneur most values.

We tend to discount the ventures of the poor because so many of them are inefficient, marginally profitable (at best), and create few jobs or innovations. Besides the fact that they support millions of families across the globe, discounting these ventures represents a gross misunderstanding of entrepreneurship and its potential. The true value of new ventures created by entrepreneurs is dependent upon the metrics being used to assess them. Rather than focusing purely on the conventional metrics used by economists and financiers, it is time for an entirely new paradigm. If new ventures give meaning to or enhance the lives of those who own them; if they are a source of dignity for those whose dignity is continually compromised; if they enable a person to feel they are part of (and a contributor to) the fabric of society; and if they enhance human freedoms through capability development, then we can conclude they are indeed valuable. Of course, entrepreneurship can also make people worse off, or do nothing to improve their quality of life. The key to generating this value lies in unlocking the potential of the venture creation process and the associated entrepreneurial ecosystems to enhance the capabilities of the poor. In the chapters ahead, we examine a range of key issues and considerations that surround the realization of this potential.

REFERENCES

Abramson, A. J., Tobin, M. S., & VanderGoot, M. R. (1995). The changing geography of metropolitan opportunity: The segregation of the poor in US metropolitan areas, 1970 to 1990. *Housing Policy Debate*, *6*(1), 45–72.

Adebayo, N. A., & Nassar, M. L. (2014). Impact of micro and small business entrepreneurship on poverty reduction in Ibadan Metropolis, South Western Nigeria. *International Review of Management and Business Research*, *3*(3), 1603–1626.

Alvarez, S. A., & Barney, J. B. (2013). Epistemology, opportunities, and entrepreneurship: Comments on Venkataraman et al. (2012) and Shane (2012). *AMR, 38*, 154–157. https://doi.org/10.5465/amr.2012.0069

Alvarez, S. A., & Barney, J. B. (2014). Entrepreneurial opportunities and poverty alleviation. *Entrepreneurship theory and practice*, *38*(1), 159–184.

Banerjee, A. V., & Duflo, E. (2011). *Poor economics: A radical rethinking of the way to fight global poverty*. Public Affairs.

Bhattacharya, J., Currie, J., & Haider, S. (2004). Poverty, food insecurity, and nutritional outcomes in children and adults. *Journal of Health Economics*, *23*(4), 839–862.

Béné, C., Newsham, A., Davies, M., Ulrichs, M., & Godfrey-Wood, R. (2014). Resilience, poverty and development. *Journal of International Development*, *26*(5), 598–623.

Boyd, R. L. (2000, December). Race, labor market disadvantage, and survivalist entrepreneurship: Black women in the urban North during the Great Depression. In *Sociological Forum* (Vol. 15, pp. 647–670). Kluwer Academic Publishers-Plenum Publishers.

Butler, J. S. (1991). *Entrepreneurship and self-help among Black Americans: A re-consideration of race and economics*. Albany: State University of New York Press.

Clark, D. A., Fennell, S., & Hulme, D. (2017). Poverty and inequality. In *Handbook of Globalisation and Development*. Edward Elgar Publishing.

Davis, J. F. (2002). Enterprise development under an economic detour? Black-owned advertising agencies, 1940–2000. *Journal of Macromarketing*, *22*(1), 75–85.

Fisher, G., Stevenson, R., Neubert, E., Burnell, D., & Kuratko, D. F. (2020). Entrepreneurial hustle: Navigating uncertainty and enrolling venture stakeholders through urgent and unorthodox action. *Journal of Management Studies*, *57*(5), 1002–1036.

Garmezy, N. (1991). Resiliency and vulnerability to adverse developmental outcomes associated with poverty. *American Behavioral Scientist*, *34*(4), 416–430.

Griskevicius, V., Ackerman, J. M., Cantú, S. M., Delton, A. W., Robertson, T. E., Simpson, J. A., . . . & Tybur, J. M. (2013). When the economy falters, do people spend or save? Responses to resource scarcity depend on childhood environments. *Psychological Science*, *24*(2), 197–205

Herring, C. (2004). Open for business in the black metropolis: Race, disadvantage, and entrepreneurial activity in Chicago's inner city. *The Review of Black Political Economy*, *31*(4), 35–57.

Horton, H., & De Jong, G. (1991). Black entrepreneurs: A socio-demographic analysis. *Research in Race and Ethnic Relations*, 6, 105–120.

John, D., & Poisner, D. (2016). *The power of broke: How empty pockets, a tight budget, and a hunger for success can become your greatest competitive advantage*. New York: Currency.

Krishna, A. (2004). Escaping poverty and becoming poor: Who gains, who loses, and why? *World Development, 32*(1), 121–136.

Light, I. (1979), Disadvantaged minorities in self-employment, *International Journal of Comparative Sociology, 20,* 30–45.

Light, I. H., & Rosenstein, C. N. (1995). *Race, ethnicity, and entrepreneurship in urban America*. Transaction Publishers.

Maldonado, L. C., & Nieuwenhuis, R. (2015). Family policies and single parent poverty in 18 OECD countries, 1978–2008. *Community, Work & Family*, *18*(4), 395–415.

Maslow, A. H. (1954) *Motivation and personality*. New York: Harper & Row.

Masten, A. S., & Reed, M. G. J. (2002). Resilience in development. *Handbook of Positive Psychology*, *74*, 88.

Matthews, P., & Besemer, K. (2015). Social networks, social capital and poverty: Panacea or placebo? *Journal of Poverty and Social Justice*, *23*(3), 189–201.

McCubbin, H. I., McCubbin, M. A., Thompson, A. I., Sae-Young, H., & Allen, C. T. (1997). Families under stress: What makes them resilient. *Journal of Family and Consumer Sciences*, *89*(3), 2.

Morland, K., Wing, S., Roux, A. D., & Poole, C. (2002). Neighborhood characteristics associated with the location of food stores and food service places. *American Journal of Preventive Medicine*, *22*(1), 23–29.

Morris, M. H. (2020). The liability of poorness: Why the playing field is not level for poverty entrepreneurs, *Poverty and Public Policy, 12*(3), 304–315.

Morris, M. H., Webb, J. W., Fu, J., & Singhal, S. (2013). A competency-based perspective on entrepreneurship education: Conceptual and empirical insights. *Journal of Small Business Management*, *51*(3), 352–369.

Morris, M. H., Santos, S. C., & Neumeyer, X. (2018). *Poverty and entrepreneurship in developed economies*. Edward Elgar Publishing.

Morris, M. H., Soleimanof, S., & Tucker, R. (2022). Drivers of fragility in the ventures of poverty entrepreneurs. *Small Business Economics*, 1–19.

Muradian, R. (2019). Frugality as a choice vs. frugality as a social condition. Is de-growth doomed to be a Eurocentric project? *Ecological Economics*, *161*, 257–260.

Nakara, W. A., Messeghem, K., & Ramaroson, A. (2021). Innovation and entrepreneurship in a context of poverty: A multilevel approach. *Small Business Economics*, *56*(4), 1601–1617.

Nussbaum, M., & Sen, A. (Eds.). (1993). *The quality of life*. Clarendon Press.

Orfield G, & Lee, C. 2005. *Why segregation matters: Poverty and educational inequality*. Cambridge, MA: Civil Rights Project, Harvard University.

Pare, P. P., & Felson, R. (2014). Income inequality, poverty and crime across nations. *The British Journal of Sociology*, *65*(3), 434–458.

Payne, R. K., Devol, P., & Smith, T. D. (2012). *Bridges out of poverty*. Highlands, TX: Aha! Process.

Reutter, L. I., Stewart, M. J., Veenstra, G., Love, R., Raphael, D., & Makwarimba, E. (2009). "Who do they think we are, anyway?": Perceptions of and responses to poverty stigma. *Qualitative Health Research*, *19*(3), 297–311.

Rönkkö, R., Rutherford, S., & Sen, K. (2022). The impact of the COVID-19 pandemic on the poor: Insights from the Hrishipara diaries. *World Development*, *149*, 105689.

Saito, M. (2003). Amartya Sen's capability approach to education: A critical exploration. *Journal of Philosophy of Education*, *37*(1), 17–33.

Sen A. (1987). *The standard of living*. (Hawthorne G). Cambridge: Cambridge University Press.

Sen, A. (1999). *Development as Freedom*. New York: Alfred A. Knopf.

Shane, S. (2009). Why encouraging more people to become entrepreneurs is bad public policy. *Small Business Economics*, *33*, 141–149.

Sheehy-Skeffington, J. & Rea, J. (2017). How poverty affects people's decision-making processes. York, UK: Joseph Rowntree Foundation. https://discovery.ucl.ac.uk/id/eprint/10186609/1/how-poverty-affects-peoples-decision-making-processes.pdf.

Silverman, R. M. (2011). Black real estate professionals' perceptions of career opportunities: The economic Detour Redux. *The Review of Black Political Economy*, *38*(2), 145–163.

Smith-Hunter, A. E., & Boyd, R. L. (2004). Applying theories of entrepreneurship to a comparative analysis of white and minority women business owners. *Women in Management Review*, *19*(1), 18–28.

Van Agt, H. M., Stronks, K., & Mackenbach, J. P. (2000). Chronic illness and poverty in the Netherlands. *The European Journal of Public Health*, *10*(3), 197–200.

Wachs, M. (2010). Transportation policy, poverty, and sustainability: History and future. *Transportation Research Record*, *2163*(1), 5–12.

Walsh, F. (1998). *Strengthening family resilience*. New York: Guilford.

Waxman, C. (1983). *The stigma of poverty: A critique of poverty theories and policies*. New York: Pergamon Press.

Wilson, W. J. (1996). *When work disappears*. New York: Vintage Books.

Wilson, W. J. (2012). *The truly disadvantaged: The inner city, the underclass, and public policy.* Chicago: University of Chicago Press.

Wiwad, D., Mercier, B., Piff, P. K., Shariff, A., & Aknin, L. B. (2021). Recognizing the impact of COVID-19 on the poor alters attitudes towards poverty and inequality. *Journal of Experimental Social Psychology*, *93*, 104083.

Chapter Three

Types of Ventures and the Poverty Entrepreneur

The preoccupation when it comes to entrepreneurship tends to be with aggressive growth businesses that scale rapidly and turn the founders into billionaires. These are ventures, such as Uber, Coinbase, and Amazon, that represent exciting success stories and which made many people rich. Scholars, educators, policy experts, and politicians are enamored with this kind of entrepreneurial activity because of its significant impact on job creation, innovation, and economic development. The roots of the focus on this type of entrepreneurship lie in the work of the economist Joseph Schumpeter in the early part of the 20th century, whose concept of the entrepreneur emphasized a kind of hero who disrupts the status quo, makes existing approaches obsolete, and creates entirely new industries (Schumpeter, 1934).

In reality, this type of entrepreneurial activity is extremely rare. Across the globe millions of people start businesses every year, and hardly any of them rapidly scale in terms of size and scope. While it is understandable that they generate a lot of excitement from those interested in economic development, they actually represent less than 1% of all startups. It is not just that they almost never happen, but it is impossible to know in advance which new startups will be the ones that achieve this kind of impressive growth. So betting on them is a huge gamble. They are high-risk undertakings which, in the instances where they actually succeed, can generate very high returns. They are started very rarely, and even more rarely by those from poverty and severely disadvantaged circumstances.

A very interesting question concerns what the other 99% of startup enterprises look like. In this chapter, we explore the four main types of businesses created by entrepreneurs: survival, lifestyle, managed growth, and aggressive growth. Characteristics of each of these are identified, including the kinds of skills and resources required for a given type. We focus extensively on which of these types of ventures tend to be created by people in poverty circumstances, and why. It is also argued that there is a path dependency, such that the type of business one starts involves decisions that make it hard to subsequently transition the business into a different type.

Finally, it is likely that the nature of the ventures launched by low-income entrepreneurs has significant implications for their individual welfare. We explore how both integral human development and personal well-being are affected in different ways and to varied degrees depending on the type of business being created.

THE FOUR TYPES OF VENTURES LAUNCHED BY ENTREPRENEURS

There is tremendous diversity among the businesses created by entrepreneurs. Even two businesses of the same type (e.g., two hair salons) can be quite different from one another. Yet, it is possible to identify general categories of new ventures based on similarities in their basic underlying characteristics. Our focus here is on ventures in their emergent stages, typically during the first five to seven years of existence. This is the period of time over which a new venture is conceptualized and created, mistakes are made, learning occurs, adjustment and adaptation take place, systems may be implemented, and a sustainable business model may take root and allow for growth. Hence, we are concentrating on ventures from inception through the point at which they become sustainable or fail, and have settled on a particular growth mode.

As illustrated in Table 3.1, we emphasize four primary types of entrepreneurial firms (Morris, Neumeyer, & Kuratko, 2015). These include survival ventures, lifestyle ventures, managed growth ventures, and aggressive growth ventures. This typology is relatively parsimonious in the number of categories included while at the same time allowing for the identification of venture types that are meaningfully different. The categories are, for the most part, mutually exclusive while also being collectively exhaustive. Further, each of these venture types has received attention from scholars, with survival ventures receiving the least amount of attention.

The differences among the four types of ventures become clearer if we compare them using fourteen key variables:

a. *annual growth rate*: to what extent does the entrepreneur seek growth and how fast do they strive to grow?
b. *time horizon:* how immediate-, short-, intermediate-. or long-term does the entrepreneur's outlook tends to be when planning and making business decisions?

Table 3.1: The Four Types of Entrepreneurial Ventures

	Survival	*Lifestyle*	*Managed Growth*	*Aggressive Growth*
Annual growth rate	Nominal	<5%	10-15%	>20%
Time commitment	Part-to full-time	40+ hours per week	60+ hours per week	70+ hours per week
Time horizon	Day to day	Monthly	1-3 years	2-5 years
Key resources	Few, limited, physical, simple	Simple, physical, basic technology	Complex, physical & intangible, technological	Complex, intangible, intellectual, technology-centric
Facilities	Home-based	Premises or home-based, 1–2 locations	Premises with 3 to 30 or more locations throughout region	Significant facilities across country or globally
Management focus	Selling whatever one has	Maintain working business model	Incremental strategic growth	Scalability at rapid pace
Management style	Reactive	Tactical	Strategic	Strategic and proactive
Innovation / risk-taking	Very low	Low	Moderate	High
Technology investment	None	Limited	Moderate	High
Source of finance	Self, family	Self, family & friends, banks	Self, family and friends, banks, private investors	Banks, angel investors, venture capital, private equity firms, IPOs
Exit approach	Close down	Close, sell, transfer	Sell, merge, transfer	Sell, merge, go public
Business skills	Making, selling	Operational skills, planning, organizing	Planning, strategizing, delegating, leveraging	Planning, innovating, cash flow management, negotiation
Structure	Little to none	Simple	Functional, centralized	Complex, product & market based
Economic motives	Sustain one's family	Make a decent living	Wealth creation, legacy	Significant wealth creation
Reward emphasis	Weekly income taken from business	Salary, bonus	Salary, performance incentives, equity	Salary, equity, capital gain

Source: Adapted from Morris, M. H., and Kuratko, D.F. (2020), *What Do Entrepreneurs Create*, Edward Elgar Publishing.

c. *key resource requirements:* how simple and inexpensive versus complex and more costly are the key resources that enable the business to create value and serve customers?
d. *nature of premises:* is the business run from home, a vehicle, a stall or from dedicated business premises, and how many locations does the business have?
e. *managerial focus:* while there are always multiple issues to be addressed, what is the primary focus of the entrepreneur in attempting to manage the business?
f. *management style:* to what extent is the entrepreneur running the business in a more reactive, tactical, strategic, or proactive manner?
g. *management skills:* what key skills are critical for successfully running the business?
h. *entrepreneurial orientation:* how much emphasis is being placed on innovation, risk-taking, and proactive behaviors in developing the business?
i. *technology investment:* to what extent are investments in technology critical for business development?
j. *sources of finance:* from where does the entrepreneur obtain capital to run the business?
k. *company structure:* how formalized, functional, and complex is the structure of the business?
l. *economic motives:* what is the entrepreneur seeking from the business in terms of income or financial return?
m. *reward emphasis:* how does the entrepreneur extract returns from the business?
n. *exit approach:* what are the primary options when the entrepreneur is ready to leave the business?

This list of variables covers multiple dimensions of the enterprise, including aspects of strategy, structure, and management. Importantly, the inclusion of firm growth rate is central, but the growth that occurs is likely a by-product of some of the other variables (e.g., motives, resources, skills, managerial orientation, investment in technology). The importance of these other variables is suggested by contemporary research in entrepreneurship (e.g., Boso et al., 2013; Bradley et al., 2011; Covin & Slevin, 1989; Langlois, 2007; Naldi & Davidsson, 2014; Perez-Luno et al., 2011). Let us further consider each of the four types, and explore their relevance when it comes to businesses started by the poor.

Survival Ventures

Survival ventures are the ones disproportionately created by those in poverty conditions. These are businesses that provide basic subsistence for the entrepreneur and his or her family, in effect allowing for little more than a hand-to-mouth type of existence. The business may or may not be formally registered, and typically has no premises, very few assets, no business banking relationship, and operates on a cash or barter basis. The entrepreneur is often the only employee, although family members may help out and casual laborers (informal workers who are paid when there is work, usually in cash) may be used when needed. The limited financial investment in the business comes from the entrepreneur, family members, and friends. Examples of survival ventures include a lawncare service, handyman, mobile automobile detailer, roadside fruit stand, street vendor, maker of crafts, small caterer, personal trainer, Uber driver, dog walker, masseuse, or a home-based childcare, laundry, or cleaning service.

The survivalist will have a lower entrepreneurial orientation and so places little emphasis on innovation or risk-taking. Their skills generally center on producing the product or service and selling it. Other business-related skills and knowledge are lacking. They attempt to sell what they can produce, and production capacity is limited as the entrepreneur is doing virtually all of the work, has little in the way of equipment, and lacks technology. The entrepreneur is so busy working "in the business" that he or she has little time to strategize or plan (i.e., working "on the business"). As a result, the managerial approach is more reactive with a focus on the short-term.

As the business exists to provide for basic personal financial needs, once costs are covered there is usually no money left to reinvest into the venture. The venture might be started out of necessity, as conventional employment opportunities are limited or unattractive, or started as an augmented source of income (sometimes referred to as a side hustle). The business typically operates in highly competitive, price-based, and largely undifferentiated markets. These tend to be microenterprises with marginal returns, and also include many unregistered or informal sector businesses (Hall et al., 2012; Sutter et al., 2019; Webb et al., 2009). When it comes to exit strategies, these businesses are usually shut down or otherwise cease to exist.

Despite their marginal nature, survival ventures often prove to be quite resilient. Not only do such ventures provide a basic income to many millions of people in both developed and developing economies, in developing nations they often produce a meaningful proportion of a country's GDP (Commission on the Private Sector and Development, 2004; Prahalad, 2005).

Lifestyle Ventures

While less prevalent than survival businesses when it comes to the poor, a number of low-income people are able to launch lifestyle ventures. These are businesses that provide a relatively stable income stream for owners based on a workable business model and a maintenance approach to management. Hence, they provide for a decent lifestyle. Although the entrepreneur is generating an income, no one is getting rich. The business produces enough profit that modest reinvestments can be made into facilities, equipment, marketing, inventory, and to hire staff. This reinvestment enables the enterprise to maintain its competitiveness in a local market where the firm is embedded. The venture frequently has premises, but could be home-based. It usually operates from one or two locations, and does not seek meaningful expansion. Hence, it is not adding locations, entering new markets, or developing major new products. Once a stable business model is established, the number of employees remains relatively constant. Given limited capacity, it is difficult for the venture to achieve economies in operations. Examples of lifestyle businesses include a local bar or restaurant, hair salon, small machining business, hardware store, auto repair shop, toy store, independent movie theatre, small accounting firm, local taxi company, or the owner of a single franchise.

A lifestyle business tends to demonstrate, at most, a moderate entrepreneurial orientation. Innovation may occur, but it is not usually an area of emphasis and tends to involve incremental improvements to existing products or services. The business sells mainstream goods and services in existing markets, and is usually not engaged in high risk (or high return) undertakings. Functional business skills (marketing, bookkeeping, logistics, customer service, operations, inventory management) are the priority. The focus tends to be on serving local markets and countering both local competitors and national players operating in local markets. The planning horizon is one to two years, and the orientation of the firm tends to be tactical, engaging in short term moves to remain competitive.

The key to a lifestyle business is that, once the entrepreneur figures things out and has a working business model that generates some modicum of consistent profits, it becomes more of a maintenance operation. For instance, the restaurant or store or small construction company identifies a formula that works, and may make periodic adjustments and improvements, but otherwise maintains the working business model. The employee base remains fairly constant. The entrepreneur finds ways to incrementally improve sales from a fairly fixed operation. In terms of exit, the business is either sold off, passed on to a family member, or shut down.

Managed Growth Ventures

Rarely launched by the poor, although often aspired to, managed growth ventures develop a workable business model and then seek steady growth over time, as reflected in occasional launches of new products or new lines of business, periodic entry into new markets, a steady expansion of facilities, locations and staff, and development of a strong local and regional brand. Ongoing reinvestment in the business and continuous but controlled growth guide ongoing business development. Examples could include a custom boat manufacturer, third-party logistics company, charter jet business, multi-location walk-in medical clinics, or a regional law firm, real estate company, marketing agency, and auto dealership.

Consider a person who earns commissions selling real estate for a large national realty. Tired of having someone else make money from her sales efforts, she quits and starts her own real estate company. Initially opening a single office and subsequently hiring a handful of other real estate agents, over time she adds additional offices in the same town. After twelve years she has fifteen locations in seven cities throughout the region, and has established both a residential and a commercial division. This is a classic case of a managed growth business, as the entrepreneur wants to expand, but at a steady pace. The entrepreneurial orientation and risk-profile are higher than with a lifestyle business, as reflected in the quest for ongoing growth. The entrepreneur is more strategic, looking for new opportunities and planning five or more years ahead.

With managed growth businesses, the key is the ability to not over-extend oneself. Steady, ongoing growth places continuous cash flow pressures on the business. There is the cost of new locations, additional employees, and increased marketing. Just as important is the ability to create the infrastructure necessary to support an expanding operation, including systems, structures, and processes. Regular incorporation of new technologies helps to enhance capabilities and improve operational efficiencies. Successful managed growth entrepreneurs are frequently able to accumulate considerable wealth. These firms are frequently targets for acquisition by larger companies.

Aggressive Growth Ventures

The discipline of entrepreneurship is preoccupied with so-called gazelles, or aggressive growth ventures, which, unfortunately, are rarely started by the poor and disadvantaged. These businesses are often technology-based with strong innovation capabilities that seek exponential growth and are funded by equity capital. Launch of the venture is opportunity-driven, with the founders (often a team) seeking to transform industries and create markets with breakthrough new products and services. The focus is typically national or international in scope. Examples include Amazon, Facebook, Under Armour, SpaceX, Applied Optoelectronics, Avedro, Baidu, Eventbrite, FITBIT, LinkedIn, Nexeon, and Restore Health.

Aggressive growth firms create large numbers of new jobs, many of them highly skilled types of positions that are well-paying. They produce tremendous amounts of intellectual property, as reflected in a large volume of patents. These are high-risk and high-return ventures that either end up losing many millions of dollars of investors' money, or making the founding team, initial employees, and investors very wealthy. They receive money from venture capitalist firms and other equity investors, often at a fairly early stage of development, without which they could not achieve the kind of explosive growth that is mandated. These investors place high expectations on the founding team to produce explosive growth, often forcing them out of the business if they fail to do so. The environment inside these firms tends to be dynamic, experimental, and highly stressful in the early years. Once an initial market position is established, the scale of operations begins to expand exponentially. Those involved are racing to develop the infrastructure needed to support this kind of growth. When successful, these firms often become candidates for initial public offerings or acquisition.

IMPLICATIONS OF THE FOUR VENTURE TYPES FOR THOSE IN POVERTY

Two of these categories experience relatively little growth or expansion, while the other two expand, but to differing degrees. Assessments of the emerging venture landscape suggest that survival and lifestyle businesses constitute as much as 85% of the new enterprises launched in developed economies, and an even higher percentage in developing economies, reinforcing the idea that most new businesses start small and remain small (Dennis, 2011; Kauffman Foundation, 2019). Managed growth ventures represent almost 15% of start-ups, while aggressive growth firms make up less than 1%. However, managed growth and aggressive growth ventures together are responsible for a disproportionate amount of employment and wealth creation (Birch, 1987; Malchow-Møller et al., 2011).

The fact that low-income entrepreneurs start an even higher proportion of survival and lifestyle businesses can be traced to a number of characteristics of the poverty experience (see Chapter 2). Getting any sort of venture off the ground is a considerable achievement when dealing with some combination of literacy challenges, severe resource scarcity, chronic health challenges, limited social networks, and food, housing, and physical insecurity, among other factors. Under such circumstances, the kinds of opportunities the entrepreneur is able to recognize, the amount of time available to focus on the business, and the ability to plan and think strategically may be severely compromised. Let us further consider the difficulties these individuals have with the creation of growth-oriented enterprises.

The creation of aggressive growth businesses requires access to resources that are far removed from a person in poverty circumstances. The technologies, talent pools, logistical capabilities, distribution channels, and legal expertise that enable a venture to scale are complex and expensive. Some of these resources are controlled by elite institutions. The poor can also experience various forms of discrimination based on their race, educational background, communication abilities, and life experiences. Most fundamentally, the limited social networks of the poor make it extremely difficult to connect with major sources of investment capital.

Poverty conditions also work against the creation of managed growth businesses. First, many of the businesses started by the poor operate in highly competitive industries, such that growth is especially challenging. Second, the steady expansion of a restaurant, accounting agency, skin care product business, or cleaning company to new locations and markets is time consuming and requires planning, strong financial management capabilities, and the ability to take on debt. It demands enhanced skills in marketing, people management, and customer service. Building upon and expanding one's network and then leveraging that network to open doors, gain access, and get approvals and support are instrumental in the steady expansion of a business.

Accordingly, the result is a disproportionate number of survival and lifestyle businesses. It is not that those in poverty and disadvantaged conditions do not aspire to create higher growth businesses. Their dreams are often quite big. Rather, conditions of scarcity lead to compromises in the resources they can muster and the manner in which these resources can be deployed. Even where they can obtain resources, the ability to convert these resources into outcomes is constrained by their capabilities.

The institutional environment also tends to work against the poor. While it may be understandable, the preoccupation among scholars, government officials, economic development professionals, and others with growth-oriented ventures has had unintended consequences for those in poverty conditions. Where the priority is technology-centric, growth-oriented entrepreneurship when designing public policies, developing local ecosystems, and managing the financial system, the needs of the ventures of the poor can be ignored. In some instances, these elements can actually discourage or work against poverty entrepreneurs (Morris & Tucker, 2021; Neumeyer, Santos, & Morris, 2019). Even educational systems can reflect a bias toward a type of entrepreneurship not generally pursued by low-income and disadvantaged individuals (Morris, Kuratko, & Cornwall, 2013).

For the person attempting to start a hair salon, junk hauling service, catering business, or roofing company, the institutional environment does less to facilitate, and sometimes more to hinder, their success (see Chapters 13 and 14). The legal and regulatory mandates, tax structures, funding mechanisms, training and mentoring programs, incubation opportunities, and forms of technical assistance are not designed to address their needs and circumstances.

DIFFERENCES BETWEEN VERSUS AMONG THE TYPES

The population of businesses that make up a particular type of venture (e.g., survival ventures) is not homogeneous. Considerable differences can be found among the ventures of a particular type. For instance, within any of the four categories, differences can usually be found in the cost structures, skills necessary to produce the products and services, market focus, revenue models, competitive intensity, and the profit potential of the venture.

These "within-type" differences can be seen if we examine three survival ventures: a cleaning business, a small shop that sells wigs and hairpieces, and a maker of artistic baby bibs. The cleaning business is home-based, labor-intensive, carries a small inventory of cleaning supplies, uses the client's equipment, has two relatives who help do the cleaning, is paid in cash, has virtually no fixed costs, and makes money from serving repeat customers on a scheduled basis. The wig shop has premises, carries inventory, involves less physical labor, has a number of one-time customers, and finds most customers paying with credit cards. The baby bib maker also works from home, has three sewing machines, no employees, is struggling to get her bibs into local stores, and so sells directly to her personal network and at farmers' markets, maintains little inventory, and spends so much of her time making the bibs she has little time for marketing, bookkeeping, sourcing, and other business activities.

Yet, despite their differences, the commonalities among these three business are far greater. All struggle with differentiation, are engaged in laborious work where the entrepreneur must do everything, have limited production capacity, and cannot afford key equipment or technology. In addition, all struggle in penetrating mainstream markets, rely on low-cost marketing (social media, fliers, word-of-mouth), and tend to price too low. They do not maintain proper bookkeeping systems, have difficulties properly costing their products or services, and experience constant cash flow problems. Further, they either work alone or have casual laborers to help out, but no formal employees. The businesses are operated in a more reactive than strategic manner, and there is little room for planning.

Alternatively, the "between-type" differences are so significant that each type represents a truly distinct phenomenon. The underlying variables that define each category, when combined, produce a unique and distinctive quality. These distinct qualities have major implications. The uniqueness becomes apparent when we examine ventures from each category operating within the same industry. Let us continue by building upon the example above of a cleaning company.

Let's call our survival business Claire's Cleaners, and compare it to Lincolnstreet Commercial Cleaning, a lifestyle business, Johnson Bio-clean Services, a managed growth business, and Mighty Maids, an aggressive growth business. We described Claire's Cleaners as home-based and cash-based. A sole proprietorship with a focus on residential clients, Claire does much of the cleaning herself and uses her own car to get to customer locations. She relies on family members when she has more work and needs help. Having little equipment of her own, Claire uses the mops, vacuum cleaners, and supplies of her clients and rents some equipment. The business serves less than ten customers each week, and has no written contracts with any of them. New business comes from referrals, and little formal marketing is done. She does the bookkeeping, although her financial records are incomplete. She has no business insurance and does not have a business bank account. Claire does not pay herself a salary, but takes money out of the business for personal use when she can. Claire is a single mom, and also has a part-time job on weekends to make ends meet.

Lincolnstreet Commercial operates in the same town as Claire, but focuses on cleaning offices, retail stores, and commercial buildings. Also founded by an entrepreneur who comes from poverty circumstances, it has taken thirteen years to get the business where it is today. Employing 13 employees (8 full-time and 4 part-time cleaners and an office manager who also keeps the books), the company is able to offer them basic healthcare benefits. With a small office, it owns two vans to transport the cleaners and a mix of basic cleaning equipment and supplies. Month-to-month, six-month, or twelve-month contracts exist with most of their customers. Marketing activities include a company website and business Facebook page (with occasional posts), brochures mailed to local businesses, some cold calls on businesses, and visits by the owner to business networking events. The company carries two insurance policies. It has a business banking account and business credit card, and many customers pay electronically. Profits are steady but moderate, but the entrepreneur pays herself a decent salary, and reinvests between $4,000 and $7,000 a year back into the business. While the founder has considered adding a third van and more cleaning crews, she is not certain the local market, which is quite competitive, would warrant this.

Johnson Bio-clean offers specialized cleaning and sanitizing services to medical facilities of all types. Created and initially financed by three partners, one of whom grew up in poverty, the business is certified as woman-owned and veteran-owned. The company has grown steadily over ten years from a single location in Claire's hometown to locations in eight cities located within 75 miles. This growth has been financed from profits and a series of bank loans. The company and its employees have multiple certifications, and the staff receive ongoing training. It has developed its own patient-centered cleaning approach, and is able to adapt to the cleaning protocols of the different medical facilities being served. JB-C has 125 employees, 115 of which are organized into multiple cleaning teams operating out of each of its locations. Some of the teams specialize in particular types of facilities and tasks. The company has a fleet of trucks and vans, and an array of basic and specialty equipment, materials, and supplies that are kept in inventory at each location. With a strong regional brand and a growing promotional budget, marketing efforts include a strategic mix of personal selling carried out by three salespeople, together with advertisements in targeted publications, appearances at regional healthcare conferences, and a strong online presence. The company has invested in technology and equipment to support job performance, scheduling, communications, hiring, training, client feedback, expense reporting, payroll, and a number of other administrative functions.

Also founded in Claire's hometown, Mighty Maids offers a range of cleaning services tailored to individual client needs and requests. The founder built the company around a unique operating model, which focuses on professionalism and consistency with a personal touch. She set the business up as a franchise system that specializes in residential cleaning. It has grown to include 50 company-owned locations and 1,150 franchises (with 400 of these based in the U.S. and the remainder in five other countries). Collectively, all the locations employ over 6,000 employees who clean over 225,000 residences each month. The company only uses eco-friendly equipment and cleaning products. Mighty Maids provides extensive training, mentoring, marketing, communications, and operations infrastructure as well as financing support to the franchisees. The company has developed its own proprietary software that integrates all facets of a franchisee's business operations, including office management, scheduling, payroll, bookkeeping, goal setting, and performance tracking. The company is an attractive acquisition candidate, and has received proposals for buyouts from three different organizations.

While operating in the same industry, these four companies could not be more different. Each is unique in terms of how they operate, with what resources, who they serve and are trying to reach, how they define success, the key challenges they confront, and where they want to go. These differences reinforce the reasons why managed growth and aggressive growth ventures are so rarely started by people in poverty.

THE DIFFICULTY IN MOVING A VENTURE FROM ONE CATEGORY TO ANOTHER

It is tempting to assume that the four categories of ventures represent a logical continuum along which a given venture can move over time. Hence, whatever type the entrepreneur starts, one assumes that, with time, it could transition into a different type, such that a survival business becomes a lifestyle business, a lifestyle venture becomes a managed growth venture, and so forth. This would be especially useful for those in poverty circumstances, as it would suggest that, with proper assistance, they can transform any type of venture into something more profitable and growth-oriented. It is our contention, however, that this happens much less often than one might assume, such that this tendency is more the exception than the rule. The reality is that ventures of a given type tend to indefinitely remain as that type.

A new business can be thought of as a combination or bundle of resources (people, skills, money, equipment, facilities, intellectual property, and so forth). A resource has properties, including how valuable, rare, and easy to duplicate by others it is, and whether it can be substituted for it (Barney & Clark, 2007). The more valuable, rare, non-replicable, and non-substitutable the resource, the more its potential to provide a firm with competitive advantage. The nature of the resources the entrepreneur is able to acquire, combine, and deploy will differ significantly across the four types of ventures. They will vary in terms of their cost, sophistication, complexity, and productivity. With poverty entrepreneurs, they are only able to access low-cost, simple resources with limited productivity.

The mix of resources that the founder can attract serves to delimit what the venture is capable of producing, the kinds of opportunities it can capitalize upon, and what it can become. A path dependency is involved, meaning that the commitment to a particular mix of resources delimits the directions or pathways the entrepreneur is able to pursue. Once one is locked into particular resources, it becomes quite difficult, although possible, to pursue a markedly different pathway, particularly in terms of the growth trajectory of the business. For example, the resources necessary to build a successful survival business also tend to restrict the enterprise to being a survival business. Limits are placed on the kinds of resources the organization is able to subsequently acquire or exploit. The resources determine not only what the venture is able to accomplish, but also the way things are done, and the underlying nature of the organization. Thus, once the venture has committed to a resource path, it struggles to recognize, understand, acquire, and/or exploit the kinds of resources that would enable it to become a different type of venture. Further, it has taken on a certain identity, and changing that identity, or what is central, distinctive, and enduring about a business, is quite complicated (Morris et al., 2018; Shah & Tripsas, 2007).

Conceptually (and practically), we believe the distance to be travelled in moving from one type of venture to another gets greater as we move from survival to lifestyle, managed growth and then aggressive growth. Hence, it is less difficult to transform a survival business into a lifestyle business, but it becomes much more challenging to transform a lifestyle business into a managed growth venture, and it is exceedingly hard to go from managed to aggressive growth. Alternatively, while one can imagine a circumstance where a lifestyle venture declines to the point that it is really more of a survival venture, we generally believe a given venture thrives or fails as a particular type.

HOW THE VENTURE TYPES IMPACT THE INDIVIDUAL ENTREPRENEUR

The type of venture being created can have significant implications for the disadvantaged individual. Using the lens of integral human development, or the holistic development of the person, what the disadvantaged entrepreneur creates is apt to be directly associated with the ability to not just improve their financial situation, but grow holistically and have a better life. Here, we are speaking of *potential* development, as the venture is a platform, and its potential may or may not be realized by a given individual.

In Table 3.2, we summarize how each of the four types of ventures has the potential to affect the development and well-being of the poverty entrepreneur. We consider financial, social cultural, political, and spiritual development. When the entrepreneur creates a survival business, the venture creation experience can have a positive, but relatively nominal, impact on some of the dimensions of integral human development. The primary impact can include a very modest financial improvement, contributions to the development of one's self-concept and identity, and an enhanced basic skill set. However, as we move across the other three types, we see meaningful improvements across all the dimensions of integral human development. Their economic well-being and security, social networks and the nature of their social engagement, ability to leverage cultural assets and give back to their communities, development of a voice and an ability to access political platforms and influence issues, and their spiritual development and ability to find deeper

Table 3.2. Impact of Venture Type on Well-being of Poverty Entrepreneur

IHD Dimension	*Survival Venture*	*Lifestyle Venture*	*Managed Growth Venture*	*Aggressive Growth Venture*
economic/ financial	Potential for modest improvement; could also make person financially worse off	Potential to create stable income, move entrepreneur out of poverty	Potential to create wealth for entrepreneur, with enhanced opportunities for family	Potential to create extreme wealth for entrepreneur, provide financial security for next generation
social	Very limited expansion of the entrepreneur's social network; is held back by lack of social ties and social capital	Moderate expansion of social network and degree of social engagement; may be seen in one's immediate network as role model	Significant expansion of social network and ties, engagement in multiple social domains, becomes role model to larger audience	Transformative impact on social connections and relationships that can be leveraged across many social spheres; becomes major role model; also faces greater social expectations
cultural	Little ability to benefit from community's cultural assets	Embedded in local community, is able to appreciate and benefit somewhat from local cultural assets	Is able to leverage cultural assets across a larger geographic region and contribute to their enhancement	Significant ability to give back to community, leverage cultural assets, contribute to cultural richness
political	Limited voice, powerlessness, under-represented, nominal political access	Entrepreneur starts to develop a local voice and be heard, can achieve greater sense of local representation	Has fairly strong voice in local and regional affairs; can influence issues affecting local and regional poverty	Development of strong voice, with extensive access to platforms & means to channel one's voice regionally and nationally
spiritual	Some ability to find more meaning, develop identity as a business owner, reflect on personal development, but also has little time to reflect	Individual is able to develop meaning and clear identity as an entrepreneur, owner, employer, creator of value and taxpaying business	As a prominent regional player, creator of personal wealth and many jobs, yet tied to and able to give back to local or regional area, entrepreneur may be able to find spiritual meaning	Strong potential to seek deeper meaning; entrepreneur has created major wealth, a strong identity and reputation, transformed an industry, and is able to generously give back

meaning are all positively affected. The potential improvements markedly increase as one creates either a managed or aggressive growth venture.

This discussion highlights the critical importance of finding ways to help low-income entrepreneurs create more than survival ventures. Some of this centers on the extent to which their ventures fall into the commodity trap, which we shall explore in more depth in Chapter 9. Morris et al. (2023) have demonstrated that the well-being of entrepreneurs who come from poverty circumstances is positively associated with their ability to create well-differentiated businesses that can earn decent margins, expand their production capacity, and hire employees.

Finally, while the venture creation process provides opportunities for holistic growth, many successful entrepreneurs fail to take advantage of the possibilities. Particularly when pursuing continuous growth, self-development can be hindered by the very high levels of pressure and stress experienced by the entrepreneur, the total preoccupation with the venture to the exception of all else, and the material riches made possible through their ventures.

CONCLUSION

This chapter has explored the four main types of ventures created by entrepreneurs, their underlying nature, and their implications for the poverty entrepreneur. The poor disproportionately create survival and lifestyle ventures, and this tendency can be directly traced to key characteristics of the poverty experience. Moreover, once they create a certain type of venture, the business does not tend to evolve into a different and more promising venture type. To the extent that they start marginal ventures with severely limited potential, they frequently get caught in a circular trap that only serves to keep them in poverty. As such, the nature of the venture being created has direct implications for the potential of entrepreneurship to not only move an individual out of poverty, but to meaningfully contribute to his or her overall development and well-being. In future chapters we will more fully elaborate upon the causes of these more marginal businesses and the elements that are critical if the poor are to capitalize on the truly empowering potential of entrepreneurship.

REFERENCES

Barney, J. B., & Clark, D. N. (2007). *Resource-based theory: Creating and sustaining competitive advantage*. Oxford, UK: Oxford University Press.

Birch, D. G. (1987). Job creation in America: How our smallest companies put the most people to work. *University of Illinois at Urbana-Champaign's Academy for Entrepreneurial Leadership Historical Research Reference in Entrepreneurship.*

Boso, N., Story, V. M., and Cadogan, J. W. (2013). Entrepreneurial orientation, market orientation, network ties, and performance: Study of entrepreneurial firms in a developing economy. *Journal of Business Venturing, 28*(6), 708–727.

Bradley, S., Wiklund, J., and Shepherd, D. (2011). Swinging a double-edged sword: The effect of slack on entrepreneurial management and growth. *Journal of Business Venturing, 26*(5), 537–554.

Commission on the Private Sector and Development (2004). Unleashing entrepreneurship: Making business work for the poor. Report to the Secretary-General of the United Nations, New York: UNDP.

Covin, J. G., & Slevin, D. P. (1989). Strategic management of small firms in hostile and benign environments. *Strategic Management Journal, 10*(1), 75–87.

Dennis Jr., W. J. (2011). Entrepreneurship, small business and public policy levers. *Journal of Small Business Management, 49*(1), 92–106.

Hall, J., Matos, S., Sheehan, L., & Silvestre, B. (2012). Entrepreneurship and innovation at the base of the pyramid: A recipe for inclusive growth or social exclusion? *Journal of Management Studies, 49*(4), 785–812.

Kauffman Foundation (2019). *America's new business plan*. https://www.kauffman.org/currents/americas-new-business-plan-expands-what-it-means-to-be-pro-business/

Langlois, R. N. (2007). The entrepreneurial theory of the firm and the theory of the entrepreneurial firm. *Journal of Management Studies, 44*(7), 1107–1124.

Malchow-Møller, N., Schjerning, B., & Sørensen, A. (2011). Entrepreneurship, job creation and wage growth. *Small Business Economics, 36*, 15–32.

Morris, M. H., & Kuratko, D. F. (2020). *What do entrepreneurs create?: Understanding four types of ventures*. Cheltenham, UK: Edward Elgar Publishing.

Morris, M. H., Neumeyer, X., Jang, Y., & Kuratko, D. F. (2018). Distinguishing types of entrepreneurial ventures: An identity-based perspective. *Journal of Small Business Management, 56*(3), 453–474.

Morris, M. H., Neumeyer, X., & Kuratko, D. F. (2015). A portfolio perspective on entrepreneurship and economic development. *Small Business Economics, 45*, 713–728.

Morris, M. H., & Tucker, R. (2021). Poverty and entrepreneurship in developed economies: Re-assessing the roles of policy and community action. *Journal of Poverty, 25*(2), 97–118.

Morris, M. H., Kuratko, D. F., & Cornwall, J. R. (2013). *Entrepreneurship programs and the modern university*. Edward Elgar Publishing.

Naldi, L., & Davidsson, P. (2014). Entrepreneurial growth: The role of international knowledge acquisition as moderated by firm age. *Journal of Business Venturing, 29*(5), 687–703.

Neumeyer, X., Santos, S. C., & Morris, M. H. (2019). Who is left out: Exploring social boundaries in entrepreneurial ecosystems. *The Journal of Technology Transfer, 44*, 462–484.

Perez-luno, A., Wiklund, J., and Cabrera, R. V. (2011). The dual nature of innovative activity: How entrepreneurial orientation influences innovation generation and adoption. *Journal of Business Venturing, 26*(5), 555–571.

Prahalad, C. K. (2005). *The fortune at the bottom of the pyramid: Eradicating poverty through profits*. Upper Saddle River, NJ: Wharton School Publishing.

Schumpeter, J. (1934). *The theory of economic development*. Cambridge, MA: Harvard University Press.

Shah, S. K., & Tripsas, M. (2007). The accidental entrepreneur: The emergent and collective process of user entrepreneurship. *Strategic Entrepreneurship Journal*, *1*(1–2), 123–140.

Sutter, C., Bruton, G. D., & Chen, J. (2019). Entrepreneurship as a solution to extreme poverty: A review and future research directions. *Journal of Business Venturing*, *34*(1), 197–214.

Webb, J. W., Tihanyi, L., Ireland, R. D., & Sirmon, D. G. (2009). You say illegal, I say legitimate: Entrepreneurship in the informal economy. *Academy of Management Review*, *34*(3), 492–510.

Chapter Four

The Underlying Nature and Importance of Ventures of the Poor

As we saw in Chapter 3, the overwhelming majority of entrepreneurs, including virtually all of those who come from poverty conditions, do not build high growth, scalable ventures. They create something far less ambitious. Yet, the distinguished scholar Scott Shane (2009) has provocatively argued that the only ventures that matter are these dynamic, rapidly expanding enterprises. He goes so far as to suggest that government policies should only support these kinds of businesses and that devoting societal resources to other kinds of start-ups is a waste of money. This perspective has been echoed by many others (e.g., Erhardt, 2022; Lee, 2014; Stenholm, Acs, & Wuebker, 2013).

These arguments lead us to a question that is central to this book: *do the ventures of the poor matter?* Shane and others would argue that such ventures are inefficient, marginal, create few jobs or growth, fail at a high rate, and do not move people out of poverty (Acs & Kallas, 2008; Adebayo & Nassar, 2014; Doering & Wry, 2022; Kiggundu, 2002; Matos &Hall, 2021; Si et al., 2021; Zhao, 2009). Yet, there are those who conclude just the opposite, namely, that these ventures play a significant and positive role in the lives of those who come from poverty circumstances, and they contribute in important ways to the overall economy of a nation (Amorós et al., 2021; Banerjee et al., 2015; Santos, Costa, & Morris, 2022).

To understand the value of entrepreneurship when it comes to those in poverty, we must further examine the nature of the ventures created by these entrepreneurs. People in poverty are arbitrarily labeled as 'necessity entrepreneurs,' where it is assumed that they start businesses because they have no choice. Their businesses are assumed to heavily fall into the informal sector, or to be formalized survival ventures that struggle to generate any income, or are what some refer to as "side hustles." It has been argued that these ventures are often unable to grow because of something called the "commodity trap" (see Chapter 8).

In this chapter, we explore each of these distinctions. Implications are drawn from each for the efficacy of entrepreneurship as a solution to poverty. We demonstrate not only the importance of these ventures but also the different roles they can play in the lives of the poor. It is argued that the promise of entrepreneurship, when realized, is both significant and multi-faceted.

NECESSITY (PUSH) AND OPPORTUNITY (PULL) ENTREPRENEURSHIP

It is popular among entrepreneurship researchers and many economic development experts to distinguish between necessity-driven and opportunity-driven entrepreneurship. Largely ignored in entrepreneurship theory, necessity entrepreneurs pursue venture creation because they have no other viable alternatives. They are *pushed* into entrepreneurship. Either jobs are not available, or the available employment opportunities do not provide enough income. The individual might have been laid off, or otherwise find themselves in economic difficulty due to a death in the family, divorce, discrimination, incarceration, refugee status, a natural disaster, or some other adverse development. While it certainly is not always the case, necessity-driven entrepreneurs are assumed to create basic survival and lifestyle ventures that generate relatively low revenues and struggle to survive. High levels of necessity entrepreneurship have been observed in both developing (rates of over 45%) and developed (rates over 20%) economies (Poschke, 2013).

Alternatively, opportunity-driven entrepreneurs recognize an opportunity and start a business to capitalize on that opportunity. They are *pulled* into entrepreneurship by its attractiveness. They see a gap or opening in the marketplace and attempt to come up with a unique approach for capitalizing on that gap or opening. This kind of entrepreneurship is associated with businesses that aggressively grow, are scalable, and generate impressive returns. Again, this is not necessarily the case, as many so-called opportunity-driven businesses are simply successful lifestyle and managed growth ventures, and many of them fail.

The biggest problem with this distinction is its tendency to arbitrarily dichotomize all entrepreneurs when the distinctions among entrepreneurs are more nuanced. This overly simplistic categorization likely misses far more than it captures and reflects a certain naiveté in our understanding and approach. There certainly are people who pursue venture creation out of pure necessity, as well as those who start a venture to capitalize on a defined opportunity. However, a large proportion of those labeled as necessity entrepreneurs actually has some sort of opportunity in mind. A person who, out of necessity, starts a cleaning company may have in mind a fairly specific target audience or market niche that is either poorly served or not being served at all.

Some might argue that necessity entrepreneurs tend to go after established opportunities where there are already a number of competitors and entry barriers are quite low, while opportunity-driven entrepreneurs capitalize on new, untapped opportunities. Again, if we consider the data gathered on these two categories of entrepreneurs, it would appear that many of those labeled as opportunity-driven are pursuing opportunities that may not be all that new or novel, and where there are often existing competitors in some form. At a minimum, though, the opportunities pursued by necessity entrepreneurs are assumed to have limited revenue and profit potential, particularly relative to the ones pursued by their opportunity-driven counterparts. At the same time, opportunity-driven entrepreneurs vary considerably in how well-specified the opportunity is, with many of them relying on a very broadly or vaguely specified (and loosely quantified) conception.

What differs about them is their dominant motive for starting the business. A complication exists even here, as many of those categorized as necessity entrepreneurs have additional motives in mind (e.g., independence, creating jobs for others, supporting the community). At issue is whether the motive for starting is associated with outcomes. Do opportunity-driven entrepreneurs have a lower failure rate than necessity entrepreneurs? Do their firms perform better? While the available evidence suggests any differences in survival rates or performance may either be insignificant or more nuanced, there are serious methodological problems. A major challenge in this regard is the questionable manner in which necessity and opportunity entrepreneurship are measured, whether through large, ongoing data collection efforts such as the Global Entrepreneurship Monitor (GEM) or the research projects of individual scholars who generate their own measurements and data.

Despite these limitations, the distinction between necessity- and opportunity-driven does offer some useful insights, particularly when it comes to those in poverty conditions. Although the substantive research is limited, Table 4.1 provides key findings regarding necessity entrepreneurship and its important role in contemporary economies. At the same time, there is a mistaken tendency to conflate necessity-driven entrepreneurship with poverty entrepreneurship when we see these as distinct but overlapping categories. Those in poverty circumstances may indeed have fewer options, but many start businesses not out of pure necessity, but based on an opportunity. Many have dreams of creating something that will grow. A number of them start ventures on the side, and once the business is doing well enough, they leave their jobs to pursue the venture full time.

Table 4.1. Findings on Necessity Entrepreneurs

Necessity entrepreneurs are not well-understood. Controversies surround how these types of entrepreneurs are defined, and measurement challenges limit the research findings that might shed more light. Based on research by Poschke (2013) using data from the Global Entrepreneurship Monitor (GEM), a number of patterns can be observed.

1. 28.4% of business involved necessity entrepreneurs across all countries;
2. 52.4% of businesses in developing countries are necessity entrepreneurs, and this is traced to the presence of fewer economic opportunities;
3. The fraction of necessity entrepreneurs in a country is positively associated with the rate of entrepreneurship;
4. The fraction of necessity entrepreneurs is negatively associated with the gross domestic product (GDP) of a country;
5. Necessity entrepreneurs are likely to be less educated (particularly those having less than twelve years of education) than entrepreneurs in general;
6. Women are more likely to be necessity entrepreneurs, particularly in developing countries;
7. Necessity entrepreneurs run smaller firms (in terms of employees) and expect them to grow less;
8. The length of time necessity entrepreneurs are able to stay in business does not differ significantly from opportunity-driven entrepreneurs.

Source: Adapted from Poschke, M. (2013), "Entrepreneurs Out of Necessity: A Snapshot," *Applied Economics Letters*, 20, 658–663.

Further, not all necessity entrepreneurs are in poverty. Consider the mother with three children who has not worked for a number of years and is suddenly divorced or her spouse is incapacitated or passes away. Absent recent work experience or an updated skill set, and potentially without a lot of flexibility in her schedule, she is pushed into entrepreneurship. Or consider the middle-aged business manager who suddenly finds himself downsized or laid off, but based on the income he is used to making, there are no jobs. Another example is the disabled person that no one will hire. A wide variety of contextual factors can help explain the pursuit of entrepreneurship out of necessity.

To the extent that many poverty entrepreneurs actually do start ventures out of necessity, work by Dencker, Bacq, Gruber, and Haas (2021) has some important implications for understanding their experiences. These researchers argue that necessity entrepreneurs are focused on venture creation as a means to address basic physiological and safety needs within Maslow's (1954) hierarchy of needs. Alternatively, opportunity entrepreneurs start ventures to fulfill higher-order needs, such as belongingness, self-fulfillment, esteem, and the need for achievement. Further, the necessity entrepreneur in a developed country may be more concerned with meeting physiological or survival needs (e.g., food, clothing, shelter), while one in a developed country (where there is more of a social safety net) might be more focused on meeting basic security and stability needs (e.g., health, safety, property, employment).

When those in poverty start businesses out of necessity, they typically lack entrepreneurial experience and may have limited education. As a result, they begin the journey not only with little money but also with low human capital endowments (i.e., knowledge, skills, abilities). This limits the kinds of opportunities these entrepreneurs are able to recognize and their ability to exploit these opportunities (Morris, Santos, & Neumeyer, 2018). These limitations will be present in both developing and developed countries but are likely more marked in developing economies.

It has been hypothesized that the entrepreneur's approach to the venture creation process (and the potential of the venture being created) will be determined by the combination of: (a) whether the individual is focused more on addressing basic physiological versus higher-order safety needs; (b) how well-developed and supportive of new venture creation the institutional environment is; and (c) the extent to which the entrepreneur begins with low versus high levels of human capital (Dencker et al., 2021). While logical, our experience working with poor and disadvantaged entrepreneurs is that things are much more complex. Each of these variables can play an important role, but what is being created, and how, is the result of interactions among a much larger set of variables. Venture creation is an emergent process where both an entrepreneur and a business are being formed over time. This emergence is a function of an unpredictable sequence of events and how the individual processes them. It involves an ongoing experience of trying things, making errors, learning and adapting, and a series of doors that open and close as the entrepreneur becomes aware of new possibilities as things unfold (Morris, Pryor, & Schindehutte, 2012). Accordingly, it is very hard to generalize what the outcomes are going to be.

INFORMAL VERSUS FORMAL SECTOR VENTURES

Poverty is also associated with businesses in the so-called informal sector of the economy. This sector has two major components: (a) workers in organizations who do not have formal contractual relationships and therefore, are not subject to income taxation, labor laws, and social protections; and (b) self-employed individuals operating what are usually very small enterprises. The latter consists of unregistered start-up ventures that generally avoid many taxes and do not comply with many of the regulations governing how business must be conducted.

To suggest the informal economy is huge would be an understatement. According to the World Bank (2021), it contributes 50% or more of the GDP in many developing countries and as much as 20% of GDP in some developed nations. The numbers could be considerably higher, depending upon how we define the sector. From the perspective of overall entrepreneurial activity, the informal sector is the single biggest source of start-up activity across the globe. These businesses employ hundreds of millions of people, generate a large volume of goods and services, can serve as an incubator for entities that may eventually formalize, and represent an economic lifeline for a significant part of the population in virtually every country.

The amount of research on the informal sector pales in comparison to its importance, and this is even more the case when we talk about empirical research. The sector is treated far too often as being less significant, as an unfortunate by-product of poverty and lack of employment opportunities, and as being full of inefficient enterprises that fail at a high rate and add little real value to an economy. Although it is certainly true that many informal sector businesses struggle to generate much profit, and that most create few jobs beyond those of the founder and family members, the sheer scope and level of economic output from this sector suggests it should be a higher priority among scholars and policymakers.

Let us further consider the nature of informal sector businesses. We are typically talking about the production of legitimate goods and services through means that do not comply with legal rules or requirements. Further, the focus is usually on non-agricultural activity. Key criteria for counting a business as informal can include whether it is formally registered with government authorities or industry governance bodies, has licenses or permits to operate, has a bank account, maintains a bookkeeping system or proper records of economic activity, and/or pays taxes. One or more of these criteria might be applied depending on the country in question. It is a sector that resists measurement because these businesses are not reporting to, and prefer to be invisible when it comes to, government authorities.

There are, of course, plenty of informal businesses engaged in criminal or illicit activities, but these are not the focus when it comes to understanding the importance and value of this sector. In a study of what he calls the "underground economy" in the inner city, Venkatesh (2006) describes a vibrant business community consisting of a wide range of "off the books" ventures ranging from back alley car repair businesses, seamstresses, and waste pickers to hustlers, street vendors, artisans, and a homeless person who is not simply sleeping behind a building but actually providing a service as a night watchman. He notes that those involved see such activity not as illegal behavior but as work or as a business.

While many observers tend to dichotomize the formal and informal sectors, Newman (2018) argues we are really talking about a continuum or degrees of informality. Hence, an entrepreneur might not be formally registered, but pays some taxes, has a proper bookkeeping system and some kind of banking relationship (see also Darbi, Hall, & Knott, 2016). She discusses the potential for considerable overlap between the two sectors, which produces what she labels the semi-formal economy.

The nature of these different criteria, together with the notion of a continuum, combine to suggest the informal sector is quite heterogeneous. Kaveri Gill (2009), in a fascinating study of the poorest of the poor in India, describes a sector that is highly fragmented and segmented. These businesses can be subdivided based on the gender of the entrepreneur, performance (some generate significant profits, and many struggle just to cover costs), level of sophistication, whether they have a banking relationship, if they employ people outside the immediate family of the entrepreneur, whether they represent the principal source of income for the family, and the extent to which they are involved in production as opposed to providing a service or retail trading, among other distinguishing characteristics. Such fragmentation suggests there are different needs and behaviors among entrepreneurs across different segments of informal enterprises.

There is, as a generalization, a preoccupation among many scholars, policy experts and economic development professionals with moving informal businesses to the formal sector. So, the concern is primarily with their needs and requirements when it comes to getting them to formalize. Various incentives and disincentives are used to encourage this transition. However, a key question is whether our focus should be on getting these ventures to formalize or simply on helping them perform better as informal entities. One might argue that improving their performance enables these businesses to move to the formal sector. However, as Newman (2019) suggests, it may be that many enterprises will, for various reasons, permanently remain in the informal (or semi-formal) sector even as their performance improves. If so, we might expect a number of societal benefits to be derived from concentrating our efforts on understanding how to improve their ability to generate profits.

This issue of performance is yet another arena that is not well-understood. We know little about the distribution of performance levels across informal sector businesses in any given country, region, community, or industry category. In addition to the general lack of performance data, we might expect the relative importance of different performance metrics (e.g., sales, sales growth rate, net income, return on sales, inventory turnover, new accounts generated, jobs created, etc.) to vary depending upon the segment of the informal sector being examined. Beyond this, new insights are needed regarding the nature of informal sector businesses that perform better over time and why. In recent years, scholars have demonstrated the critical differences in performance based on such variables as gender (Olamide & Ogbechie, 2021), social capital (Akintimehin et al., 2019), amount of innovation (Avenyo & Kraemer-Mbula, 2021; Sharma & Kumar, 2019), and mastery of entrepreneurial competencies (Ibidunni, Ogundana, & Okonkwo, 2021). However, more work is needed to explore the roles of variables at different levels of analysis in driving performance. Examples of such variables include:

Individual level—how does success with an informal sector business vary based on demographics, place of birth, motives, literacies (functional, financial, technological), experience (including serial informal entrepreneurship), earnings and credit history, identity, networks, entrepreneurial alertness, and openness to learning among informal business founders?

Organizational level—do the entrepreneurial orientation, customer orientation, management practices, principal products and services, business models, differentiation strategies, and technologies employed within informal businesses make a difference?

Ecosystem level—does the availability of training, incubation, mentoring, microcredit, and other local resource support services affect outcomes for informal sector entrepreneurs?

Larger Institutional level—how do the educational, regulatory, taxation, rule of law, cultural, financial, technological, and religious environments in a given country affect informal sector firms?

We also need to better understand the nature of the disadvantages and advantages when operating within the informal sector and the extent to which these vary by national and local context. Researchers and others tend to focus on the obvious advantages (e.g., avoidance of taxation, fees and regulations) and disadvantages (e.g., access to capital and markets, conditions of insecurity and vulnerability). Yet, informality may offer subtler advantages that are not well understood. There is also a temporal dimension here because perceptions regarding the extent of particular advantages and disadvantages should be expected to change as an informal sector business evolves, establishes a stable customer base, builds its network, and involves more or fewer family members. Advancements in this area require that we develop new approaches to measuring the (economic and non-economic) benefits associated with advantages and costs associated with disadvantages.

In the final analysis, our interest in the performance of informal enterprises is tied to the ability of these ventures to provide a level of income that actually changes the entrepreneur's poverty circumstances for the better. However, the relationship between poverty alleviation and the informal sector is not well established. Canelas (2019) has demonstrated a dual relationship, where poverty both causes and results from informal sector activity. Hence, running an informal sector business could serve to keep a person in poverty. Alternatively, Malik (1996) argues the sector plays an important role in poverty alleviation, while Truong (2018) suggests the effect may be positive but is quite nominal. Another view is the informal enterprise serves to augment wages from employment (Tipple, 2005). Missing from the extant literature is sufficient evidence regarding longer-term patterns of the effect of informal businesses on family well-being.

The informal sector is a complex and dynamic phenomenon. We must avoid the tendency to over-simplify and over-generalize when it comes to this vibrant sector. Rather than denigrate these firms, marginalize their importance, or discourage their informal existence, it is time to celebrate and empower them. The sector represents a vast incubator. Empowering the sector to improve the lives of more people means improving the ability of these businesses to perform. Some may view this as a fool's errand and others may conclude that these businesses can only perform better if they formalize. Yet, as observers have come to recognize the potential of these "under the radar" businesses, a philosophy of encouraging them rather than forcing them to shut down or formalize has, to differing degrees, emerged in a number of countries (Bromley, 2013; Potts, 2008). Realizing the true potential of this sector requires both advancements in theory about informal entrepreneurship and rigorous research into the contextual factors that explain the outcomes generated by these ventures. This kind of evidence must guide the design and implementation of public policies, entrepreneurial support mechanisms, and intervention approaches.

SURVIVALIST VENTURES AND THE POOR

Chapter 3 distinguished four types of ventures: survival, lifestyle, managed growth, and aggressive growth. The poor disproportionately start survival ventures. These are the easiest ventures to start, and compared to the other venture categories, involve the lowest risk while generating the smallest returns. A study featuring 1,000 microbusiness owners in the United States found that half of them could survive just one month or less (i.e., 55% could cover just one month or less of business expenses using current savings), 30% had no savings, and 15% would be unable to cover a $1,000 emergency business expense (McKay, 2014). Despite their vulnerable nature, they can prove to be resilient in the face of adverse circumstances. They are able to make the most out of relatively little and can be quite creative at bootstrapping, bartering, sharing, and leveraging resources.

Survivalist ventures take a variety of forms. Common examples include: a vendor who sells goods (e.g., fresh vegetables, prepared foods, crafts, clothing) on the street or at public forums such as fairs and farmers' markets; people with skills related to a basic trade (e.g., house painting, massage, or graphic design) or that have knowledge related to some task (e.g., tour guide, math tutor, makeup artist, disk jockey) that they try to build a business around; providers of less-skilled but broadly demanded tasks (e.g., cleaning homes, lawn care, driving a vehicle); those with a hobby or personal interest (e.g., sewing quilts, designing logos, making candles) that find others will pay them for their product or service; and individuals owning an under-utilized asset (e.g., person who has a van and decides to provide transport

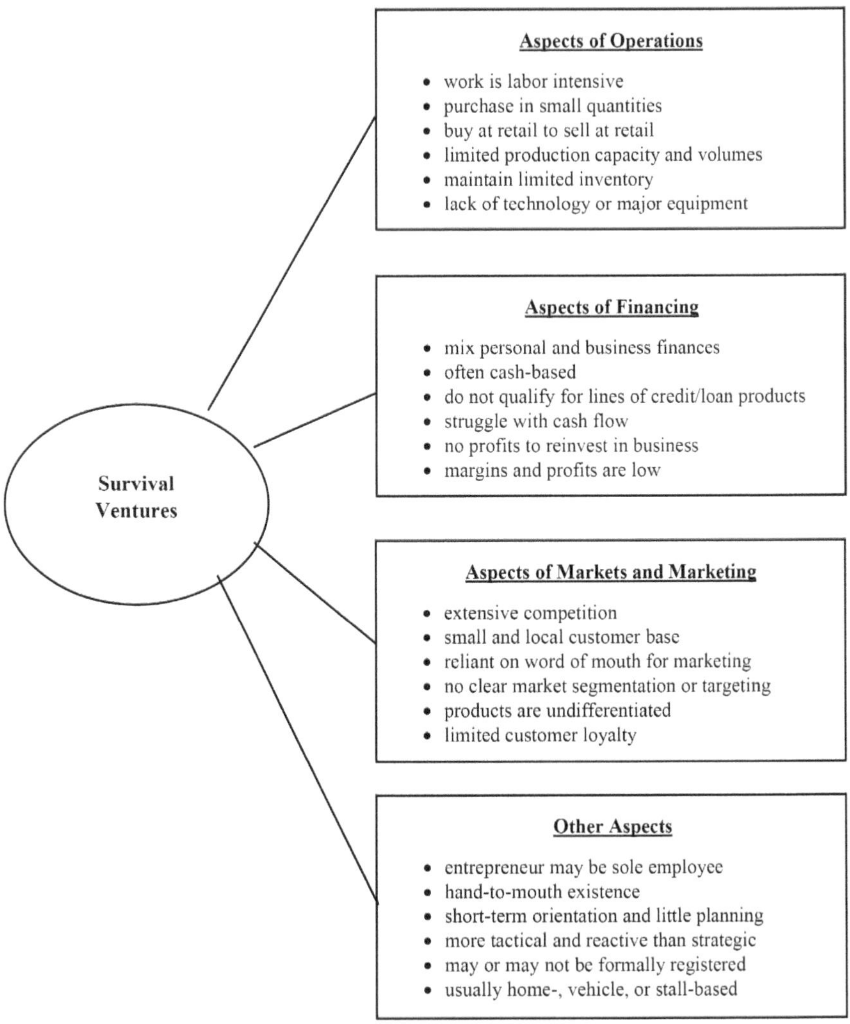

Figure 4.1. Understanding the Nature of Survival Ventures
Created by Authors

services; someone who is homebound but provides call center services to small businesses).

Although quite diverse, survivalist ventures share a number of critical characteristics (see Figure 4.1). They depend on the entrepreneur to run the business, but also to be the primary person doing the (labor-intensive) work of the business. Because of this dependency, if the entrepreneur is ill, has to travel, experiences a family emergency, or is otherwise unavailable, the business simply may not operate. As the revenue coming in is primarily used to pay the expenses necessary to operate the business, it is hard to get ahead. A lack of cash makes it difficult to purchase raw materials or supplies in bulk quantities. Survival ventures do not tend to have permanent premises. Marketing efforts are generally very basic and heavily rely on word of mouth. These are often cash-based businesses, unable to take credit cards or engage in electronic funds transfers. This can complicate the abilities to track revenues and expenses and minimize employee theft. To a greater or lesser degree, many of these entrepreneurs mix personal finances with business finances.

Scarcity is a core aspect of the survival venture—scarcity of money, labor, inventory, time, and customers. Scarcity can lead the entrepreneur to concentrate on the most pressing tasks at hand. Immediate problems consume a disproportionate amount of one's time, effort, and limited financial resources. There is less time to plan or focus on strategic issues. As the survivalist entrepreneur is usually scrambling to get by, the managerial approach tends to be more reactive and tactical than strategic (Tirado, 2015). It is harder for them to understand how key decisions impact one another and must be coordinated. With reactive management, the entrepreneur can become a victim of circumstances. An extensive amount of time is spent on responding to emergencies or critical demands from customers, suppliers, employees, or some unforeseen development. Being reactive suggests a lack of planning or preparation for unexpected events.

The survivalist is often unable to hire people (and especially qualified people) and so must rely on temporary labor or family members and friends. As a result, they have to be able to do everything in the business themselves. They are involved in negotiation with suppliers, producing the product or service, doing marketing, keeping the books, raising money, cleaning equipment, and dealing with customer complaints. These realities can turn the entrepreneur into a micromanager. Being preoccupied with all these tasks, he or she does not develop the bandwidth to think and act strategically.

Like most entrepreneurs, the survivalist will engage in a trial-and-error approach in order to figure things out, particularly in the early days of the venture. Prices are modified, operating hours or locations are changed, a promotion is run, or some other change is made to see if it stimulates sales or reduces costs. However, with survival ventures, these experiments may be more random than systematic, do not reflect particular goals, and can be inconsistent with other decision areas in the business. There are no clear criteria for determining whether or not the tactic worked. Alternatively, the entrepreneur may observe something another business is doing and try to mimic the approach, without considering differences in context. Although such tactical moves sometimes result in a positive outcome, they often waste time and money, and send mixed or inconsistent messages to customers. All too often, tactics are attempted, do not appear to produce results, and are discarded, with no real learning taking place as to why the approach did or did not work.

For the most part, survivalists receive little support from society. There are few training or mentoring programs available to them, and they often do not qualify for tax incentives, supplier diversity initiatives, or other forms of small business support. Most are unable to access traditional debt or equity sources of funding. They are largely excluded from the entrepreneurial ecosystems in their communities, where the focus tends to be on fostering growth-oriented businesses.

SIDE HUSTLES VERSUS FULL-TIME BUSINESSES

When they have jobs, which tend to be low paying, or their time is filled with other responsibilities such as being a caregiver for a family member or relative, those in poverty often engage in what are called "side-hustles" (Scott, Edwards, & Stancyk, 2020). These are defined as income-generating work where a person is otherwise employed or engaged full-time. An example might be an Uber driver or a person who makes money singing at weddings and funerals. This type of work is associated with the gig economy, where more people are pursuing temporary or freelance work on an informal or when-needed basis. For the poor, having some sort of gig on the side to supplement their incomes has long been a common practice.

As the side hustle is usually pursued at the same time as a full-time job or personal commitment, it can be a source of stress, health challenges, and reduced time with loved ones. Yet, the benefits may well outpace any costs. Beyond their positive impact on the economic well-being of the poor (Scott et al., 2020), side hustles allow individuals to develop and practice new skills and learn new routines (Sessions et al, 2021). As the person is working independently, they typically must not only produce a product or service, but also deal with a variety of other tasks with which they may have little experience, such as pricing, billing, selling, and customer service. The person is creating value for a client and typically receiving feedback. In addition, they may be developing an identity around the work they are providing.

Sessions et al. (2021) argue that side-hustles can be a source of individual empowerment, as the experience can reinforce self-determination, agency, impact, competence, and meaning. In fact, the individual may sense these things to a greater degree than they do from a full-time job. This impact on empowerment is likely greater when more task complexity is involved in the side-hustle. Further, the more meaning one finds through the side-hustle, the more engaged they are likely to be with this work.

Beyond serving as a training ground where someone can learn basic business skills, a side hustle represents a risk management strategy for low-income and disadvantaged entrepreneurs. They can effectively keep their day job, and hence some kind of income stream, while experimenting with a venture on the side. Learning from trial and error and establishing an initial customer base, their confidence grows regarding the ability to generate an income from the side hustle. With time, they may feel comfortable pursuing the entrepreneurial venture on a full-time basis. Mwaura (2022) demonstrates how side hustles enabled young Kenyan farmers to reconfigure their imagined futures.

DRAWING SOME IMPORTANT DISTINCTIONS

The poor are often assumed to be necessity entrepreneurs operating survival ventures in the informal sector, and many of these may begin as side hustles. Yet, it is important that we do not stereotype the poor, particularly when it comes to entrepreneurial behavior. A low-income or disadvantaged entrepreneur could start a venture that fits into none of these categories, or could fall into one category but not any of the others. Let us further examine distinctions among these categories.

First, necessity entrepreneurship is not the same thing as creating a survival venture. There are plenty of necessity-driven entrepreneurs who create lifestyle and managed growth ventures, and plenty of opportunity-driven entrepreneurs who create survival ventures. With this latter point, researchers seem to assume that if you are opportunity-driven, then whatever gets created must be a growth-oriented venture, or at least a lifestyle venture. It is simply not true, particularly because what one starts out to create is rarely what actually gets created. Entrepreneurship is not controllable or predictable—it is emergent. It is probably true that most necessity-driven entrepreneurs create survival ventures, but many do not. The reality is that necessity-driven entrepreneurs can create different types of ventures, and survival ventures can be created by literally anyone, not just those in poverty or disadvantaged conditions.

Second, necessity entrepreneurs often operate in the informal sector, but large numbers of them do not. If pushed into entrepreneurship by sheer necessity, one is typically so resource-constrained that they may resist registering their business, incurring the fees associated with a business bank account, creating a formal bookkeeping system, or paying taxes. However, the advantages of formalization, together with pressures from government agencies, serve as incentive for many to formalize.

Third, survival ventures are not the same thing as informal ventures. Certainly, the informal sector is filled with survival businesses, as both have low entry barriers and can require little in the way of resources or complex skills. Yet, while representing a much smaller percentage than can be found in the formal sector, many informal sector businesses are lifestyle and even managed growth ventures.

Fourth, necessity entrepreneurs start both side hustles and full-time businesses. Although businesses that are side hustles tend to start as informal ventures, many are registered and pay taxes. Similarly, because they are generally part-time efforts that represent a supplemental source of income, side hustles will most often fall into the survival category of enterprises. At the same time, there are any number of side hustles that prove to be quite lucrative for the entrepreneur.

For venture creation to serve as a pathway out of poverty, it is critical that we develop richer insights into each of these categories of entrepreneurial activity. The nature, functioning, needs, and outcomes of necessity entrepreneurship, the informal sector, survival ventures and side hustles have important implications for understanding how the poor can successfully navigate the journey to a sustainable enterprise.

WHY ALL VENTURES MATTER

There may be a tendency among some academics, public policy makers, economic development professionals, and members of the public to denigrate the ventures of the poor—or to treat them as somehow less worthy than other types of entrepreneurial activity. The reality is that these businesses, even where they generate few jobs per venture and relatively little income, matter very much for economies, communities, and individuals. They make six important contributions:

- They employ millions of impoverished individuals, providing an economic lifeline to their families, and constitute a sizeable contribution to the gross domestic product (GDP), particularly in developing economies;

- They are sources of human capital development as the entrepreneur develops attitudes, skills, competencies, and self-efficacy from real-time venture creation experiences;
- They create unique sources of value in the marketplace;
- They fill market niches—often under-served niches that are not attractive to incumbent firms;
- They tend to be deeply embedded in the fabric of local communities, giving back in various ways, and providing an important source of local stability; and,
- They can produce spillover benefits, such as reduced crime rates, increased school completion rates, and neighborhood pride.

Unfortunately, data on entrepreneurship and its effects on poverty is limited. In the U.S., Slivinski (2015) found a relationship between a state's rate of entrepreneurship and the change in the state's poverty rate (between 2001 and 2007). Those states with the highest rates of entrepreneurship demonstrated the largest reductions in poverty, while lower rates of entrepreneurship corresponded to increases in poverty (Slivinski, 2012, 2015). Separately, the Self-Employment Learning Project of the Aspen Institute followed over 405 individuals running microbusinesses for five years, of which 133 were poor at the time of the study (Clark et al., 1999). They found that 72% of poor micro-entrepreneurs increased their household income over five years (the average increase was $8,484), enough to move 53% of these entrepreneurs out of poverty. Because of these household family gains, poor microentrepreneurs were able to reduce their dependence on public assistance programs by 61% on average. A different perspective can be found in the work of Amorós and Cristi (2011). Using data from twenty-nine developed and thirty-seven developing countries, their findings indicate higher levels of entrepreneurship are associated with greater reductions in poverty in *both* developed and developing countries—with a higher relative impact in developing countries. Overall, there is a growing pattern around the world of people with severely limited resources starting businesses, building something that is sustainable, and making a living (Banerjee & Duflo, 2007). In the process, hundreds of millions of people are being pulled out of poverty (Abraham, 2012).

In addition to these contributions, counter-arguments can be made to some of the criticisms levied at the ventures of the poor. For instance, while it has been suggested that the ventures of the poor are inefficient, the reality is that many of these entrepreneurs are able to do much more with considerably less. While they often cannot afford the kinds of equipment and technology that would make them even more efficient, they typically do not require much in the way of resources. Further, as they rely on the ongoing abilities of the entrepreneur to bootstrap, leverage, and stretch resources, while engaging in bricolage, these ventures can prove to be quite resilient in overcoming obstacles, dealing with setbacks, and surviving the ups and downs of the marketplace.

Further, the argument that these types of ventures tend to fail at a high rate and incur entry and exit costs that burden society is debatable. The new venture failure rate tends to be between 45 and 55% in the first five years. The reality is that relatively little data is available on the actual start-up and failure rates of poverty entrepreneurs and the extent to which they differ from those of all new businesses. On entry and exit costs, ongoing changes in technology, market structures, supply chains, labor practices, social patterns, and abilities to outsource have significantly lowered these costs over the last few decades. Today, with little in the way of fixed assets or permanent resources, it is easier than ever to start and stop a business and run it from virtually anywhere. In fact, the average firm has gotten smaller in size and requires less resources to get going. Meanwhile, the highest rates of productivity growth are in regions having large numbers of very small businesses (Robbins et al., 2000).

Others are concerned about the over-concentration of these businesses in certain sectors (e.g., retail trade, personal care, food service). This is a challenge with low-income entrepreneurs and is traceable to low entry barriers in these industries and the limited opportunity horizons of these individuals (see Chapter 6). There is actually a fair amount of diversity to be found among these ventures, ranging from manufacturers of basic goods (furniture, clothing, concrete blocks, skin care products), to providers of transportation and basic financial services to owners of media companies and entrepreneurs involved in arts and crafts. At the same time, these entrepreneurs are significantly under-represented in high-tech, heavy construction, high volume goods manufacturing, medical products, energy production, mining, and other industries requiring high fixed cost investments and advanced technical skills. They also are much less likely to be involved in exporting goods and services to other countries.

Another criticism of these ventures concerns the quality of the jobs they create. The assessment of quality depends upon the object of comparison. Certainly, a high tech firm may be creating skills-based jobs that pay well and offer attractive employee benefits. However, as with an Amazon warehouse worker or delivery truck driver, many of these jobs may not be that different from those created by the poverty entrepreneur, and work conditions are not always any better. More importantly, the job of an entrepreneur and business owner is frequently superior on a number of criteria when compared to other kinds of jobs (if any) they were able to find prior to starting their venture. Being an entrepreneur can provide autonomy, freedom, intellectual challenge, personal growth, skills development, pride, and other benefits, while the alternative may be a low-paying (or non-existent) job that is labor-intensive and involves little employment security or opportunity for development and advancement.

Morris, Neumeyer, and Kuratko (2015) go further in arguing that all ventures matter and should be encouraged. However, different venture types play fundamentally different roles in the economy. As such, they should be approached from a portfolio perspective. Thus, the survival business can serve to move people out of poverty and joblessness into a mode where they are able to meet basic economic needs. A lifestyle business can play a stabilizing role in local economies, providing markets for locally made goods, paying local taxes, and reinvesting in the community. A managed growth firm can serve a similar role, but here the market reach is greater, more jobs are created, efficiencies are greater, and the potential for innovation is stronger. The aggressive growth firm can produce dynamic breakthroughs and major innovations that create new markets, create large numbers of jobs, and enhance the global competitiveness of a nation. These four types are independent. Hence, there could be no Uber without independent (survivalist) drivers. As a balanced portfolio, these ventures vary in terms of risk and return to society, and their shorter- versus longer-term payoffs.

While the poor do disproportionately create survival and lifestyle types of businesses, it is important to recognize that ventures are emergent (Morris, Pryor, & Schindehutte, 2012). What one sets out to create is rarely what actually gets created. How a new business emerges is not predictable or controllable. With poverty, certain factors may limit the possibilities. Yet the poor have created all four types of ventures. With a supportive ecosystem and tailored types of interventions, many ventures of the poor can emerge as sustainable lifestyle, managed growth, and even occasionally aggressive growth ventures.

ROLES PLAYED BY ENTREPRENEURSHIP WHEN IT COMES TO PEOPLE IN POVERTY

In addition to their importance, it is vital that we recognize the different roles that these ventures play in the lives of the poor. If we view entrepreneurship from a more holistic vantage point, consistent with our discussion of integral human development in Chapter 1, venture creation can convey a reservoir of vital benefits to the disadvantaged individual.

Source of Dignity

We have noted that poverty is a characteristic of a situation, not a person. Yet, people and organizations can place a stigma on those in poverty circumstances, as if they were somehow less worthy. Their sense of dignity can be compromised when there are no decent jobs available, they cannot feed or properly clothe their families, access to all kinds of resources and opportunities is denied, their opinions and needs are ignored, and they are forced to compromise their values and beliefs in order to get any support or assistance. Having one's own business, obtaining sales, earning profits, becoming sell-sufficient, and hiring others can reinforce one's sense of dignity.

Source of Personal Development

The building of a business, particularly when the founder is doing everything from production and purchasing to marketing and bookkeeping, is a significant vehicle for personal development. The individual must learn how to organize, keep records, manage money, make sales, supervise, maintain inventory, and serve customers. Beyond this, lessons are learned about dealing with setbacks, overcoming obstacles, experimentation, negotiating, leveraging resources, and planning ahead. The experience can build self-efficacy and self-discipline.

Source of Identity

A considerable volume of research has focused on how individuals develop an identity through the process of developing a business (Fauchart & Gruber, 2011; Hoang & Gimeno, 2010). Whether that identity is rooted in being a creator, builder, innovator, job creator, winner, or some other aspect of the entrepreneurial experience, it can be a source of pride and self-worth and can give one a sense of purpose and meaning. Particularly for those who come from poverty and disadvantaged circumstances, identifying themselves as entrepreneurs can be an important source of value and self-worth.

Source of Income

For the person who struggles to support a family, even when the returns are relatively marginal in objective terms, the income can be meaningful. Often, it represents a source of income that supplements money received from a job, government transfer payment, pension, or some other income stream. Yet, very frequently, it is the family's primary source of income. Depending on whether the business is registered, the entrepreneur keeps records, and the income is reported to authorities, the entrepreneur may or may not pay taxes on this income.

Source of Well-being

Creation of a business has been tied to enhanced well-being (Stephan, Rauch, & Hatak, 2023; Wiklund et al., 2019). Well-being is a holistic construct that transcends financial well-being to include psychological, emotional, and physical elements. It is a subjective notion as it occurs within a person's experiences and reflects an evaluation of one's life (Diener & Ryan, 2009). Morris and colleagues (2023) have demonstrated that entrepreneurs in poverty conditions who can build sustainable businesses demonstrate a strong sense of personal well-being and one that is significantly higher than those who build more marginal businesses.

Source of Voice

Poverty can be a source of disenfranchisement. The individual can perceive that they have no voice and do not count. Not only is one's social network constrained, but one's ability to influence or be listened to by community leaders, fellow citizens, and representatives of government organizations, key institutions, stakeholder groups, and those who control access to resources of all kinds, is compromised. As an entrepreneur, the individual can build relationships and establish legitimacy with key stakeholders. People may be more likely to seek their opinions, ask for their advice, include them in decision-making, and respect their concerns.

Source of Ability to Give Back

In our work with those experiencing poverty, we find a common motive for starting a business is to give back to one's community and provide opportunities for others who come from disadvantaged circumstances. This sense of community responsibility is strong among the poor, and it affects how they run their businesses. It can be reflected in what they sell, who they hire, how much they pay employees, who they source from, where they locate their premises, how they price, the causes and community initiatives they support, and other key decision areas. It is not that profit and personal gain do not matter, but performance in these areas is often balanced against the need to do things in ways that uplift one's community (Debrah, 2007).

Source of Community Pride

Building a successful enterprise can be a source of pride to the poverty entrepreneur, but also to those in the community from where the entrepreneur originates, where social and economic disparities are the norm (Morris et al.,

2011). Particularly where the entrepreneur has located the business within a challenged neighborhood, hired local people, and supported local causes, he/she can serve as a role model—one that reinforces what the community is capable of producing and how others can build their own successful paths without abandoning where they came from. In addition, such success stories reinforce the importance of recycling local money back into the economy of the community rather than having it flow out.

As every entrepreneur experiences venture creation in a different way, the roles it plays in their lives can be expected to also differ considerably. Here, we have focused on positive roles and benefits. It must be kept in mind that a person in poverty might not realize most, or even any, of these benefits. However, recognition of these roles is critical for understanding the poverty entrepreneur's motives, providing the proper kinds of interventions and support, and evaluating the actual impact and functionality of entrepreneurship.

CONCLUSION

In this chapter, we have examined the tendency of those in poverty and disadvantaged circumstances to create businesses that may start as side hustles, are sometimes motivated by necessity, often start in the informal sector, and frequently operate as survival ventures. Some of the misunderstandings and controversies surrounding each of these distinctions have been examined. We have explored the implications of each distinction for the experiences of these entrepreneurs while also noting that any number of poverty entrepreneurs are not survivalists, never operated informally or as a side hustle, and/or were driven more by the perception of opportunity than sheer necessity.

The value of the businesses launched by those in poverty would appear to be under-appreciated by many scholars, government officials, economic development professionals, and entities that play important roles in local entrepreneurial ecosystems. The reality is that these businesses employ many millions of people across the globe, and these businesses provide an important source of human capital development and income to people who live in poverty and find many doors to opportunity are closed to them. There is a limited but growing body of evidence to suggest entrepreneurship can reduce rates of poverty and improve standards of living.

All too often with the poor, running one's own business, particularly as a solo operator, is simply viewed as a job. Instead of cooking, or hauling, or laboring for someone else, the individual does it for themselves (sometimes for less money). Such a view misses the many potential roles venture creation can play in the lives of people in poverty. It can be a source of dignity, pride, self-development, voice and well-being, among other roles. Only by appreciating such roles can we begin to understand the real potential of entrepreneurship.

Yet, such is not always the case. Creating a venture can keep a person in poverty, detract from their dignity, and sometimes make them worse off. Further, the entrepreneurial journey is often one of stress, anxiety, frustration, ambiguity, confusion, and uncertainty. It can take people away from their families, and create divisions with friends and neighbors. In the chapter to come, we will further explore the conditions and contextual factors that can enable entrepreneurship to serve as a pathway out of poverty.

REFERENCES

Abraham, R. (2012). Doing business at the base of the pyramid: The reality of emerging markets. *The Journal of Field Actions: Field Actions Science Reports, Special Issue 4: Fighting Poverty, Between Market and Gift.*

Acs, Z. J., & Kallas, K. (2008). State of literature on small- to medium-sized enterprises and entrepreneurship in low-income communities. In G. Yago, J. R. Barth and B. Zeidman (Eds.), *Entrepreneurship in Emerging Domestic Markets* (pp. 21–45). New York: Springer.

Adebayo, N. A., & Nassar, M. L. (2014). Impact of micro and small business entrepreneurship on poverty reduction in Ibadan Metropolis, South Western Nigeria. *International Review of Management and Business Research*, *3*(3), 1603–1626.

Akintimehin, O., Eniola, A., Alabi, O. J., Eluyela, D., Okere, W., & Ozordi, E. (2019). Social capital and its effect on business performance in the Nigeria informal sector. *Heliyon, 5*(7), e02024.

Amorós, J. E., & Cristi, O. (2011), Poverty and entrepreneurship in developing countries. In M. Minniti (ed.), *Dynamics of entrepreneurship*. Oxford, UK: Oxford University Press, 209–230.

Amorós, J. E., Cristi, O., & Naudé, W. (2021). Entrepreneurship and subjective well-being: Does the motivation to start-up a firm matter? *Journal of Business Research*, *127*, 389–398.

Avenyo, E. K., & Kraemer-Mbula, E. (2021). Innovation and the performance of informal enterprises in developing countries: a gender perspective. *International Journal of Gender and Entrepreneurship*, *13*(4), 277–301.

Banerjee, A. V., & Duflo, E. (2007). The economic lives of the poor. *Journal of Economic Perspectives*, *21*(1), 141–167.

Banerjee, A., Duflo, E., Goldberg, N., Karlan, D., Osei, R., Parienté, W., . . . & Udry, C. (2015). A multifaceted program causes lasting progress for the very poor: Evidence from six countries. *Science*, *348*(6236), 1260799.

Bromley, R. (Ed.). (2013). *The urban informal sector: critical perspectives on employment and housing policies*. Amsterdam: Elsevier.

Canelas, C. (2019). Informality and poverty in Ecuador. *Small Business Economics, 53*, 1097–115.

Clark, P., Blair, A., Zandiniapour, L., Soto, E., & Doyle, K. (1999, January 1). Microenterprise and the poor: Findings from the Self-Employment Learning Project five-year survey of microentrepreneurs. The Aspen Institute, accessed June 7, 2018, https://www.aspeninstitute.org/publications/microenterprise-poor-findings-self-employmentlearning-project-five-year-survey-microentrepreneurs/.

Darbi, W. P. K., Hall, C. M., &Knott, P (2018). The informal sector: A review and agenda for management research. *International Journal of Management Reviews, 20*(2), 301–324.

Debrah, Y. A. (2007). Promoting the informal sector as a source of gainful employment in developing countries: Insights from Ghana. *The International Journal of Human Resource Management, 18*(6), 1063–1084.

Dencker, J. C., Bacq, S., Gruber, M., & Haas, M. (2021). Reconceptualizing necessity entrepreneurship: A contextualized framework of entrepreneurial processes under the condition of basic needs. *Academy of Management Review*, *46*(1), 60–79.

Diener, E., & Ryan, K. (2009). Subjective well-being: A general overview. *South African Journal of Psychology*, *39*(4), 391–406

Doering, L., & Wry, T. (2022). The challenges of supporting necessity entrepreneurs: Understanding loan officer exit in microfinance. *Journal of Business Venturing, 37*(2), 106189.

Erhardt, E. C. (2022). Prevalence and persistence of high-growth entrepreneurship: Which institutions matter most? *Journal of Industry, Competition and Trade*, *22*(2), 297–332.

Fauchart, E., & Gruber, M. (2011). Darwinians, communitarians, and missionaries: The role of founder identity in entrepreneurship. *Academy of Management Journal*, *54*(5), 935–957.

Gill, K. (2009). *Of poverty and plastic: Scavenging and scrap trading entrepreneurs in India's urban informal economy*. New Delhi: Oxford University Press.

Hoang, H., & Gimeno, J. (2010). Becoming a founder: How founder role identity affects entrepreneurial transitions and persistence in founding. *Journal of Business Venturing*, *25*(1), 41–53.

Ibidunni, A. S., Ogundana, O. M., &Okonkwo, A. (2021). Entrepreneurial competencies and the performance of informal SMEs: The contingent role of business environment. *Journal of African Business, 22*(4), 468–90.

Kiggundu, M. N. (2002). Entrepreneurs and entrepreneurship in Africa: What is known and what needs to be done. *Journal of Developmental Entrepreneurship, 7*(3), 239.

Lee, N. (2014). What holds back high-growth firms? Evidence from UK SMEs. *Small Business Economics*, *43*, 183–195.

Malik, M. H. (1996). Urban poverty alleviation through development of the informal sector. *Asia Pacific Development Journal, 3*(2), 31–48.

Maslow, A. H. (1954). *Motivation and personality*. Harper and Row.

Matos, S., & Hall, J. (2021). An exploratory study of entrepreneurs in impoverished communities: When institutional factors and individual characteristics result in non-productive entrepreneurship. In *Business, entrepreneurship and innovation toward poverty reduction* (pp. 134–155). Routledge.

McKay, K. L. (2014, August). Achieving financial security through entrepreneurship: Policies to support financially vulnerable microbusiness owners. Federal Policy Proposal, Corporation for Enterprise Development, accessed June 7, 2018, https://prosperitynow.org/files/PDFs/financial_capability_planning_guide/Entrepreneurship_policy_proposal.pdf.

Morris, M. H., Neumeyer, X., & Kuratko, D. F. (2015). A portfolio perspective on entrepreneurship and economic development. *Small Business Economics*, *45*, 713–728.

Morris, M. H., Pryor, C. G., & Schindehutte, M. (2012). *Entrepreneurship as experience: How events create ventures and ventures create entrepreneurs*. Cheltenham: Edward Elgar Publishing.

Morris, M. H., Santos, S. C., & Neumeyer, X. (2018). *Poverty and entrepreneurship in developed economies*. Cheltenham, UK: Edward Elgar Publishing.

Morris, M. H., Schindehutte, M., Edmonds, V., & Watters, C. (2011). Inner city engagement and the university: Mutuality, emergence and transformation. *Entrepreneurship & Regional Development, 23*(5–6), 287–315

Mwaura, J. (2022). Silicon Savannah or digitising marginalisation? In T. Chari and U. Akpojivi (Eds.), *Communication rights in Africa: Emerging discourses and perspectives* (pp. 38–54). New York: Taylor & Francis.

Newman, A. (2018). Informality conceptualized: The continuum of formality. In *Academy of Management Proceedings*, 2018(1), 14419. Briarcliff Manor, NY: Academy of Management.

——— (2019). Stuck in the middle theorizing on the permanence of the semi-formal economy. In *Academy of Management Proceedings,* 2019(1), 18223. Briarcliff Manor, NY: Academy of Management.

Olamide, A., & Ogbechie, R. (2021). Social capital and business performance: A study of female-owned SMEs in the Nigerian informal sector. *Small Enterprise Research*, *28*(2), 190–205.

Poschke, M. (2013). "Entrepreneurs out of necessity": A snapshot. *Applied Economics Letters*, *20*(7), 658–663.

Potts, D. (2008). The urban informal sector in sub-Saharan Africa: from bad to good (and back again?). *Development Southern Africa, 25*(2), 151–167.

Ravenelle, A. J., Kowalski, K. C., & Janko, E. (2021). The side hustle safety net: Precarious workers and gig work during COVID-19. *Sociological Perspectives*, *64*(5), 898–919.

Robbins, D. K., Pantuosco, L. J., Parker, D. F., & Fuller, B. K. (2000). An empirical assessment of the contribution of small business employment to US State economic performance. *Small Business Economics, 15*, 293–302.

Santos, S. C., Costa, S., & Morris, M. H. (2022). Entrepreneurship as a pathway into and out of poverty: A configuration perspective. *Entrepreneurship & Regional Development*, *34*(1–2), 82–109.

Schumpeter, J. A. (1934), *The theory of economic development*, Harvard University Press, Cambridge, MA.

Scott, J., Edwards, K., & Stanczyk, A. (2020). Moonlighting to the side hustle: The effect of working an extra job on household poverty for households with less formal education. *Families in Society*, *101*(3), 324–339.

Sessions, H., Nahrgang, J. D., Vaulont, M. J., Williams, R., & Bartels, A. L. (2021). Do the hustle! Empowerment from side-hustles and its effects on full-time work performance. *Academy of Management Journal*, *64*(1), 235–264.

Shane, S. (2009). Why encouraging more people to become entrepreneurs is bad public policy. *Small Business Economics*, *33*, 141–149.

Sharma, G., & Kumar, H. (2019). Commercializing innovations from the informal economy: The grassroots innovation ecosystem in India. *South Asian Journal of Business Studies*, *8*(1), 0–61.

Si, S., Ahlstrom, D., Wei, J., & Cullen, J. (2021). Introduction: Business, entrepreneurship and innovation toward poverty reduction. In *Business, entrepreneurship and innovation toward poverty reduction* (pp. 1–20). Routledge.

Slivinski, S. (2012). Increasing entrepreneurship is a key to lowering poverty rates. Policy Report No. 254, Goldwater Institute, accessed June 7, 2018, http://www.realclearmarkets.com/docs/2012/11/PR254%20Increasing%20Entrepreneurship.pdf.

Slivinski, S. (2015). Policy report no. 252: Bootstraps tangled in red tape: How state occupational licensing hinders low-income entrepreneurship. Goldwater Institute, accessed June 7, 2018 at https://goldwaterinstitute.org/article/bootstraps-tangled-in-red-tape/.

Stenholm, P., Acs, Z. J., & Wuebker, R. (2013). Exploring country-level institutional arrangements on the rate and type of entrepreneurial activity. *Journal of Business Venturing*, *28*(1), 176–193.

Stephan, U., Rauch, A., & Hatak, I. (2023). Happy entrepreneurs? Everywhere? A meta-analysis of entrepreneurship and wellbeing. *Entrepreneurship Theory and Practice*, *47*(2), 553–593.

Tipple, G. (2005). The place of home-based enterprises in the informal sector: Evidence from Cochabamba, New Delhi, Surabaya and Pretoria. *Urban Studies*, *42*(4), 611–32.

Tirado, L. (2015). *Hand to mouth: Living in bootstrap America.* New York: Penguin.

Truong, V. D. (2018). Tourism, poverty alleviation and the informal economy: The street vendors of Hanoi, Vietnam. *Tourism Recreation Research*, *43*(1), 52–67.

Van Metre, L. (2016). Fragility and resilience. Policy Brief, Fragility Study Group. Washington, DC: U.S. Institute of Peace. Retrieved June 6, 2020, www.jstor.org/stable/resrep12256.

Venkatesh, S. A. (2006). *Off the books: The underground economy of the urban poor*. Cambridge, MA: Harvard University Press.

Wiklund, J., Nikolaev, B., Shir, N., Foo, M. D., & Bradley, S. (2019). Entrepreneurship and well-being: Past, present, and future. *Journal of Business Venturing*, *34*(4), 579–588.

World Bank (2021). www.worldbank.org/en/research/brief/informal-economy-database

Zhao, W. (2009). The nature and roles of small tourism businesses in poverty alleviation: Evidence from Guangxi, China. *Asia Pacific Journal of Tourism Research, 14*(2), 169–182.

PART II

Understanding the Poverty Context

Chapter Five

The Liabilities of Poorness

How does poverty affect the ability of someone to start a business? This is a question that has received surprisingly little attention from scholars, economic development professionals, or public policy officials. The assumption is that the lack of financial resources keeps many of those in poverty circumstances from launching a business, and/or leads them to start marginal businesses that are unable to generate meaningful returns. Yet, the story is much more complex than this.

Virtually anyone who starts a business faces significant challenges, as reflected in what have been called the "liability of newness" and "liability of smallness" (Hannan & Freeman, 1984; Stinchcombe, 1965). Here, because the business is new and quite small, it struggles to compete and generate a profit. Newness and/or smallness can result in a lack of legitimacy, inadequate resources and capabilities, misunderstood roles and unclear role definitions, few established routines and procedures, an ambiguous identity, and no bargaining power with suppliers, distributors, and other stakeholders. As such, the entrepreneur is at a disadvantage, especially relative to incumbent organizations.

However, the poor face an additional set of challenges when launching a venture. Poverty is a multi-dimensional phenomenon that represents a complex set of interwoven elements which transcend a lack of income or wealth. Factors such as an inferior educational background, chronic health problems, inadequate housing, food scarcity, physical insecurity, and social exclusion, among others, can combine to affect how an individual perceives the environment, processes information, makes decisions, and takes action. We know relatively little regarding how this complex mosaic comes into play as the individual attempts to navigate the many steps involved in developing a viable business enterprise.

In this chapter, we introduce the "liabilities of poorness" as a means of capturing the additional obstacles poverty entrepreneurs must overcome. The multi-dimensional nature of poverty can be translated into four key liabilities: literacy gaps, a scarcity mindset, intense non-business pressures, and lack of a safety net. As we shall see, the collective impact of these elements has profound implications for the number and nature of the ventures created by the poor, how the liabilities of newness and smallness are addressed, and the overall performance and sustainability of these businesses. Critically, each of them contributes to the fragility of the enterprises created by the poor. This fragility, in turn, explains why these ventures are more significantly impacted than others by external shocks and major setbacks. It helps explain their failure rates, and the extent to which they struggle to generate enough income to move the entrepreneur and his/her family out of poverty.

The presence of the liabilities of poorness suggests the playing field is not level for entrepreneurs who come from poverty and disadvantaged environments. To level the playing field, we must re-think the kinds of support needed by these entrepreneurs from community ecosystems, as well as the types of public policies that can facilitate entrepreneurship as a viable pathway out of poverty.

DIFFICULTIES IN SUCCESSFULLY LAUNCHING A BUSINESS

While starting a business is reasonably straightforward, launching one that is profitable and sustainable is a difficult undertaking regardless of who is involved, but is especially challenging for those in poverty. Failure rates differ internationally, but it is generally estimated that between 45 and 55% of new ventures fail within the first five years of operation (Stangler; 2010; Watson & Everett, 1999). We know less about the outcomes of the ventures of the poor, but there is evidence to suggest a significantly higher failure rate (Bekele & Worku, 2008; Fairlie & Robb, 2008).

Two major reasons for new venture failure are the liabilities of newness and smallness. The liability of newness is concerned with the inherent disadvantages new firms face when competing with incumbent organizations (Lefebvre, 2020). Newness suggests that those involved must learn new roles with which they are unfamiliar. The organization lacks the routines, standardized procedures, and problem-solving strategies that could increase efficacy and ensure consistency in operations. Externally, new firms lack a clear identity and struggle to establish legitimacy with customers, suppliers, financing agents, regulators, and competitors. Here, legitimacy refers to "a generalized perception or assumption that the actions of an entity are desirable, proper or appropriate within some socially constructed system of norms, values, beliefs and definitions" (Suchman,1995, p. 211).

The liability of smallness refers to the vulnerability of an entrepreneurial venture based on its limited resources and capabilities (Aldrich & Auster, 1986; Hannan & Freeman, 1984). The business has a paucity of internal resources and difficulties in accessing what it needs. Smallness makes it harder to attract and retain skilled employees. It limits the bargaining power of the entrepreneur in dealing with resource suppliers and makes it difficult to realize the economies necessary to be competitive. Limited working capital hinders operations and results in missed opportunities. Further, Anderson and Ullah (2014) have found that the condition of being small results in attitudes and behaviors that serve to reinforce smallness.

We know little regarding how the liabilities of newness and smallness affect those who come from a poverty background. This is due, in part, to our failure to consider the unique nature of poverty and how it informs the entrepreneurial experience.

HOW POVERTY CREATES ITS OWN LIABILITIES

While all entrepreneurs must overcome the liabilities of newness and smallness, and most start with insufficient resources, the ability of the poor to deal with these challenges is complicated by the enduring effects of the poverty experience. In Chapter 2, we discussed the complex mosaic of the poverty experience, noting that it is far more than a lack of income. Poverty is a dynamic phenomenon that involves complicated interactions among a host of conditions, from weak educational backgrounds, underemployment, and chronic health problems to single parenthood, limited social networks, and food, housing and physical security. At the same time, we need more clarity on exactly *how* these poverty conditions work against the entrepreneur. What is it about these particular conditions that makes it more difficult to accomplish critical entrepreneurial tasks? To address this question, we introduce the concept of "liabilities of poorness," defined as *the potential for failure of a new venture due to difficulties traceable to characteristics and influences deriving from a poverty background* (Morris, 2020).

As illustrated in Figure 5.1, the mix of variables that constitute the poverty experience combine to produce four major obstacles to a successful entrepreneurial journey. First, where the entrepreneur comes from a background that includes a lower quality education, underemployment in less attractive jobs where there is little training or room for self-development, teenage child-bearing which results in absenteeism or dropping out of school, and a limited social network, he or she is likely to suffer from *literacy gaps*. Second, lack of income, low-end jobs, food and housing insecurity, health problems, being a victim of crime, teenage childbearing, and related conditions mean

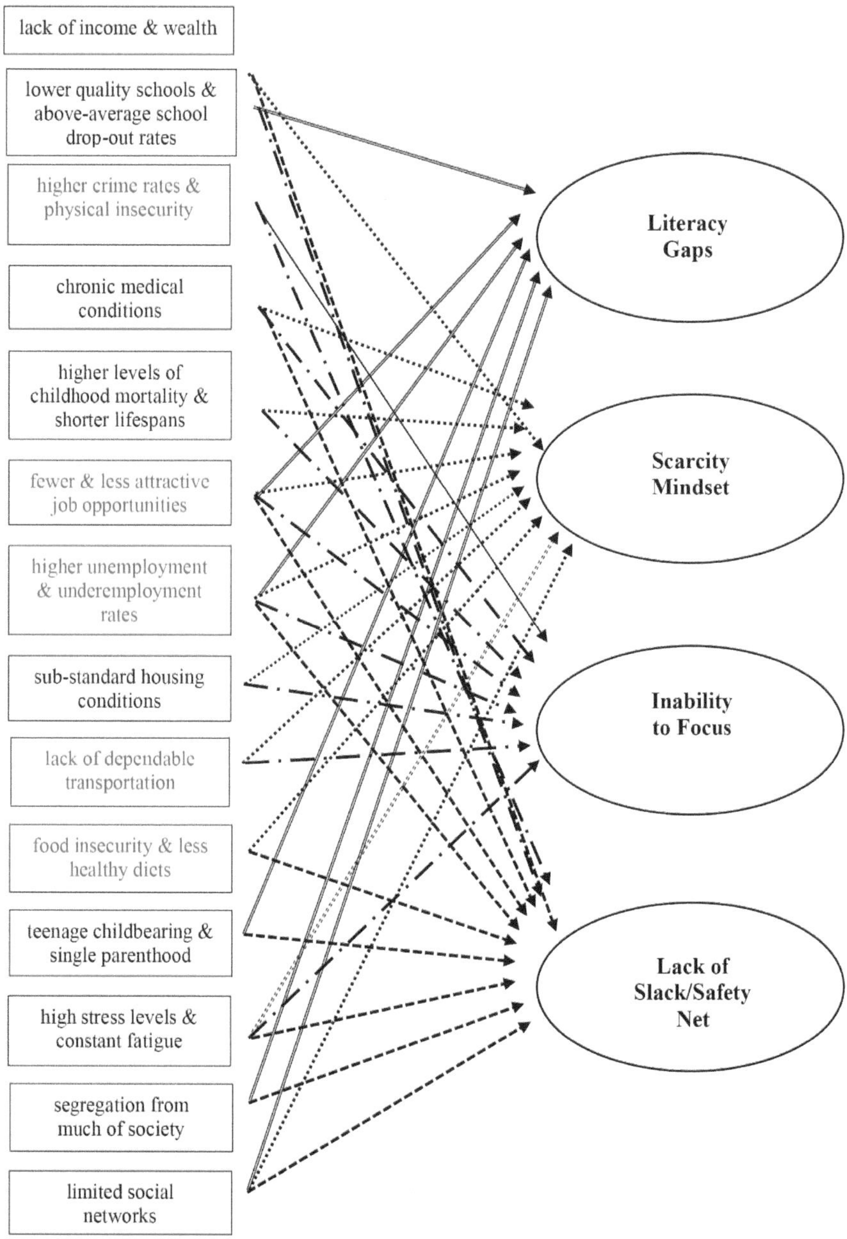

Figure 5.1. Implications of Poverty Conditions for Factors Affecting Ability to Start a Business.

Created by Authors

that money, time, and other resources are always in short supply, and can create a *scarcity mindset* that affects how the entrepreneur thinks and makes decisions. Third, chronic health problems among family members, high crime rates, food insecurity, inadequate housing, teenage childbearing, lack of dependable transportation, and both stress and constant fatigue can combine to create distractions that hinder *the ability of the entrepreneur to focus* on key operational and developmental needs of the business. Finally, factors such as lack of savings, chronic health problems, unemployment and under-employment, sub-standard housing, undependable transportation, segregation and limited social networks find the entrepreneur with *no resource slack and lack of any safety net* when encountering both setbacks or new opportunities.

Individually and collectively, these four liabilities can significantly add to the burdens that must be overcome by entrepreneurs experiencing poverty. They can put these individuals at a relative disadvantage when compared to entrepreneurs in general. To appreciate the nature of this disadvantage, let us consider each of them in more detail.

EXPLORING THE LIABILITIES OF POORNESS

Understanding the liabilities of poorness is the key to unlocking the potential of entrepreneurship as a vehicle for poverty alleviation. These liabilities have important implications for the kinds of ventures started by those in poverty, how these ventures perform, and the extent to which they contribute to the integral human development of the entrepreneur. Each of the liabilities has a number of underlying components (see Figure 5.2), which are further explored below.

Literacy Gaps: UNESCO (2005, p. 21) defines literacy as "the ability to identify, understand, interpret, create, communicate and compute using printed and written materials associated with varying contexts. Literacy involves a continuum of learning in enabling an individual to achieve his or her goals, develop his or her knowledge and potential, and participate fully in community and wider society." Morris, Santos, and Neumeyer (2018) emphasize the roles of five inter-related literacies when launching a business: *functional* (reading, writing, numeracy, communication); *financial* (understanding how to budget, save, manage credit and debt obligations, make financially responsible decisions); *economic* (understanding economic incentives and disincentives, supply and demand conditions, and the costs and benefits of alternative courses of action); *business* (mastering the language of business and how to effectively interact with various stakeholders); and *technological* (appreciation for the significance of key technologies impacting a business, how they are used, and issues raised by their use). Arguably, these five

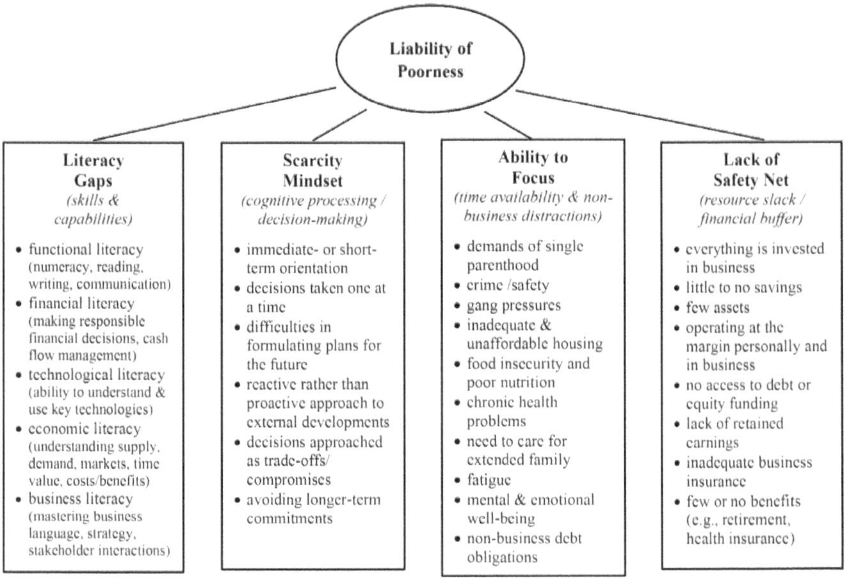

Figure 5.2. Underlying Components of the Liabilities of Poorness.
Created by Authors

literacies are more important than any other resource when starting a business. Yet, the evidence is clear that, across the globe, the poor suffer from low literacy levels (Ahmed, 2011; Hernandez, 2011; Wilson, 1996).

Scarcity Mindset: An endemic characteristic of poverty is scarcity. Lack of resources forces the poor individual to make trade-off decisions in determining which bills to pay. Do they buy medicine for a sick child or cover this month's rent? Beyond this, the poor face a scarcity of options and choices, and can also experience a dearth of time and energy, such as when attempting to work two part-time jobs while also launching a venture. Shah, Shafir, and Mullainathan (2015) demonstrate that those with limited resources will more exclusively focus on accomplishing the most pressing tasks at hand while ignoring other critical tasks—even when doing so takes away from the ability to achieve larger goals. Immediate problems, where scarcity is most salient, consume a disproportionate amount of their time, effort, and limited financial resources (Mani et al., 2013). By allocating attention to immediate needs, the individual frequently ignores other needs and engages in actions that prove to be costlier or detrimental in the longer term. Shah, Mullainathan, and Shafir (2012, p. 682) argue that "resource scarcity creates its own mindset, changing how people look at problems and make decisions." In an entrepreneurial context, this mindset can undermine the ability to think holistically and strategically. It becomes more difficult to plan ahead, especially in a manner that anticipates and prepares for unexpected occurrences and emerging threats. Attentional shifts and reliance on locally convenient responses can serve to harm the long-term potential of the venture.

Ability to Focus: The ability of a poor individual to run a business is also compromised by constant and sometimes extreme personal demands (unrelated to the business) placed on the entrepreneur. Time pressures on the poor have been explored by various authors (e.g., Chatzitheochari & Arber, 2012; Dermott & Pomati, 2016). If one's family is exposed to more chronic medical problems, difficulties paying for basic needs, threats of foreclosure or eviction, high crime rates and gang violence, unexpected job losses, and similar everyday pressures, large amounts of time can be consumed. Such developments can distract the entrepreneur from addressing critical business needs and they can be quite exhausting. The ventures of the poor are frequently labor-intensive operations heavily dependent on the entrepreneur to both manage the business and also perform the core work (e.g., construction, cleaning, cooking) of the business. A major personal or family problem can require that operating hours be reduced, key decisions be compromised or deferred, and resources be taken out of the business. Similarly, the quality of business operations may suffer as the entrepreneur is distracted by these outside developments.

Lack of Safety Net: The final contributor to the liabilities of poorness is the lack of any sort of safety net or resource slack when major obstacles are encountered or unexpected developments occur. The entrepreneur typically puts all of his/her financial resources into the business, leaving no remaining savings to draw upon (Barr & Blank, 2009). Friends and family members lack resources to help out should the business get in trouble. Beyond this, the entrepreneur's limited social network contributes to the lack of a safety net. The kinds of connections that might enable the venture to weather a storm typically do not exist. Further, he or she struggles to qualify for any sort of bank debt or outside financial support, and if they have credit cards, these are at their limit (Littwin, 2008). The business fails to contribute to the entrepreneur's safety net, as it frequently operates at the margin (Morris, Santos, & Neumeyer, 2018). Capacity is limited, as the entrepreneur may work from home, a truck, or a stall, and is not able to employ much equipment or technology in operations. Competitive conditions keep prices low, and when combined with relatively high unit costs, result in little to no profit. Marginal operations limit the ability to build cash reserves or generate retained earnings that can be reinvested in the business or flow back to the entrepreneur.

Beyond their individual effects, the four liabilities of poorness can interact with one another in a variety of ways. For instance, a short-term focus and the struggle to plan or think strategically resulting from a scarcity mentality are reinforced by distractions posed by intense non-business pressures that make it hard to focus. Failure to plan can also contribute to the lack of a safety net, which in turn leads to more conservative and short-term decision making. Literacy shortcomings are likely to encourage a focus on the immediate needs while hindering the ability to create slack in the organization through investments in equipment and technology. When combined, these four factors can impose a burden on the entrepreneur that influences the ability to address the liabilities of newness and smallness, the kind of venture that emerges, and the ultimate venture outcomes.

Others who have not experienced poverty can certainly encounter aspects of these dimensions. However, for the person in poverty, the degree and length of prolonged exposure to all four factors are high. They are conditions in which the poor tend to be immersed prior to and during the launch of a venture, often for all of their lives. As a result, overcoming them once the business is operating places unique demands on the entrepreneur, and for some can represent an insurmountable challenge.

THE LIABILITIES OF POORNESS AND VENTURE FRAGILITY

The ventures of the poor tend to be more vulnerable when confronting adverse circumstances (Bekele & Worku, 2008; Fairlie & Robb, 2008; McMullen, 2011), and the liabilities of poorness are a key contributor. Vulnerability is related to fragility, although the distinction between the two has not received sufficient attention from entrepreneurship scholars. While the former term suggests a potential weakness that could result in loss, the latter concerns how easily (the likelihood that) something could be damaged or broken and a loss incurred (Porter, 2015). A venture is fragile when it is vulnerable to poor internal decisions and threatening external developments, and there is a high likelihood of loss of value or outright failure. Without a buffer that allows them to withstand the adverse impact of shocks, the organization becomes unable to fulfill its core functions.

The burdens posed by the liabilities of poorness vary. The poor differ in terms of the extent to which they experience lower levels of literacy, an immediate-term orientation, personal pressures that are not business-related, and little safety net. Additionally, certain types of businesses may perform adequately in spite of one or more of these risk factors. However, for most new ventures started by the poor, as this burden increases, so does their fragility. They become more vulnerable to major setbacks, their ability to provide core functions declines, and the likelihood of failure increases.

To better appreciate how the liabilities of poorness affect an entrepreneur's ability to succeed, Table 5.1 summarizes ways in which these four dimensions

Table 5.1. How the Liabilities of Poorness Affect Ability to Overcome Other Liabilities

	Challenges Produced by Venture Newness and Smallness							
Liability of Poorness Dimension	Lack of legitimacy	Weak bargaining power	Lack of routines/ procedures	Non-familiarity with roles	Inability to achieve economies	Inefficiency in operations	Lack of resources/ capital access	Lack of established capabilities
Literacy gaps	Deficiencies undermine relationships with key stakeholders	Problems understanding and using bargaining position	Learning that would facilitate routines is hindered	Less understanding of roles due to literacy problems	Multiple literacies are needed to optimize order output quantities	Literacy problems limit the use of technology in venture	Functional & financial literacies needed to work resource providers	Literacy shortcomings take away from developing key capabilities
Scarcity mindset	With little strategic thinking stakeholders question legitimacy	Focus on immediate problems & needs lessens ability to bargain	Short-term problems take focus away from establishing routines	Focus on immediate problems means less learning of key roles	Economies suffer with reactive management & without longer-term planning	Lack of focus on all facets of business leads to inefficiency in some areas	Resource providers expect to see projections, plans and a forward focus	New skills difficult to develop if preoccupied with immediate needs
Ability to Focus	Stakeholders question dedication of entrepreneur to business	Less focus on business can undermine bargaining power	Insufficient time for creating routines & procedures	Outside demands distract the entrepreneur from learning key roles	Distractions make it difficult to build sales, production volumes	Failure to recognize efficiency opportunities due to distractions	Less time for and focus on identifying & leveraging resources & relationship-building	Difficult to learn new capabilities if continually distracted
Lack of financial slack/ safety net	Stakeholders more aware of entrepreneur's financial vulnerability	Lack of safety margin lessens bargaining power	Money, staff & time (and learning) not available to establish routines	Key roles may not receive attention due to leanness of operations	Lack of safety net discourages growth that would enable economies	Under-investment in labor-saving mechanisms & technology	Resources harder to attract due to lack of savings, assets, margins	No extra time or money to invest in personal development

make it difficult to address conventional problems associated with newness and smallness. Consider the implications of gaps among the poor in the five literacies. Gaps in functional and business literacies can make it difficult to communicate effectively with prospective employees, suppliers, distributors and others, increasing the difficulties in establishing legitimacy with stakeholders. Even fundamental tasks such as obtaining permits, registering the business, and tax compliance can seem overwhelming. Organizational learning and the entrepreneur's understanding of how to develop routines and procedures can be hindered. A person with less functional, technological, and financial literacy may have limited capabilities when it comes to addressing particular organizational tasks. These literacy gaps can mean less familiarity with roles, and an inability to incorporate basic technologies into how things are done, which can produce inefficiencies in operations. These combined literacy gaps can make it harder to realize how to achieve economies in procurement, production, and distribution.

With a scarcity mindset, the entrepreneur is focused on immediate problems and short-term needs, in effect ignoring or putting off other business decisions. The result can be inefficiencies in the areas not receiving attention, particularly if deferring things results in higher unit costs. A lack of strategic thinking can result in legitimacy problems, especially when stakeholders are aware of emerging challenges for which the entrepreneur appears unprepared. A preoccupation with immediate problems can also mean the entrepreneur is not developing knowledge and capabilities associated with key roles that must be filled within the enterprise, particularly when these roles are unrelated to the problems at hand. Without the planning that comes with a longer-term focus, the firm cannot begin to achieve economies in procurement and production. Such planning is also critical for the development, over time, of effective routines and procedures.

When intense personal pressures distract the entrepreneur and make it difficult to attend to the needs of the venture, legitimacy can suffer as stakeholders question the entrepreneur's dedication to the enterprise. Lack of complete focus on the enterprise is likely to produce inefficiencies in operations, less learning, reduced planning, and weaker bargaining power with external stakeholders. Key activities do not receive proper attention. In addition, such distractions could undermine the ability of the entrepreneur to ensure that key routines have been formalized and adhered to.

The absence of any financial slack or a safety net can make it more difficult to attract financial resources, particularly when the organization has had to under-invest in assets, and financial statements indicate little in the way of owner's equity. Without any cushion in terms of personal savings or cash on hand, stakeholders become more aware of the financial vulnerability of the enterprise, especially with regard to a major threat or setback, which can detract from its legitimacy. Suppliers may use such vulnerability as a reason to impose more restrictive terms on purchases. Operating on a thin margin with no reserves, the entrepreneur can be forced to limit inventory levels and make smaller purchases. Overly conservative spending then reduces bargaining power and limits the firm's ability to achieve economies in operations.

As the liabilities of poorness raise the hurdles that must be overcome, the ventures of the poor can become especially fragile. This fragility is most evident when an entrepreneur makes a questionable decision that proves to be costly or encounters a major setback caused by some external development. It is not simply the case that the entrepreneur has greater exposure when such events occur. Fragility means the negative impact of these developments on the venture is likely to be more severe.

An example can be found in the high vulnerability of these businesses during the economic crisis that accompanied the COVID-19 pandemic. For many businesses, orders quickly dried up, contracts were canceled, and sources of supply became problematic. For poverty entrepreneurs, the implications were even more dire. Their fragility was reflected in an inability to afford inventory, pay bills, meet payroll demands, serve customer needs, retain employees, maintain marketing efforts, and sustain relationships with external stakeholders. Outside sources of support disappeared. Lack of cash flow ultimately forced many of these businesses to reduce capacity, sell off assets, and otherwise lessen the venture's ability to create value. They become less competitive and less economically viable. Even as the crisis passed and new opportunities began to appear, these firms were often unable to capitalize upon them. Many poor entrepreneurs failed, and only a percentage will ever regain ground that has been lost.

Alternatively, a resilient venture is one able to absorb, adapt and transform in ways that allow it to continue providing the core functions of the business when confronting shocks and stresses (Van Metre, 2016). Elements that can make a venture more resilient include things like planning for contingencies, developing social networks for support, having financial slack, developing a loyal customer base, building strong supplier relationships, being adaptable, and establishing problem-solving routines that allow for flexibility (Avery & Bergsteiner, 2011; Dahles & Suilowati, 2015; Linnenluecke, 2017). In the COVID scenario above, elements that might enable a venture to withstand the economic crisis are directly compromised by the liabilities of poorness. As we have seen, the liabilities of poorness can result in the very kinds of operational weaknesses that work against these elements and serve to limit resiliency. With the ventures of the poor, fragility and resiliency arguably co-exist, while also working against one another (De Boer, Muggah, & Patel, 2016). When the risk factors that cumulatively produce fragility become so great, they take away from and eventually overwhelm elements that contribute to resiliency.

Finally, we should note that aspects of the poverty experience can also help an individual learn to be more resilient, in effect offsetting the liabilities of poorness. Individuals in poverty can learn to mobilize resources as they are exposed to hardship in ways that better prepare them for subsequent risks (Fergus & Zimmerman, 2005). Zolkoski and Bullock (2012) explain that "with continued exposure to adversity as youth age and mature, their capacity to thrive despite risks increases." Development of this capacity appears more likely when confronting moderate, as opposed to extreme, risks although its effects have not been examined in a new venture context.

THE NEED TO LEVEL THE PLAYING FIELD

Poverty entrepreneurs will vary in the extent to which they must overcome the liabilities of poorness. Some will start a venture with relatively higher literacy levels, less of a scarcity mentality, fewer outside pressures, or more reserves they can draw upon. Others may experience all of these elements to such an overwhelming extent that they make little progress in getting a venture off the ground. They remain stalled in writing a business plan, getting permits and licenses, or figuring out how to attract customers.

All aspects of the business creation process are potentially affected by the liabilities of poorness. Its effects can be found in decisions ranging from what is being sold, the prices charged, and the customers targeted to purchases of equipment, where the business operates from, whether it is formally registered, and how much money is taken out for personal use. The liabilities can have a compounding effect, as decisions in one area delimit the possibilities in another area, in turn constraining yet other aspects of business operations. Perhaps the greatest implication of the liabilities of poorness lies in the potential for these factors to become reinforcing and have a circular effect. Hence, a person who is struggling to get by creates a survival venture that lacks assets and generates only enough revenue to pay this week's bills, and feed his or her family. The entrepreneur fails to develop key business competencies, struggles to build a positive reputation, and the business remains highly fragile. The marginal status makes it harder to attract customers, employees, and suppliers. Stated differently, the venture does not provide a pathway out of poverty and may ultimately serve to worsen the individual's financial and personal situation.

The liabilities of poorness may also produce a fear of growth in the entrepreneur, despite the fact that growth is critical for overcoming the liabilities of newness and smallness. Consistent with prospect theory (Tversky &

Kahneman, 1979), poverty entrepreneurs can become more concerned with avoiding loss when faced with opportunities for gain. Because they must overcome a greater set of challenges to get a venture up and running, the priority is to hold onto whatever gains or progress the individual has already made. This makes the entrepreneur hesitant to buy major equipment, consider new markets, or take on larger or more complex orders.

Another issue concerns how temporal the effects of the liabilities of poorness prove to be. While these are burdens that some entrepreneurs never completely overcome, many in poverty build ventures that become sustainable, achieve growth, and prove to be quite resilient. It would seem likely that the entrepreneurs who succeed become more self-aware over time of their literacy gaps, their failure to adequately plan or think beyond the immediate, and the need to better prepare for and manage personal distractions and create a margin for safety. For some, as they work in the venture, intentionally or unintentionally they are able to remove risk factors associated with the liabilities of poorness. They improve their financial literacy by focusing on patterns with costs or studying simple financial statements. They enhance their technological literacy by experimenting with new software products or technical equipment. They learn to save and put money back into the business and begin to create annual budget plans for the next year or two. They find ways to address non-business demands without compromising the needs of the business. They employ entrepreneurial hustle to overcome unexpected uncertainties (Fisher et al., 2020). They steadily learn from trial and error. And, while fragility remains such that one major shock can destroy the venture, poverty entrepreneurs find ways to become more resilient.

Several other factors can contribute to resilience in a poverty context. Family variables represent a case in point. There is evidence that businesses run by families with more functional integrity, where there is clear separation of family tasks and issues from those related to work, are more resilient when faced with crises (Amann & Jaussaud, 2012). Family trust, family social capital, and strong social networks have also been tied to resiliency (Danes et al., 2009). Separately, having a repertoire of adaptive responses to disruptions that derive from facing frequent financial problems or stress can contribute to resilience (Jang, 2005). Another contributor is the psychological capital (including optimism and self-efficacy) of the entrepreneur and any employees (Luthans et al., 2010). Others emphasize improvisation and bricolage (making use of the resources at hand) capabilities (Duchek, 2019; Yang & Danes, 2014), both of which can be motivated by poverty circumstances (Busch & Barkjema, 2017; Linna, 2013).

Finally, as the liabilities of poorness place the poverty entrepreneur at a relative disadvantage, it is important that we find ways to level the playing field. Unfortunately, the unique context of poverty is not well-reflected in the design of public policies or community action initiatives that seek to foster entrepreneurship (Morris & Tucker, 2020). Instead, many of the existing policies and programs prioritize the needs of those who are launching growth-oriented or scalable enterprises (Morris & Kuratko, 2020). Thus, the initial challenge is to make venture creation by the poor a priority both in terms of policy formulation and in the activities of local entrepreneurial ecosystems. These are topics to which we shall return in Chapters 12 and 13.

CONCLUSION

Poverty can impose an additional set of burdens on an entrepreneur, which we have labeled the liabilities of poorness. The disadvantages resulting from a combination of literacy shortcomings, a scarcity mindset, intense non-business pressures, and lack of a safety margin place the poverty entrepreneur at a disadvantage. Where these liabilities are greater, the entrepreneur is left with reduced capabilities and less room to maneuver. It becomes more difficult for them to address the challenges of newness and smallness. Their ventures are likely to be more fragile and suffer higher failure rates. They become especially vulnerable when faced with external threats and disruptive shocks.

For entrepreneurship to become a viable part of the poverty-fighting toolkit, we must fundamentally rethink how the poverty experience can be reconciled with the nature of the entrepreneurial process. Such a reconciliation requires that we systematically address the liabilities of poorness while simultaneously capitalizing on the creativity, tenacity, adaptability, resilience, and other qualities that are often endemic to the experience of poverty.

REFERENCES

Ahmed, M. (2011). Defining and measuring literacy: Facing the reality. *International Review of Education*, *57*(1–2), 179.

Aldrich, H., & Auster, E. (1986). Even dwarfs started small: Liabilities of age and size and their strategic implications. In L. L. Cummings and Barry M. Staw (eds.). *Research in Organizational Behavior, 8,* 165–198. Greenwich, CT: JAI Press.

Amann, B., & Jaussaud, J. (2012). Family and non-family business resilience in an economic downturn. *Asia Pacific Business Review, 18*(2), 203–223.

Anderson, A. R., & Ullah, F. (2014). The condition of smallness: How what it means to be small deters firms from getting bigger. *Management Decision, 52*, 2, 326–349.

Avery, G. C., & Bergsteiner, H. (2011). Sustainable leadership practices for enhancing business resilience and performance. *Strategy & Leadership, 39*(1), 5–15.

Barr, M., & Blank, R. (Eds.) (2009). Savings, assets, credit, and banking among low-income households: Introduction and overview. In R. Bland and M. Barr (Eds.), *Insufficient funds: Savings, assets, credit, and banking among low-income households* (pp. 1–22). New York: Russell Sage Foundation.

Bekele, E., & Worku, Z. (2008). Women entrepreneurship in micro, small and medium enterprises: The case of Ethiopia. *Journal of International Women's Studies*, *10*(2), 3–19.

Busch, C., & Barkema, H. G. (2017). Scaling bricolage in the context of deep poverty. In *Academy of management proceedings* (Vol. 2017, No. 1, p. 11768). Briarcliff Manor: Academy of Management.

Chatzitheochari, S., & Arber, S. (2012). Class, gender and time poverty: A time-use analysis of British workers' free time resources. *The British Journal of Sociology*, *63*(3), 451–471.

Dahles, H., & Susilowati, T. P. (2015). Business resilience in times of growth and crisis. *Annals of Tourism Research, 51*, 34–50.

Danes, S. M., Lee, J., Amarapurkar, S., Stafford, K., Haynes, G., & Brewton, K. E. (2009). Determinants of family business resilience after a natural disaster by gender of business owner. *Journal of Developmental Entrepreneurship, 14*(4), 333–354.

De Boer, J., Muggah, R., & Ronak P. (2016). Conceptualizing city fragility and resilience. New York: United Nations University Centre for Policy Research.

Dermott, E., & Pomati, M. (2016). "Good" parenting practices: How important are poverty, education and time pressure? *Sociology*, *50*(1), 125–142.

Duchek, S. (2019). Organizational resilience: A capability-based conceptualization. *Business Research, 13*, 215–246.

Fairlie, R. & Robb, A. (2008), *Race and entrepreneurial success*. Cambridge, Massachusetts: The MIT Press.

Fergus, S., & Zimmerman, M. A. (2005). Adolescent resilience: A framework for understanding healthy development in the face of risk. *Annual Review of Public Health, 26*(4), 399–419.

Fisher, G., Stevenson, R., Neubert, E., Burnell, D., & Kuratko, D. F. (2020). Entrepreneurial hustle: Navigating uncertainty and enrolling venture stakeholders through urgent and unorthodox action. *Journal of Management Studies, 57*(5), 1002–1036.

Hannan, M. T. & Freeman, J. (1984). Structural inertia and organizational change. *American Sociology Review, 49*, 149–164.

Hernandez, D. J. (2011). *Double jeopardy: How third-grade reading skills and poverty influence high school graduation.* Baltimore, MD: Annie E. Casey Foundation.

Jang, L. (2005). The 921 earthquake: A study of the effects of Taiwanese cultural factors on resilience. Unpublished dissertation, University of Denver, Denver, CO. Accessed on July 10, 2020, www.riskinstitute.org/peri/images/file/LJ_dissertation.pdf.

Lefebvre, V. (2020). Performance, working capital management, and the liability of smallness: A question of opportunity costs? *Journal of Small Business Management.* https://doi.org/10.1080/00472778.2020.1735252

Linna, P. (2013). Bricolage as a means of innovating in a resource-scarce environment: innovator-entrepreneurs at the BOP. *Journal of Developmental Entrepreneurship, 18*(3), 1–23.

Linnenluecke, M. K. (2017). Resilience in business and management research: a review of influential publications and a research agenda. *International Journal of Management Reviews, 19*(1), 4–30.

Littwin, Angela. 2008. Beyond usury: A study of credit-card use and preference among low-income consumers. *Texas Law Review, 86,* 451–506.

Luthans, F., Avey, J. B., Avolio, B. J., & Peterson, S. J. (2010). The development and resulting performance impact of positive psychological capital. *Human Resource Development Quarterly, 21*(1), 41–67.

Mani, A., Mullainathan, S., Shafir, E., & Zhao, J. (2013). Poverty impedes cognitive function. *Science, 341*(6149), 976–980.

McMullen, J. S. (2011). Delineating the domain of development entrepreneurship: A market–based approach to facilitating inclusive economic growth. *Entrepreneurship Theory and Practice, 35*(1), 185–215.

Morris, M. H., & Kuratko, D. F. (2020). *What do entrepreneurs create?: Understanding four types of ventures*. Edward Elgar Publishing.

Morris, M. H., Santos, S. C., & Neumeyer, X. (2018). *Poverty and entrepreneurship in developed economies*. Edward Elgar Publishing.

Morris, M.H., Santos, S. C., & Neumeyer, X. (2020). Entrepreneurship as a solution to poverty in developed economies, *Business Horizons*, doi: 10.1016/j.bushor.2020.01.010.

Morris, M. H., & Tucker, R. (2020). Poverty and entrepreneurship in developed economies: Re-assessing the roles of policy and community action. *Journal of Poverty, 24*, 1–22.

Morris, M. H. (2020). The liability of poorness: Why the playing field is not level for poverty entrepreneurs. *Poverty & Public Policy, 12*(3), 304–315.

Morris, M. H., Kuratko, D. F., Audretsch, D. B., & Santos, S. (2022). Overcoming the liability of poorness: Disadvantage, fragility, and the poverty entrepreneur. *Small Business Economics, 58*, 41–55.

Porter, K. (2015). A beginner's guide to fragility, vulnerability, and risk. *Encyclopedia of earthquake engineering, 2015*, 235–260.

Shah, A. K., Mullainathan, S., & Shafir, E. (2012). Some consequences of having too little. *Science, 338*(6107), 682–685.

Shah, A. K., Shafir, E., & Mullainathan, S. (2015). Scarcity frames value. *Psychological Science, 26*(4), 402–412.

Stangler, D. (2010). *High growth firms and the future of the American economy.* Kansas City: Kauffman Foundation.

Stinchcombe, A. L. (1965). Social structure and organizations. In J. G. March (Ed.), *Handbook of organizations* (pp. 142–193). Chicago: Rand McNally.

Suchman, M. C. (1995). Managing legitimacy: Strategic and institutional approaches. *Academy of Management Review, 20*, 571–610.

Tversky, A., & Kahneman, D. (1979). Prospect theory: an analysis of decision under risk. *Econometrica, 47*(2), 263–291.

UNESCO. (2005). Aspects of literacy assessment: topics and issues from the UNESCO expert meeting. June 2003. Paris: United Nations Educational, Scientific and Cultural Organization.
Watson, J., & Everett, J. (1999). Small business failure rates: Choice of definition and industry effects. *International Small Business Journal, 17*(2), 31–47.
Wilson, N. & Summers, B. (2002). Trade credit terms offered by small firms: Survey evidence and empirical analysis. *Journal of Business Finance and Accounting, 29*(3), 317–351.
Wilson, W. J. (1996). *When work disappears*. New York: Vintage Books.
Yang, Y., & Danes, S. M. (2015). Resiliency and resilience process of entrepreneurs in new venture creation. *Entrepreneurship Research Journal, 5*(1), 1–30.
Zolkoski, S. M., & Bullock, L. M. (2012). Resilience in children and youth: A review. *Children and Youth Services Review, 34*(12), 2295–2303.

Chapter Six

Opportunity Horizons and Poverty

In our work with low-income and disadvantaged entrepreneurs, we find they frequently create ventures based on what they see and experience in their daily lives. They start businesses involved in lawn care, residential and commercial cleaning, hair care, retail sales of clothing, catering and food service, transport/delivery, and wedding planning. They create products such as candles, baby bibs, skin lotions, lip balms, decorative wreaths, cakes, and chocolates. Their businesses fail to incorporate much in the way of technology and equipment and are severely capacity constrained. These are often ventures in highly competitive markets where sustainable differentiation is difficult to achieve. As a result, they find themselves attempting to compete solely on price. Such businesses frequently cannot generate enough profit to move the entrepreneur out of poverty.

A successful venture begins with the recognition of a marketplace opportunity by the entrepreneur. Opportunities are favorable circumstances in the external environment that create an opening for a new product, service, or process. They emerge from tapping unfilled gaps in the marketplace and exist in a specific context, community, or place. They can come in the form of unmet needs, dissatisfaction with current solutions in the marketplace, or the potential to improve or be more efficient with a product or service. Further, once a business is launched, the alert entrepreneur can encounter a stream of additional opportunities. The recognition and pursuit of some of these opportunities ultimately lead to the kinds of adaptations and adjustments that result in a sustainable enterprise.

The process of identifying opportunities is one of the most challenging and intriguing processes in entrepreneurship. It depends on human agency and emerges from complex cognitive processes in interaction with (and dependent on) the environment and context in which an individual is embedded. Attempts to answer the critical question "*Why do some people, and not others, discover a particular opportunity?*" generally emphasize cognitive biases and decision-making processes (Sarasvathy, 2001), resources that individuals control (Baker & Nelson, 2005), and social construction processes with the environment (Alvarez & Barney, 2007), such as recognizing patterns (Baron, 2006) or being alert to market imperfections (Tang, Kacmar, & Busenitz, 2012), in an ongoing process of discovery.

While opportunities may be one of the most explored topics in entrepreneurship research, the idiosyncrasies of uncovering business opportunities when experiencing poverty have received much less attention. Yet, a limited ability to find attractive opportunities is a key factor explaining why poverty entrepreneurs launch ventures having little profit potential. The liabilities of poorness (see Chapter 5) play a critical role here.

Opportunities are identified by recognizing patterns, interpreting trends, challenging assumptions, discerning needs that are not well-served, and seeing ways a solution can be improved or enhanced. When one experiences prolonged poverty and adversity, the ability to discern market opportunities on a timely basis can be severely constrained. This is due to a range of factors, from literacy gaps and weak educational backgrounds to lack of mobility, a preoccupation with immediate needs, lack of choice, segregated social status, and limited social networks. Being exposed to opportunities helps an individual see additional possibilities, while being closed off from opportunities limits the range of possibilities one can discern.

Suppose one is struggling with paying medical bills or constantly worrying about eviction from their home or the physical safety of their children. How much cognitive bandwidth is there to be alert and perceive opportunities in the environment? If one has never crossed outside the boundaries (psychologically and physically) of the community where they grew up, how novel are the opportunities they can recognize? If one has difficulty using a smartphone and navigating the internet, how can they understand opportunities to tap into online and virtual markets? In this chapter, we reflect on these issues and focus on the challenges and idiosyncrasies of business opportunities in the context of poverty.

RECOGNITION, DISCOVERY, AND CREATION OF BUSINESS OPPORTUNITIES IN POVERTY

Finding a business opportunity is the beginning point of entrepreneurship. One cannot start a new business, in either the formal or informal sector, without there being a potential source of demand for the products and services produced by the business. Opportunities fuel entrepreneurial behaviors, and bring into existence new products, services, materials, artifacts, and/or organizing methods that can produce a profit (Grégoire, Shepherd, & Lambert, 2010). The attractiveness of a given opportunity is based upon four criteria: the economic value it can generate (how much profit can be made from selling the product/service), the novelty of the idea (how unique, different, and new is the product or service), its perceived desirability (how prominent is the need for the product or service and how large is the set of potential customers), and the durability of the market need (how long the opportunity will endure) (Baron, 2006).

Three main approaches describe how business opportunities are uncovered. The first approach argues that opportunities are just out there waiting to be observed by an entrepreneur—what we call *simple recognition*. In this approach, individuals recognize everyday changes, spot trends, or identify connections between developments in their environments (e.g., social and demographic patterns, technological developments, political and regulatory changes, etc.) that may represent a possible opportunity for a new business (Morris, Santos, & Neumeyer, 2018). For example, the coronavirus pandemic brought several political and regulatory changes, such as the mask mandate requiring individuals to use face-covering masks. At the same time, a new social movement, or the passing of a significant figure, may lead people to want to display and voice support for causes and things they believe in. Connecting these changes, an individual recognizes opportunities for sewing and selling face masks with political or social statements. This basic approach requires active cognitive processes, such as pattern recognition (Baron & Ensley, 2006) and structural alignment (Grégoire, Barr, & Shepherd, 2010), along with the important role of entrepreneurial alertness (Kaish & Gilad, 1991; Gaglio & Katz, 2001). Although individual functioning is driven by economic principles (Rosch, 1978), being inundated with a range of daily distractions (financial pressures, job uncertainty, childcare demands, food scarcity, etc.) can constrain the ability to perceive even the most apparent market opportunities.

The second approach can be labeled the *discovery* process. Here, the process is more complicated than simple discovery, as it involves back and forth interactions between the individual and the opportunity until its nature is discovered (Shane & Venkataraman, 2000). Opportunities come to be uncovered based on interactive and complex cycles between the individual and the surrounding context, such as by interactions with potential customers, suppliers, competitors, or exogenous shocks (Alvarez & Barney, 2007). Hence, it is an iterative process where the opportunity emerges from trial and error, learning, and adaptation (often when the individual is not necessarily looking for an opportunity). The types of opportunities developed in the discovery process are not self-evident for everyone because they are shaped along the way and require learning and prior knowledge (Corbett, 2007; Shane, 2000). They are contingent on how individuals perceive and interpret unmet needs, trends, as well as their knowledge and observation of the environment and competition. When the individual is immersed in the context of poverty, discovery approaches come with additional challenges as there is limited access to information and technology, lack of knowledge of the competition, and the limited resources (including time) to experiment and go through interactive cycles of discovery.

Finally, the *creation* approach suggests the entrepreneur is taking actions that actually generate the opportunity, usually based upon some sort of technological breakthrough. This approach is grounded in the notion of evolutionary realism (Alvarez, Barney, & Anderson, 2013), and assumes that opportunities constitute subjective social constructions dependent on the individuals' enactment. Specific actions of entrepreneurs bring these opportunities into existence (Alvarez & Barney, 2007), and opportunities do not exist prior to endogenous efforts by entrepreneurs. For example, the development of breakthrough medical technology allowed for the creation of laser eye surgery, where the entrepreneur leveraged the emerging technology to drive the creation of an entirely new market. Prior to this, new opportunities were defined by better approaches to making eyeglasses or contact lenses. For the low-income or disadvantaged individual, the breakthroughs that led to the creation of an otherwise non-existent opportunity are typically beyond their reach, especially when they suffer from literacy gaps, significant non-business distractions, and a shorter-term focus resulting from a scarcity mindset.

Overall, the recognition, discovery, or creation of business opportunities involves both subjective and objective dimensions. It is subjective and idiosyncratic because it is contingent upon an individual's alertness—an "antenna" that recognizes stimuli that represent opportunities, together with underlying cognitive, motivational, and identification processes (Tang, Kacmar, & Busenitz, 2012). Any opportunity is perceived based on how individuals look at and process stimuli in the environment (their lenses and mindset), the social situations in which they are embedded, and the depth and breadth of their information, knowledge, and expertise. Interestingly, it is not just the rational or cognitive side of things that matters in uncovering opportunities. An important role is played by emotion, as one will recognize opportunities in domains, spaces, and contexts they care most about—areas they are passionate about, or where they have a stronger personal interest (Cardon et al., 2009). At the same time, opportunities are also objective in the sense that they are "*out there*" and everywhere in the external environment. They derive from imperfections in the market and changes in the external environment (Baron, 2006). An objective perspective suggests that, at any point in time, there are innumerable opportunities in any community, context, or social system, waiting to be recognized and capitalized upon. This perspective includes impoverished and low-income contexts. However, individuals in poverty contexts tend to struggle when it comes to identifying highly attractive opportunities. Why is this and how can it be changed? To address these questions, we must consider the notion of the individual's *opportunity horizon*.

HOW POVERTY LIMITS OPPORTUNITY HORIZONS

Consider two young men who grow up in an urban slum. All they have known in their early lives is scarcity, deprivation, discrimination, and lack of access. At age 18 one of them joins the military and is stationed in posts around the country or the world. The other remains in the local neighborhood working a series of low=paying jobs with little opportunity for self-development or advancement. The two young men come back together at age 25. Which of them is able to recognize a more diverse range of interesting opportunities?

The answer is likely to be the individual who encountered a wider range of novel stimuli, had a greater diversity of experiences, and was exposed to more occasions for personal and professional development. When one is exposed to different approaches for solving the same problem or need, alternative technologies, solutions that vary in scale and scope, or divergent assumptions and norms, there is likely to be an expansion of what we refer to as the individual's "opportunity horizon." This horizon refers to the range of possibilities a person is able to perceive at a given point in time (Morris, Santos, & Neumeyer, 2018).

Opportunities are tied to particular approaches to addressing a need. The ability to recognize both the need and different approaches for addressing it depends upon the individual's life experiences, the knowledge base they can draw upon, and their cognitive processing abilities, among other considerations. The notion of an opportunity horizon accounts for both individual and contextual factors that can place boundaries on how one views the world and its possibilities. We can identify four sets of factors that serve to define one's horizon. They include:

- demands of the multiple roles that an individual is assuming: parent, provider for a family, caregiver, employee with one or more jobs, employer, friend, mentor, student, volunteer, community activist, and so forth;
- skills, abilities, knowledge, and expertise acquired through schooling, training, work experiences, and life experiences, as well as access to information and related resources to promote continued learning;
- the interpersonal or social context in which one is embedded, including individuals (e.g., family, friends, peers, colleagues, neighbors, supervisors) and organizations (e.g., schools, churches, workplaces, venues where one volunteers, clubs and organizations to which one belongs);

- the larger environment to which one is exposed (e.g., cultural influences, norms, expectations, values, pressures, threats, sources of support).

In a poverty context, these sets of factors can have an interactive relationship and a cumulative impact. They influence one another in complex and varied ways, with the net effect being a reduced ability to recognize potential opportunities (Müller, 2002). As Berkman (2015) concludes, poverty conditions restrict a person's vision of what might be possible. The ability to recognize the set of factors that indicate a gap or opening may exist in the marketplace, and then formulate a unique approach to filling this gap, is constrained. In essence, blinders are placed on the individual, constricting the scope of what they can see and how different phenomena are interpreted. The result is a cumulative disadvantage effect (Vandecasteele, 2011), in which inequalities accumulate from one set of factors to the others (Leseman & Slot, 2014). These cumulative effects are both bottom-up and top-down.

Let us begin with top-down effects. The opportunity horizon is largely determined by what we are familiar with. The environment and personal circumstances within which the individual is embedded serve to delimit what she or he is able to perceive, recognize, and act upon (Morris et al., 2002). Individuals living in segregated conditions in ghettos or low-income neighborhoods are exposed to a very specific range of possibilities characterized by social exclusion and isolation. In such a context, the poor are often marginalized and deprived of opportunities to meaningfully participate in societal structures. There are limited employment opportunities, high uncertainty and turnover in jobs, scarcity of resources, poor housing conditions, difficulties in accessing healthcare, problematic school absenteeism, low academic and behavioral expectations for students, and limited co-curricular opportunities (see Chapter 2). In such an adverse context, relationships between peers and groups can be tense and victimization of children and teenagers is frequent due to the pressure to fit in with or adopt group norms. As children and adolescents from poor families may lack the resources to participate in stimulating co-curricular activities, they may have more difficulties creating and maintaining positive relationships with peers (Hjalmarsson, 2018) and thus can engage in deviant behavioral patterns. The characteristics of such social interactions also influence family dynamics, as conflicts and discussions between parents and children can arise, which in turn have implications at the individual level. In low-income conditions, harsh and less supportive parenting behavior may influence children's behavior (Conger et al., 2010), and, consequently, their relationships with peers and the self (Curtner-Smith et al., 2006). This series of phenomena illustrates what can be termed cumulative chains of determination, where conditions in the individual's social environment strongly influence and determine the scope of the social interactions and family and individual dynamics.

Similarly, cumulative chains of determination may continually emerge from the bottom-up. Individuals born and raised in poverty are also exposed to families facing constraints and hardships. In these families, affect can be flat and silent, tension can be high, and generally, there is less space for the finer emotions (Sarbin, 1970). Children are very likely to attend schools with high rates of academic absenteeism, a limited curriculum, less talented instructors, and fewer resources to support personal and academic growth. In such low-income conditions, social systems are characterized by intense peer pressure and influences to fit in with the group. Overall, these conditions reinforce the social exclusion of individuals in poverty, leaving the poor secluded, marginalized and powerless in the face of threatening barriers to inclusion.

In Figure 6.1, we provide a graphical representation of these cumulative chains of determination, displaying the bottom-up and top-down paths. Overall, these chains help explain why poverty can become a multigenerational struggle (Shlonsky, 1984; Garrity & Martin, 2018). As we will see, entrepreneurship can be a mechanism to provide better educational opportunities for children and break the cumulative effect of poverty (Shepherd, Parida, & Wincent, 2021).

THE DEPTH AND BREADTH OF OPPORTUNITY HORIZONS

The cumulative chains of determination in the poverty context have important implications for one's opportunity horizon. For example, if an individual is not familiar with the use of a computer or smartphone, it is unlikely that the person will recognize opportunities in the areas of software, hardware, networks, or information and technology systems. In the poverty context, overcoming technology barriers is a significant hurdle that entrepreneurs face (Neumeyer, Santos, & Morris, 2020). Similarly, if one's life circumstances find him or her simultaneously performing various complex demanding roles that absorb most of the mental space that one has to devote to deciphering opportunities, this will limit the ability to find multiple opportunities. Another example is a single mother who is also the main family provider for the household and at the same time has elderly parents that require healthcare support—how is there spare mental space to recognize opportunities? Imagine a person segregated in a geographical area, being born and raised in the same neighborhood in the skirts of a major city, interacting with peers that are also exposed to the same constraints and pressures, where there is crime, drugs, distrust, anxiety, and few job opportunities. The opportunity horizon of

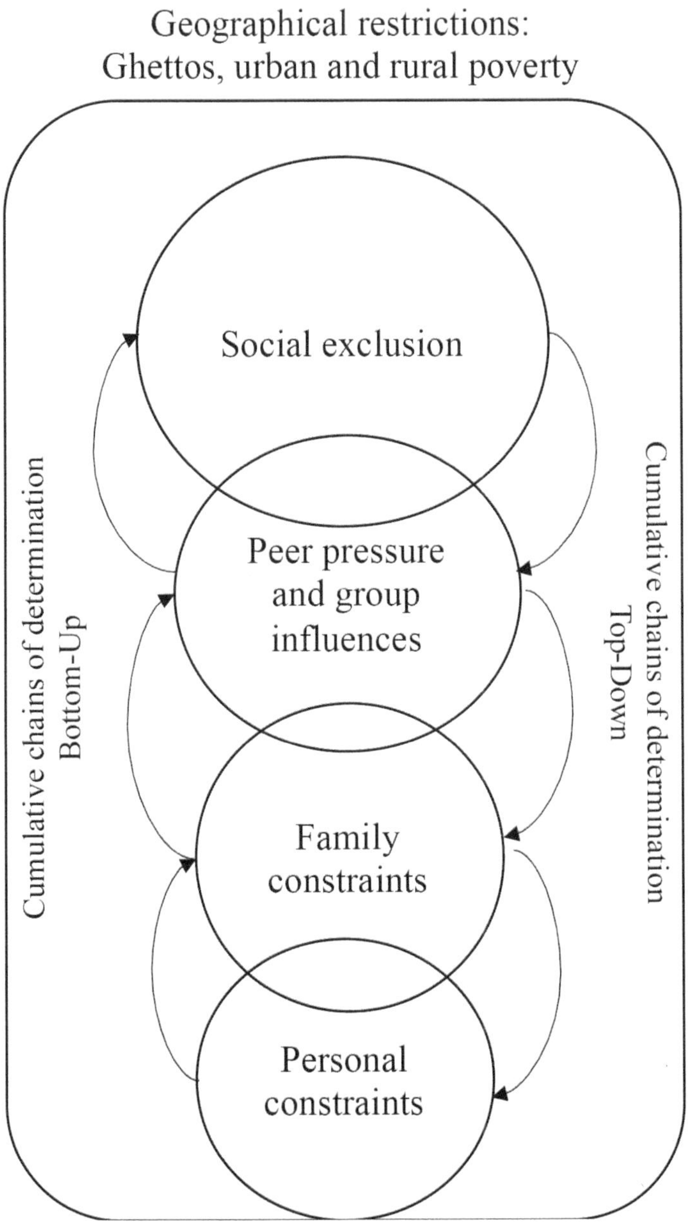

Figure 6.1. Cumulative chains of determination in poverty context.
Created by Authors

such an individual is often bounded by the array of possibilities he or she has been exposed to in that neighborhood or community.. It can be problematic to recognize high potential opportunities that reflect needs in other markets.

These examples lead to the conceptualization of one's opportunity horizon in terms of two dimensions: *breadth*, that is, the range of different opportunity domains within which the entrepreneur is able to perceive or recognize possibilities; and *depth*, that is, the number of possibilities that are apparent within the specific opportunity domains apparent to the entrepreneur.

In poverty contexts, the *breadth* of the opportunity horizon is comprised of the types of industries and fields of endeavor that the individual is familiar with. For example, one may see opportunities in personal care, cleaning, food and beverage, or construction, which constitute a relatively narrow breadth that likely generates businesses that often fall into the commodity trap (see Chapter 8). On the other side of the continuum is a wide opportunity horizon that can capitalize on such diverse opportunities as genetic engineering of crops, design of drones to assist first responders, use of artificial intelligence within patient healthcare, or safety applications to protect women and minorities in foreign countries. A wider breadth in the opportunity horizon is likely to create businesses with more robust competitive advantages.

The *depth* dimension of the opportunity horizon is related to the number of possibilities that the entrepreneur may perceive within a given domain, such as possibilities of new markets, customer segments, technologies, or business applications. For example, within house cleaning, one may see the opportunity to provide cleaning services to households (limited depth), but a greater depth would be to offer cleaning services to businesses or to offer specialized cleaning services, for example, medical, laboratory and biotech. Greater depth is associated with more specialized opportunities, where the entrepreneur may be able to charge a higher price, achieve greater differentiation, and develop a more sustainable business model.

While the opportunity horizon for each individual is unique, considerations of depth and breadth combine to shape four main types of horizons. These horizons, in turn, have important implications for the types and potential of the businesses pursued by individuals. Our four types include:

- *bounded commodity*—an opportunity horizon characterized by a limited depth and narrow breadth, typically leading to survival types of ventures selling commodity-like products, with limited to no competitive advantage and low barriers to entry;
- *bounded aspirant*—an opportunity horizon characterized by a greater breadth but limited depth, where more generic products are offered and potential exists to expand the offering of the commodity business to integrate other basic products (sometimes in unrelated categories). The

additional breadth may expose the entrepreneur to alternative technologies or approaches that can be used within the business. This kind of diversification may (or may not) offer competitive advantage;
- *commodity breaker*—an opportunity horizon characterized by narrow breadth but greater depth. In this case, opportunities offer more room for differentiation or uniqueness. For example, it can include exploring, within a particular business domain, new market segments, more specialized niches, or integrating basic technologies to improve efficiency. Competitive advantage is achievable but may be difficult to maintain over time, as competitors mimic the firm's advantage and the narrow breadth limits the range of new products and services that are explored; and,
- *visionary maker*—an opportunity horizon characterized by greater depth and broad breadth. In this case, the entrepreneur perceives opportunities in multiple domains with wide market potential and multiple customer segments. There is considerable room for sustainable differentiation and uniqueness. One of the main characteristics of such a visionary maker opportunity horizon is its openness to change, continuously in search of new possibilities.

Figure 6.2 provides a graphic representation of the two dimensions of the opportunity horizon and the four main types of opportunity horizons that emerge.

For those experiencing poverty conditions, a bounded commodity type of opportunity horizon is likely to be the most common. The cumulative chains of determination constrain the depth and breadth of opportunity horizons in such contexts, limiting the ease of broadening the scope of opportunities and stretching boundaries. The psychological boundaries in low-income neighborhoods inhibit exposure to out-group socialization, reaching new geographic areas even at relatively close distances, interacting with individuals from other socio-economic backgrounds, or looking for employment opportunities in other contexts. There are no rules that one cannot rise above the geographic space and challenge the components of the chains of determination, excepting the hidden rules implicit in the poverty context (Payne, 2005) which can serve as solid and anchored barriers. For many, moving out of such a context can seem like a myth (Quillian, 1999), as one key study found 70% of the families living in high-poverty neighborhoods in 1972 were still living in equivalent conditions 40 years later (Sharkey, 2013). This strong social anchoring can contribute to a very constrained opportunity horizon among the poor. Limits are placed on the kinds of demographic, social, technological, competitive, regulatory, or other developments of which one is aware and understands.

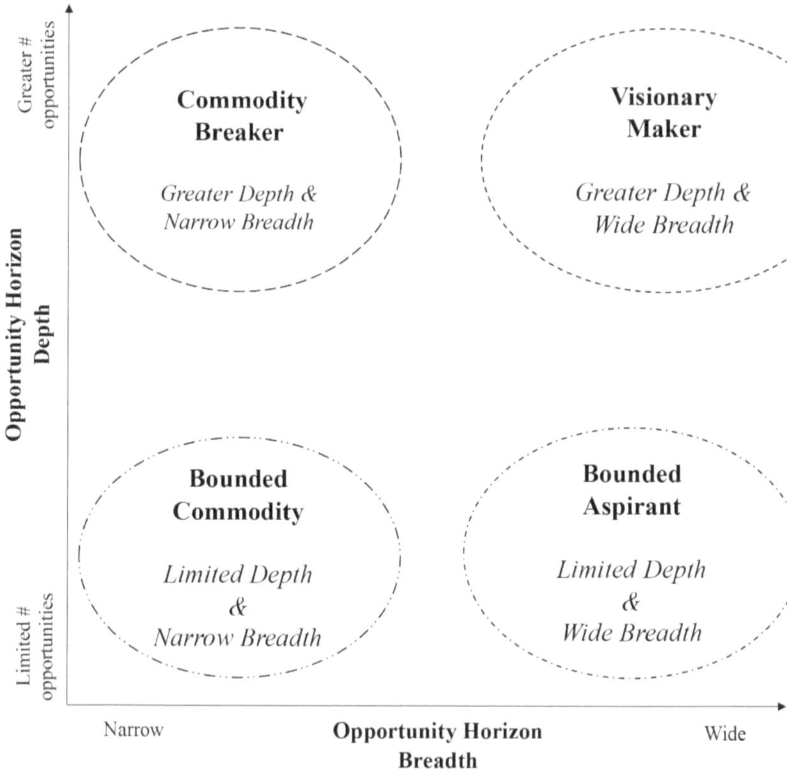

Figure 6.2. Depth and Breadth of Opportunity Horizons.
Created by Authors

Often, the entrepreneur is able to perceive only minor and relatively short-lived pockets of disequilibrium in the marketplace.

However, opportunity horizons are not static or predetermined by a postal code. While the starting conditions may help to define the kind of access an individual has at a given point in time, where they find themselves is not where they must remain. Opportunity horizons are flexible, dynamic, and elastic, such that the biggest issue for those in poverty conditions concerns how to move the boundaries that have been placed upon them.

STRETCHING THE OPPORTUNITY HORIZON IN POVERTY CONTEXTS

How can we overcome the constraints on opportunity recognition engendered by the poverty experience? Poverty is a condition experienced by individuals, not a personal characteristic. As such, we must focus on the limiting nature of poverty conditions. Any individual is capable of seeing more in terms of opportunities. The narrow depth and shallow breadth of one's horizon are circumstantial and can be broadened if we adopt a process-based perspective on poverty, grounded in empowerment and development, where the acquisition of new perspectives and capabilities fosters a pathway out of poverty. Enlarging one's opportunity horizon is one of several factors that can help individuals break the cumulative chains of determination.

Our basic premise is that exposure to other contexts and associated content (individual, social, and geographic) can serve to alleviate the invisible boundaries of segregation in poverty. This can be enabled by cultivating an entrepreneurial mindset (Morris & Tucker, 2021), fostering network development, and exposure to a broad set of novel contexts and events (see Figure 6.3), as we shall explore.

Opportunity horizons can be enlarged as the individual is exposed to new sources or types of information, influences, and experiences. In line with the principles of socially situated cognition (Smith & Semin, 2006), exposure to other external realities shapes a person's cognitive or mental frameworks. The challenge is to both introduce the individual to a different array of possibilities and enable them to process and make sense of these possibilities.

Broadening an opportunity horizon from a limited and narrow quadrant (bounded commodity) to a greater and wide quadrant (visionary maker) (Figure 6.2) is a significant leap, but exposure to various kinds of triggers at different levels of analysis helps to incrementally stretch the cognitive scope of one's horizon. Smith and Semin (2006) stress the role of cognition in the adaptive regulation of action, where mental representations are action-oriented. Here, the emphasis is placed on the *embodied* (drawing on one's brain, sensorimotor abilities and surrounding environment) and *socially situated* (an emergent outcome of dynamic interactions between the individual and environment) nature of cognition. For instance, exposing the individual to incrementally more complex levels of information, networks and institutional contexts can contribute to progressively enlarging their opportunity horizon.

There are three kinds of overlapping and interacting levers that can be manipulated to broaden the depth and breadth of horizons for those in poverty circumstances: knowledge, information, and educational levers; interpersonal and social levers; and institutional and political levers. These are illustrated in Figure 6.4 and expanded upon below.

Knowledge, Information, and Educational Levers

At a core level, opportunity horizons among the poor can be expanded by exposure to new knowledge, information, education, personal experiences,

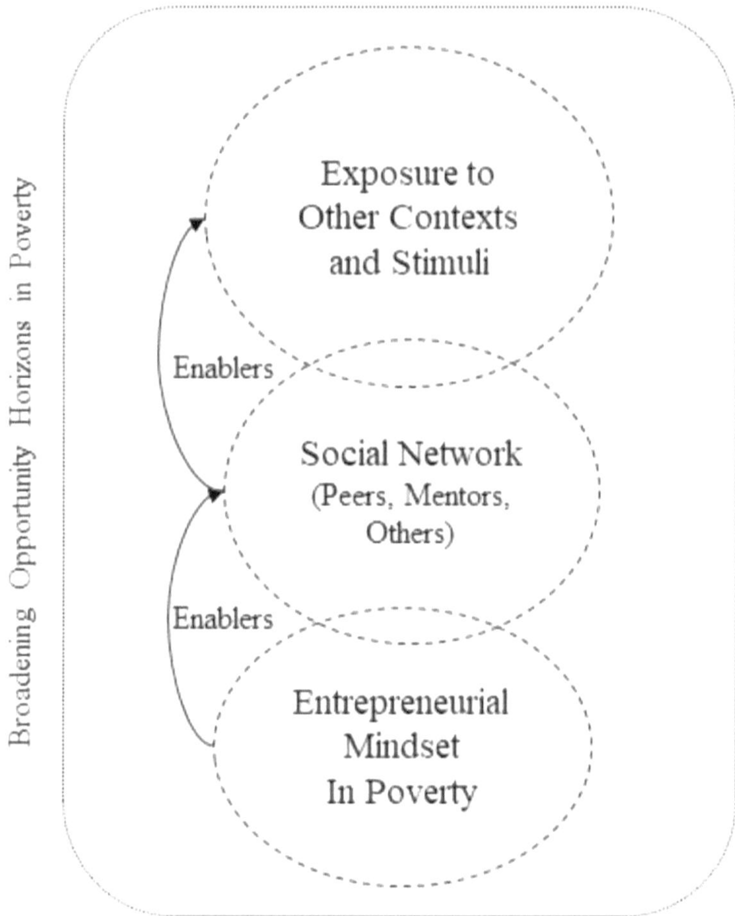

Figure 6.3. Broadening Opportunity Horizons in Poverty.
Created by Authors

and observation of other realities. This primary lever is high in agency, meaning it is dependent on the individual and their personal efforts. While poverty circumstances can condition one's scope and array of recognizable

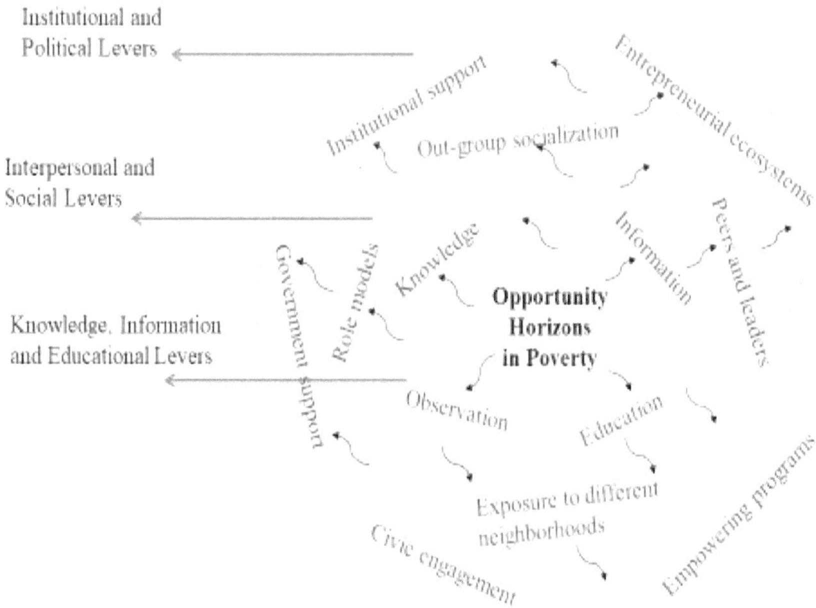

Figure 6.4. Extending the Entrepreneurs Horizon at Three Levels.
Created by Authors

opportunities, it is also true that the individual's intention to break the self-reinforcing chains of determination starts with their own actions and behaviors.

Searching for new knowledge, being curious and pursuing actions (even small or micro) that expose oneself to other realities is the key. Agency is applied as the individual pursues activities outside what is required in his or her daily existence. Examples include:

- hobbies
- exchange programs
- internships and apprenticeships
- volunteer activities
- membership in self-development organizations, clubs or groups
- entering competitions
- enrollment in free online courses and webinars
- church-sponsored travel or mission trips
- joining the military
- organizing events and inviting diverse participants
- frequenting establishments and events that are not part of one's normal routine.

Consider a teenager studying in an under-privileged school who decides to attend a free after-school workshop on internet search techniques that is taking place at a community center (where there is more dependable bandwidth). This micro action can be the first step in expanding one's opportunity horizon as enhanced digital literacy and awareness about digital tools and resources resulting from the workshop are put into action. The student applies these capabilities in looking for part-time job opportunities and discovers a range of job categories he or she otherwise would never know existed (breadth of his/her horizon), including jobs requiring a certain kind of basic skill, or that can be done remotely, or completed at certain times or days of the week (depth of the horizon). As the student's field of vision (or cognitive scope) is enlarged, it becomes possible to identify patterns in terms of types of part-time jobs in higher demand, or requiring certain skills, which in turn leads to the recognition of an opportunity to create some type of youth training and placement service.

Importantly, knowledge, access and usage of digital resources are a particularly valuable lever to stretch opportunity horizons, as this is increasingly a primary vehicle for learning new skills (e.g., DIY solutions, alternative approaches to accomplishing a task) and establishing connections outside of the geographical, psychological, and social boundaries of the local neighborhood or community. Micro actions, such as attending this after-school activity, can have a cumulative effect over time, such that the individual later in life has evolved from operating within a bounded commodity frame of reference to being a commodity breaker. While this may not be a significant leap in a more privileged context, for someone in disadvantaged circumstances, this vertical transition in the depth axis can be a game changer in creating the kind of business that can actually move them out of poverty. Again, it all started with agency that resulted in exposure to novel information, content, technologies, and processes.

Alternatively, there is evidence that knowledge limitations and their associated bounded commodity opportunity horizons can result in the creation of survival ventures—ventures that keep the individual in poverty. A study involving entrepreneurs from low-income regions in Spain found that knowledge deficiencies represented one of the most severe constraints in developing a business that proves to be financially sustainable (Fernández-Serrano, Martínez-Román, & Romero, 2019). This stretching of one's cognitive scope can happen in formal contexts such as schools, jobs, and volunteering activities, but also in informal contexts, like observing others' behavior in social settings or being inspired by role models.

While knowledge, information and educational levers help expand opportunity horizons, those in poor communities cannot always uncover higher potential opportunities by themselves, no matter how driven and organized they are. They require the support of others. This brings us to interpersonal and social levers.

Interpersonal and Social Levers

In addition to what the individual knows, opportunity horizons can be expanded based on who one knows and/or is exposed to. One of the greatest constraints on low income entrepreneurs is their extremely limited social networks. The person who is primarily exposed to people similar to themselves, especially when they also come from poverty and disadvantage, tends to adopt a shared set of beliefs, norms, expectations, and assumptions. This represents a type of social segregation.

Social capital constitutes the set of resources that exist within relationships of trust and cooperation between and among people (Bourdieu & Wacquant, 1992). It tends to be quite limited in poor communities, yet it is one of the most important vehicles for escaping poverty. One's pool of social capital includes the networks of people they know or have access to, but also the willingness and ability of significant others to serve as a resource for the low-income individual. They do so in a variety of ways, such as by opening doors, making connections, eliminating obstacles, providing access, giving endorsements, and sharing information.

In poverty contexts, the individual typically relies on the support of extended family relationships, close friends, and formal organizations such as schools, churches, and neighborhood associations. While these are relevant, they are unlikely to expose the individual to novel realities as these social agents share the same experiences, worldviews, assumptions, and expectations as the poverty entrepreneur. Relationships with outside groups, social structures, and networks are more effective in stretching one's horizon to a broader range of needs, markets, and industries. But how does one break through the boundaries of their immediate network? For the person in poverty, it entails proactive efforts that are often outside of their comfort zones, frequently requiring courage as the individual attempts to connect to people who might otherwise ignore or spurn them.

Some of the activities mentioned above as methods for expanding one's knowledge base also represent vehicles for increasing the pool of social capital. When joining community organizations, pursuing volunteer activities, or participating in internships, it is easy for someone from disadvantaged circumstances to be inhibited or low-key in their approach to others. The entrepreneur must learn to become visible to critical individuals within these social contexts. Visibility comes not only from making contributions to the activity or task at hand (e.g., the volunteer activity), but also by sharing one's story, conveying one's dreams, and letting people know of one's accomplishments.

It involves investing efforts in building relationships with key influencers, finding ways to communicate with them, asking for advice and guidance, and giving them reasons to, in turn, invest in the individual. These can be difficult new roles for those from disadvantaged circumstances to master.

The possibilities can be illustrated with two examples. With the first of these, Taelor is a single mother who comes from a disadvantaged context, and, based on a part-time job in high school, has launched a mobile car detailing business. She reads a story about a community project to disburse winter coats organized by the local Rotary club, an international service organization, and decides to contact the Rotary member cited in the story as project leader. She offers to volunteer to help with the project, and in doing so, gets to know the project leader and shares her story. She is then invited to attend the next Rotary luncheon as a guest, and to give a three-minute pitch on her business. As a result, she meets another member who is the CEO of a chain of car wash facilities. The CEO becomes her mentor, and helps her see an opportunity to use technology to adapt the business from doing the car detailing herself to being a marketing platform that gets jobs for a whole network of outsourced car detailers. In our second example, Lethabo starts a cleaning business as an outgrowth of cleaning for his local church, gaining customers primarily by word of mouth. During COVID, he was cleaning a property one evening and meets the general manager of the property management company who is working late. Asking why he is working so late, the general manager explains frustration at the difficulty of finding people to handle the various facility management issues they were facing, such as painting and repairs. The entrepreneur explains that he knows a number of people with those skills. With the manager's coaching, he pivots to become a virtual property manager, providing maintenance services which allowed companies to receive critical services for their properties at a lower cost.

Role models can also play a major part. Those in poverty often lack entrepreneurial role models and have limited exposure to successful entrepreneurs (Fairlie & Robb, 2007). Learning about the life stories of other individuals who came from adverse contexts and successfully started a business can broaden one's opportunity horizon and, at the same time, build self-confidence and motivation. Consider Cathy Hughes, founder and chairperson of Urban One, Inc. Cathy is an example of a black single mom living in poverty who started and grew a leading broadcast media company. Hughes expressed the importance of role models in setting up a legacy for others facing such hardships: "*I was determined that he* [her son] *wouldn't be a Black statistic. I was determined that he and I would not grow up in the public housing that I had grown up in. I was determined that he was going to have an opportunity which meant that I had to be very serious of purpose*" (NPR, 2016). Stories of individuals in poverty who successfully started businesses and created a prosperous life are examples of interpersonal levers that build role models and thus expand opportunity horizons. Importantly, these role models often cannot be found in one's social context or neighborhood, suggesting to expose individuals to out-group stories and examples.

New interpersonal and social connections are important as they introduce alternative behavioral patterns and expose the individual to real-life contexts outside the poverty culture (Lewis, 1959). This conclusion is based on the notion of a beneficial synergistic effect of the impact of out-group relationships and socialization on poverty. A study with low-income entrepreneurs in India found that establishing a position in a market outside one's local confines led to an organic expansion of people's networks, extending the breadth of their opportunity horizons (Wierenga, 2020).

Communities of practice represent another example of social contexts that are important in stretching the boundaries of opportunity horizons. These are "groups of people informally bound together by shared expertise and passion for a joint enterprise, who interact regularly to learn about or improve their practice" (Nicolini, Pyrko, Omidvar, & Spanellis, 2022, p. 1). They can be local and in-person, but many of them are available online. Participation in these social contexts can promote self-efficacy, builds positive role modeling, and promotes the construction of a different identity. Such interpersonal and social contexts constitute levers to stretch the depth and breadth of the opportunity horizon as they facilitate knowledge sharing, allow an exchange of pockets of expertise and assets, and can eventually support and foster value creation.

Institutional and Political Levers

Our third set of levers is less dependent upon individual agency and more driven by institutional elements in the macro environment. Institutions can provide the necessary level of formality to push for, negotiate, implement, and monitor actions to expand opportunity horizons (Nason & Bothello, 2022). This is accomplished based on the programming and support from government organizations, education institutions, community-based programs, and local entrepreneurial ecosystems.

Government policies and programs represent an important lever in this category. While public sector agencies tend to focus on addressing the basic needs of the poor, well-conceptualized and executed programs can have spillover benefits in terms of the opportunities a person is exposed to. For instance, where governments offer low-income housing in nicer neighborhoods, subsidies for students to attend better schools, easily accessible public transportation that can get people to diverse locations on a timely basis, assistance with child care, and mentor-protégé programs for government contracting, they are creating vehicles for those in poverty to encounter new realities and see new possibilities when it comes to opportunity. Moreover, in some cases, the government can actually create new opportunities for the poor, such as with new types of procurement set-asides for women- or minority-owned businesses.

Schools represent another case in point. When they require students to travel, compete, volunteer, join networks, or connect with diverse individuals outside their normal social milieu, they are introducing new stimuli into the world of the person who grows up in poverty. Similarly, when schools offer formal entrepreneurship programs, business pitch competitions, facilities where students can make or build things, and related programming, students are exposed to a range of new possibilities.

In many communities around the world, there has been a focus in recent decades on the development of entrepreneurial ecosystems (Isenberg, 2010). These ecosystems are connected sets of organizations and individuals that foster local entrepreneurial activity. They can include financial institutions and private investors, universities and colleges, research parks, incubators and accelerators, networking events, specialized service providers, and other sources of support for various facets of the entrepreneurial journey. While there is evidence that these ecosystems tend to prioritize ventures other than the types typically launched by those in poverty conditions (Neumeyer, Santos, & Morris, 2019), some of them offer programs and resources that low-income individuals can access.

An example of an ecosystem program that specifically addresses constrained opportunity horizons is the *Urban Poverty and Business Initiative* coordinated by the University of Notre Dame in the USA. Operating in over forty cities around the world, the program works with low-income and disadvantaged entrepreneurs with a multi-staged, 11-month engagement that takes participants through eighty steps as they move from a business concept to a sustainable enterprise. An important philosophy that guides the program is captured in the phrase "we are not in the idea killing business!" Rather than criticize the entrepreneurs' business ideas, highlighting the inherent faults and shortcomings, or emphasizing why the idea won't work, the UPBI focuses on assisting the entrepreneur to realize whatever profit potential there is in their business ideas. By doing so, while also reinforcing the emergent nature of entrepreneurship, sharing a range of success stories of poverty entrepreneurs, and introducing the entrepreneur to a network of other disadvantaged people attempting to develop businesses, participants begin to see additional opportunities.

Beyond these local ecosystems, other types of community initiatives can play an important role. Examples include financial literacy programs at public libraries, coding schools for disadvantaged youth offered by nonprofit organizations, pop-up markets coordinated by neighborhood groups, and community groups that sponsor public forums featuring highly successful people from different professions who come from poverty circumstances. The challenge with many such community initiatives is to explicitly draw linkages between the activity or event and a new set of opportunities for entrepreneurs.

In closing, agency that results in enhanced knowledge, capabilities, and social connections must be coupled with proactive efforts from institutions and related macro-level influences if the poor are to see a broader range of possibilities. Unfortunately, many of these institutions and organizations are viewed by those in poverty with skepticism, suspicion, and frustration. They can be perceived as out of touch entities that reinforce the status quo and erect barriers to engagement and participation outside of one's immediate context. Their ability to serve as a bridge that connects those in poverty to other worlds, and to demystify those worlds, requires that they recognize this role as part of their mission, approach it purposefully, and establish trust and legitimacy among those they seek to serve.

CONCLUSION

Entrepreneurship begins with opportunity recognition. The nature and size of the market opportunity determine the potential of the business being created. Further, once a business is launched, additional opportunities can emerge. While scholars place considerable emphasis on the need to be alert to opportunities when they arise (e.g., Eckhardt & Shane, 2003), with the poor, the bigger challenge is limited opportunity horizons. The poor start businesses having less potential in markets where it is more difficult to compete, in part because of the types of opportunities they pursue. In this chapter, we have explored the boundaries that the poverty experience can place on these horizons, directions in which these boundaries can be expanded, and mechanisms for achieving this expansion. Those in poverty circumstances are inherently capable of transcending existing boundaries. Through individual, social and macro level levers, and a combination of personal agency and institutional intervention, the doors to opportunity can be unlocked.

REFERENCES

Alvarez, S. A., & Barney, J. B. (2007). Discovery and creation: Alternative theories of entrepreneurial action. *Strategic Entrepreneurship Journal*, *1*(1–2), 11–26.

Alvarez, S. A., Barney, J. B., & Anderson, P. (2013). Forming and exploiting opportunities: The implications of discovery and creation processes for entrepreneurial and organizational research. *Organization Science*, *24*(1), 301–317.
Baker, T., & Nelson, R. E. (2005). Creating something from nothing: Resource construction through entrepreneurial bricolage. *Administrative Science Quarterly, 50*(3), 329–366.
Baron, R. A. (2006). Opportunity recognition as pattern recognition: How entrepreneurs "connect the dots" to identify new business opportunities. *Academy of Management Perspectives, 20*(1), 104–119.
Baron, R. A., & Ensley, M. D. (2006). Opportunity recognition as the detection of meaningful patterns: Evidence from comparisons of novice and experienced entrepreneurs. *Management Science, 52*(9), 1331–1344.
Berkman, E. (2015). Poor people don't have less self-control. Poverty forces them to think short-term. *New Republic*.
Bourdieu, P., & Wacquant, L. P. D. (1992). *An invitation to reflexive sociology.* Chicago: University of Chicago Press.
Cardon, M. S., Wincent, J., Singh, J., & Drnovsek, M. (2009). The nature and experience of entrepreneurial passion. *Academy of Management Review*, *34*(3), 511–532.
Conger, R. D., Conger, K. J., & Martin, M. J. (2010). Socioeconomic status, family processes, and individual development. *Journal of Marriage and Family*, *72*, 685–704.
Corbett, A. C. (2007). Learning asymmetries and the discovery of entrepreneurial opportunities. *Journal of Business Venturing*, *22*(1), 97–118.
Curtner-Smith, M. E., Culp, A. M., Culp, R., Scheib, C., Owen, K., Tilley, A., et al. (2006). Mothers' parenting and young economically disadvantaged children's relational and overt bullying. *Journal of Child and Family Studies, 15*, 177–189. https://doi.org/10.1007/s10826-005-9016-7
Eckhardt, J. T., & Shane, S. A. (2003). Opportunities and entrepreneurship. *Journal of Management, 29*(3), 333–349.
Fairlie, R. W., & Robb, A. M. (2007). Why are black-owned businesses less successful than white-owned businesses? The role of families, inheritances, and business human capital. *Journal of Labor Economics*, *25*(2), 289–323.
Fernández-Serrano, J., Martínez-Román, J. A., & Romero, I. (2019). The entrepreneur in the regional innovation system. A comparative study for high and low-income regions, *Entrepreneurship & Regional Development, 31,* 5–6, 337–356.
Gaglio, C. M., & Katz, J. A. (2001). The psychological basis of opportunity identification: Entrepreneurial alertness. *Small Business Economics, 16*(2), 95–111.
Garrity, P., & Martin, C. (2018). Developing a microfinance model to break the cycle of poverty. *Business Horizons*, *61*(6), 937–947.
Grégoire, D. A., Barr, P. S., & Shepherd, D. A. (2010). Cognitive processes of opportunity recognition: The role of structural alignment. *Organization Science, 21*(2), 413–431.
Grégoire, D. A., Shepherd, D. A., & Schurer Lambert, L. (2010). Measuring opportunity-recognition beliefs: Illustrating and validating an experimental approach. *Organizational Research Methods, 13*(1), 114–145.

Hjalmarsson, S. (2018). Poor kids? Economic resources and adverse peer relations in a nationally representative sample of Swedish adolescents. *Journal of Youth and Adolescence, 47*, 88–104. https://doi.org/10.1007/s10964-017-0747-8

Isenberg, D. J. (2010). How to start an entrepreneurial revolution. *Harvard Business Review*, *88*(6), 40–50.

Kaish, S., & Gilad, B. (1991). Characteristics of opportunity search of entrepreneurs vs executives: Sources, interests, general alertness. *Journal of Business Venturing, 6*(1), 45–61.

Leseman, P. P., & Slot, P. L. (2014). Breaking the cycle of poverty: Challenges for European early childhood education and care. *European Early Childhood Education Research Journal*, *22*(3), 314–326.

Lewis, O. (1959). *Five families: Mexican case studies in the culture of poverty*. New York: New American Library.

Morris, M. H., & Tucker, R. (2021). The entrepreneurial mindset and poverty. *Journal of Small Business Management*, 1–30.

Morris, M. H., Santos, S. C., & Neumeyer, X. (2018). *Poverty and entrepreneurship in developed economies*. Edward Elgar Publishing.

Morris, M. H., Schindehutte, M., Walton, J., & Allen, J. (2002). The ethical context of entrepreneurship: Proposing and testing a developmental framework. *Journal of Business Ethics*, *40*(4), 331–361.

Morris, M. H., Kuratko, D. F., Audretsch, D. B., & Santos, S. C. (2020). Overcoming the liability of poorness: Disadvantage, fragility and the poverty entrepreneur. *Small Business Economics*. https://doi.org/10.1007/s11187-020-00409-w

Müller, G. P. (2002). Explaining poverty: On the structural constraints of income mobility. *Social Indicators Research*, 301–319.

Nason, R. S., & Bothello, J. (2022). Far from void: How institutions shape growth in the informal economy. *Academy of Management Review.* https://doi.org/10.5465/amr.2019.0170

Neumeyer, X., Santos, S. C., & Morris, M. H. (2019). Who is left out: Exploring social boundaries in entrepreneurial ecosystems. *The Journal of Technology Transfer*, *44*(2), 462–484.

Neumeyer, X., Santos, S. C., & Morris, M. H. (2020). Overcoming barriers to technology adoption when fostering entrepreneurship among the poor: The role of technology and digital literacy. *IEEE Transactions on Engineering Management*, *68*(6), 1605–1618.

Nicolini, D., Pyrko, I., Omidvar, O., & Spanellis, A. (2022). Understanding communities of practice: Taking stock and moving forward. *Academy of Management Annals,* https://doi.org/10.5465/annals.2020.0330

NPR (2016, September 27). "How I built this": Cathy Hughes on Radio One. *Morning Edition*, NPR. Accessed December 4, 2023. https://www.npr.org/2016/09/27/495595080/how-i-built-this-radio-one

Payne, R. K. (2005). *A framework for understanding poverty*. Highlands, TX: Aha! Process Inc.

Quillian, L. (1999). Migration patterns and the growth of high-poverty neighborhoods, 1970-1990. *American Journal of Sociology*, *105*(1), 1–37.

Rosch, E. (1978). Principles of categorization. In E. Rosch & B. B. Lloyd (Eds.), *Cognition and categorization* (pp. 27–48). Hillsdale, NJ: Lawrence Erlbaum.
Sarasvathy, S. (2001). Causation and effectuation: Toward a theoretical shift from economic inevitability to entrepreneurial contingency. *Acad. of Management Review, 26*(2), 243–263.
Sarbin, T. (1970). The culture of poverty, social identity, and cognitive outcomes. *Psychological Factors in Poverty.* Chicago: Markham Publishing Co., 29–47.
Shane, S. (2000). Prior knowledge and the discovery of entrepreneurial opportunities. *Organization Science*, *11*(4), 448–469.
Shane, S. A. (2003). *A general theory of entrepreneurship: The individual-opportunity nexus.* Northhampton, MA: Edward Elgar Publishing.
Shane, S., & Venkataraman, S. (2000). The promise of entrepreneurship as a field of research. *Academy of Management Review*, *25*(1), 217–226.
Sharkey, P. (2013). *Stuck in place: Urban neighborhoods and the end of progress toward racial equality*. University of Chicago Press.
Shepherd, D. A., Parida, V., & Wincent, J. (2021). Entrepreneurship and poverty alleviation: The importance of health and children's education for slum entrepreneurs. *Entrepreneurship Theory and Practice*, *45*(2), 350–385.
Shlonsky, H. R. (1984). Continuity in poverty along family lines: A reexamination of the intergenerational cycle of poverty. *Human Relations*, *37*(6), 455–471.
Smith, E. R., & Semin, G. R., 2006. Socially situated cognition as a bridge. In Van Lange, P. A. M. (Ed.), *Bridging social psychology: Benefits of transdisciplinary approaches* (pp. 145–150). Mahwah, NJ: Lawrence Erlbaum Associates.
Tang, J., Kacmar, K. M. M., & Busenitz, L. (2012). Entrepreneurial alertness in the pursuit of new opportunities. *Journal of Business Venturing, 27*(1), 77–94.
Vandecasteele, L. (2011). Life course risks or cumulative disadvantage? The structuring effect of social stratification determinants and life course events on poverty transitions in Europe. *European Sociological Review, 27*(2), 246–263.
Wierenga, M. (2020). Uncovering the scaling of innovations developed by grassroots entrepreneurs in low-income settings. *Entrepreneurship & Regional Development, 32*(1–2), 63–90. DOI: 10.1080/08985626.2019.1640478

Chapter Seven

Rethinking the Entrepreneurial Mindset

The entrepreneurial mindset lies at the heart of entrepreneurship theory and practice (Accion, 2020; Bosman & Fernhaber, 2018; McGrath & MacMillan, 2000; Turner, 2015). In essence, it suggests that to be a successful entrepreneur, one must think and act entrepreneurially. Yet, what this exactly means is less clear, with disparate views regarding the nature and underlying elements of the mindset and how it is manifested within a venture (Davis, Hall, & Mayer, 2016; Mauer, Neergaard, & Linstad, 2017; Kuratko, Fisher, & Audretsch, 2020).

New ventures tend to emerge over time through a process that is, in varying degrees, unpredictable, ambiguous, chaotic, messy, and characterized by mistakes and unexpected setbacks (Morris et al., 2012; Lichtenstein, 2014; Lichtenstein, Dooley, & Lumpkin, 2006). The entrepreneurial mindset is viewed as a vehicle for navigating such circumstances by emphasizing innovation, continuous learning and adaptation, creative problem-solving, and resilience (Morris & Tucker, 2023). It is generally assumed that people vary in terms of how strong their mindset is and that this way of thinking and acting can be developed within people (Franzén, Heljakka, & Nieminen, 2020).

Among the many things we do not know about the mindset concerns how it applies in different contexts. More specifically, is it a universal concept, or does it have different meanings in different circumstances or situations? The context of poverty represents a case in point. As we have seen, the poor frequently create survival and lifestyle ventures that struggle to produce the kind of income and wealth that can change their poverty circumstance. This is a very different context when compared to an individual starting a technology-based, scalable venture that seeks to grow aggressively, and requires millions of dollars in venture capital. The question becomes one of determining how the mindset can be a tool, weapon, or source of advantage for an entrepreneur attempting to overcome disadvantaged circumstances.

To explore these issues, this chapter first synthesizes some of the more prominent views regarding the nature of an entrepreneurial mindset while also examining key questions surrounding this way of thinking and acting. We then investigate how poverty conditions may require a different conceptualization of the entrepreneurial mindset. We argue that, while certain elements of the mindset are fairly universal, particular elements play a more prominent role in the entrepreneurial journeys of those in poverty. Further, it is posited that the ability of entrepreneurship to actually move an individual out of poverty is directly tied to their adoption of this mindset. Implications are drawn for the training, development, and support these entrepreneurs need.

WHAT IS AN ENTREPRENEURIAL MINDSET?

A mindset is as a way of "being in the world" (Stenros, 2015). It concerns the assumptions and mental methods that guide how a person views and approaches a problem, activity, or issue (Mercer & Ryan, 2010; Sinclair, Doelle, & Duinker, 2017). Think of a person with a more global mindset or a more playful mindset. These orientations shape how the individual interprets personal circumstances and the broader environment and then chooses to act, and it is associated with certain competencies or capabilities (Rhinesmith, 1992). Once developed, these capabilities tend to become automatic and the individual is not conscious of them (Stenros, 2015).

With an entrepreneurial mindset, we are concerned with the lens a person adopts as he/she navigates the ups and downs of venture creation. It includes elements that are cognitive (ways of thinking), affective (ways of feeling), and behavioral (ways of acting) (Morris & Tucker, 2023). Figure 7.1 provides a synthesis of key elements in each of these three interacting areas.

From a cognitive perspective, the individual tends to be more opportunity-driven, seeing possibilities where others only see threats or limitations (McGrath & Macmillan, 2000; Van Vuuren & Dhliwayo, 2007). They have a positive orientation toward innovation and change, are willing to experiment and try new ways, and learn quickly from mistakes (Gibb, 1997; Haynie & Shepherd, 2007; Manso, 2016). This suggests an adaptive orientation, where one is not locked into a singular view of how the business creates value, who it sells to, and how resourcing and operations are approached.

With the affective dimension, the person with this mindset brings more optimism, enthusiasm, and pleasurable engagement to the way in which developments are interpreted, new information is processed, and decisions are made (Kuratko, Fisher, & Audretsch, 2020; Morris, Santos, & Neumeyer, 2018). A number of researchers have emphasized the role of passion toward the venture and what it does for the customer (Li et al., 2017). Schumpeter

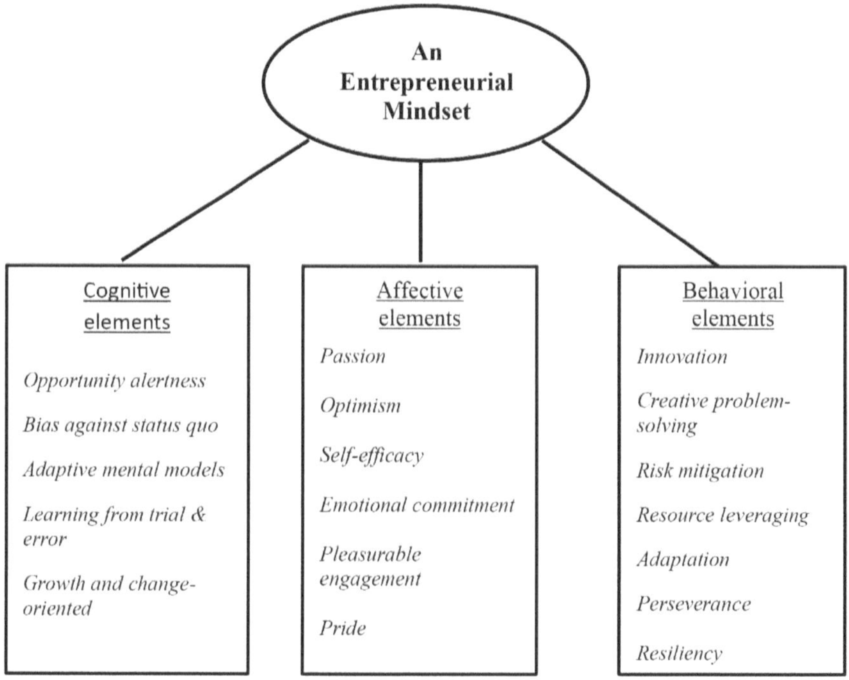

Figure 7.1. Elements Generally Associated with an Entrepreneurial Mindset.
Created by Authors

(1938) emphasizes a will to win and a joy that derives from creation and problem-solving. Goss (2005) notes the role of pride.

From the perspective of one's behavioral orientation, the individual continually recognizes and acts upon opportunities (Amato et al., 2017; McMullen & Kier, 2016) and is inclined toward innovation (Ireland & Webb, 2009; Secundo, Vecchio, & Passiante, 2015). Rather than emphasizing ownership and control of resources, they are inclined toward leveraging the resources of others (Baker & Nelson, 2005; Stinchfield, Nelson, & Wood, 2013) and risk-mitigation (Boermans & Willebrands, 2017). When faced with obstacles, they are prone to improvise and adopt creative approaches to problem-solving and risk-mitigation (Morris & Kuratko, 2020). Instead of a fixed plan, they will pursue actions that reflect flexibility and adaptation as things change (Ireland, Hitt, & Sirmon, 2003; Uy et al., 2015). Finally, the entrepreneur demonstrates tenacity and resiliency, particularly when confronting setbacks (Markman, Baron, & Balkin, 2005).

The elements cited in Figure 7.1 are interdependent (Morris & Tucker, 2023). Hence, passion can fuel tenacity and resilience, while being more opportunity-driven can help the entrepreneur identify resources that can be leveraged, and an orientation towards trial and error provides inputs that enable adaptation. However, while it is argued that all these elements comprise the entrepreneurial mindset (Kuratko, Fisher, & Audretsch, 2020), it is less clear whether all of them are necessary in a given circumstance or context, such as poverty. As such, it may help to further explore the underlying properties of the mindset.

HOW THE ENTREPRENEURIAL MINDSET WORKS

While there is much we do not know, people can be expected to vary in terms of how strongly or weakly they internalize or personally adopt each of these elements as well as the overall mindset. Further, one can demonstrate degrees of the mindset without adopting all of the elements in Figure 7.1. In a sense, then, the entrepreneurial mindset is an umbrella concept, consisting of elements that are internally consistent with one another and tend to reinforce one another, but a given element could be missing, or less developed. As an example, the entrepreneur could be quite resilient and adept at risk mitigation, but less growth-oriented.

Depending upon the context, the ability to succeed may require a stronger or weaker mindset. In particular, in contexts where there is greater uncertainty, more severe resource constraints, more adversity is encountered, and where the entrepreneur confronts more complexity and novelty, there is a need for a stronger mindset (Haynie & Shepherd, 2007; Shepherd & Patzelt, 2018). Further, the relative importance of a given element, such as being innovative or change-oriented, may well depend on the context and conditions under which one operates.

The mindset is also triggered by events and circumstances. As one is developing a venture, it may be that the entrepreneurial mindset is brought to bear when addressing particular tasks (e.g., obtaining resources, trying to win a key customer) but not others (e.g., bookkeeping). In addition, certain elements of the mindset may be more salient depending on the entrepreneurial task in question (e.g., ideation or opportunity discovery versus resourcing and operational problem-solving) (Mathisen & Arnulf, 2013).

Critically, it is possible to nurture or cultivate the entrepreneurial mindset in individuals (Dweck, 2006; Gupta & Govindarajan, 2002). Entrepreneurship educators have devoted considerable effort to finding ways to develop the mindset among students (Castaldi et al., 2020; Corbett, 2005; Pittaway & Cope, 2007; Politis, 2005). A key to this development is helping individuals master particular competencies or capabilities associated with elements of the mindset (Morris et al., 2013; Zupan, Cankar, & Setnikar Cankar, 2018). For instance, teaching skills and techniques related to recognizing opportunities, mitigation of risks, or leveraging resources, and giving them opportunities to practice these capabilities, can reinforce the mindset. Mastery of competencies means the person is not only inclined toward elements of the mindset but has the confidence regarding how to approach them.

POVERTY CIRCUMSTANCES AND THE ENTREPRENEURIAL MINDSET

As we saw in Chapter 2, poverty is a multi-dimensional phenomenon. It represents a complex mosaic of factors that create unique obstacles when a person tries to develop a business. In Chapter 5, we translated the dimensions of poverty into four major liabilities that the entrepreneur must overcome. These included *literacy gaps, a scarcity mindset, difficulties in focusing due to intense non-business pressures,* and *the lack of any sort of safety net.* The entrepreneurial mindset represents a different way of thinking and looking at one's circumstances. Each of the liabilities of poorness works against or can be at odds with the mindset, as illustrated in Table 7.1.

Let's begin with literacy. For entrepreneurs suffering from significant gaps in functional, financial, economic, technological, and/or business literacies, there are aspects of emerging opportunities that they may not perceive or understand (Alvarez & Barney, 2014; Morris, Santos, & Neumeyer, 2018). Similarly, where one's abilities to read, communicate, use numbers, assess the financial implications of an action, grasp technologies and their applications, or evaluate costs and benefits are limited, it becomes much more difficult to learn from mistakes and adapt, or to understand and mitigate risks (Hampton, 2009). In addition, certain literacies have proven to be instrumental in success when attempting to develop new products and services and develop process innovations (Marín-García, Pérez-Peñalver, & Watts, 2013; Sun et al., 2012). Further, gaps in key literacies can undermine self-confidence and self-efficacy while heightening stress levels experienced by the entrepreneur (Ahmed, 2011; Hernandez, 2011).

Similarly, a scarcity mentality can produce significant conflicts when it comes to adopting an entrepreneurial mindset. It produces a short- or immediate-term focus, making it difficult to properly consider new opportunities as they emerge. The entrepreneur lacks the ability to be forward-looking. He/she struggles to recognize emerging trends and draw longer term-implications (Dyer, Gregersen, & Christensen, 2008). As important tasks are delayed to address immediate needs, the entrepreneur is always trying to catch up (Griskevicius et al., 2013; Mani et al., 2013). With a limited cognitive bandwidth and a preoccupation with trade-offs, or what one must give up in order to get by, the propensity to develop innovative new products,

Table 7.1. Sample Challenges Posed by Liabilities of Poorness for Adoption of Entrepreneurial Mindset

Liability of Poorness	*Entrepreneurial Mindset*		
	Cognitive Elements	*Affective Elements*	*Behavioral Elements*
Literacy gaps	Gaps can make it difficult to recognize & understand opportunities, while limiting willingness to experiment with novel approaches or learn	Literacy gaps can undermine self-efficacy and make venture creation much more ambiguous and stressful	Lack of literacy can limit the ability to innovate, leverage resources, or understand risk factors and how they can be mitigated
Scarcity mentality	Short-term orientation works against developing adaptive mental models and the ability to consider emerging opportunities	A focus on immediacy and constant tradeoffs can make the future more uncertain, negatively impacting self-confidence, optimism, and pleasurable engagement	The ability to anticipate developments, adapt business models and managerial approaches, and innovate over time are hindered by a short-term orientation
Inability to focus	Distractions can undermine abilities to learn, discern emerging opportunities, or concentrate on growth	Intense external pressures can lessen one's passion, heighten stress, and make engaging in business activities less pleasurable	Lack of time to focus on creative problem-solving and identifying novel approaches to bootstrapping, bricolage, and resource leveraging
No safety net	Lack of slack can make one more conservative when considering new opportunities, ways to adapt or pivot	High vulnerability can make one less optimistic about outcomes and the future, and contribute to stress	With no safety margin one is less apt to invest in innovation, try new approach, or adapt in approaches that require resource commitments

services and processes is compromised (Shah, Shafir, & Mullainathan, 2015). Beyond this, a lack of planning for the future can contribute to uncertainty and ambiguity, potentially undermining self-confidence and optimism (Radel & Clement-Guillotin, 2012).

Significant non-business distractions related to the poverty experience find the entrepreneur struggling to keep up with daily operations. He or she is reacting to, rather than anticipating and preparing for, problems and threats as they occur. Under such circumstances, there is little room for engaging in creative problem-solving, experimenting with different approaches, or recognizing untapped resources that can be leveraged (Amabile, Hadley, & Kramer, 2002; Haynie et al., 2010). The presence of intense non-business pressures can distract the entrepreneur, limiting the time available to identify, evaluate and implement novel solutions addressing business needs (Livingston, 2010). Distractions crowd out the ability to reflect as one attempts to imagine better ways to accomplish tasks, serve customers, and create additional sources of value (Cohen & Ferrari, 2010). Instead, the simplest or most expedient solution to a problem takes precedence over the creative solution. There is less room to explore growth possibilities or pursue innovation.

Finally, without any sort of safety net, or excess resources to fall back on, the poverty entrepreneur is likely to be more conservative in pursuing new opportunities or adopting new or novel approaches to how things are done (Desai, 2008; Fafchamps, 2003). In the absence of personal savings or cash on hand, and with no access to debt or equity financing, there is less room for error (Barr & Blank, 2009). The entrepreneur is more apt to rely on tried and true approaches, while avoiding experimentation and innovation. Caution can also result in a desire to maintain the status quo rather than grow (Haushofer & Fehr, 2014; Voss, Sirdeshmukh, & Voss, 2008). As the business is continuously vulnerable to adverse developments, the entrepreneur can experience greater stress and more negative emotions, undermining optimism and further limiting the motivation to adapt one's business approach or seek growth (Dawson, 2017; Dercon & Christiaensen, 2011).

These liabilities of poorness factors also tend to interact with one another, creating even greater barriers to the adoption of an entrepreneurial mindset. For instance, literacy gaps can encourage a focus on immediate needs and a lack of planning, while the struggle to plan is exacerbated by the distractions produced by intense non-business pressures. Lack of planning makes it harder to build a safety net. The absence of any resource slack combined with literacy gaps discourages investments in the kinds of equipment and technology that could enable the entrepreneur to create resource slack. These and other interactions leave the person in poverty at a relative disadvantage compared to other entrepreneurs when it comes to thinking and acting in ways that enable one to navigate the ups and downs of the entrepreneurial journey.

Finally, as the magnitude of these liabilities of poorness factors becomes greater, the difficulties in adopting such a mindset also become greater. Yet, poverty only enhances the central importance of an entrepreneurial mindset. The mindset becomes critical for overcoming literacy shortcomings, lack of adequate resources, and the setbacks encountered because of the conditions of poverty.

MIGHT ASPECTS OF POVERTY FOSTER THE MINDSET?

While the effects of living in poverty can undermine the adoption of an entrepreneurial mindset, there are also aspects of poverty that might be expected to contribute to, or facilitate, the development of the mindset. When immersed in poverty on a day-by-day basis, the individual becomes acclimated to certain ways of thinking and acting in order to protect themselves and survive (Garmezy, 1991). They learn survival skills that can be directly applied to the creation of a venture.

A prevalent example is resilience. Those in poverty routinely encounter deprivation, setbacks, rejection, and unexpected obstacles. A family member gets a chronic illness even as family finances are just covering basic expenses. A child is suspended from school, one's house is broken into, or one's health insurance just doubled in cost. Despite outstanding performance ratings, a person is laid off from a job. One is not accepted to a key program or awarded an important grant that they were counting on. Resilience is the ability to positively adapt in the presence of significant adversity and recover from difficult developments (Masten & Reed, 2002). The evidence suggests that the poverty experience can help people learn to be resilient—able to survive despite a lack of resources, limited opportunity, and regular setbacks, with a capacity to rebound from adversity, misfortune, and trauma (Bene et al., 2014; Walsh, 1998). One perspective suggests that, as the individual learns to survive by suppressing hopes, wants, and aspirations, this suppression can foster more clearly defined goals and, consequently, the resilience and drive to achieve these goals (Clark, 2007; Nussbaum & Sen, 1993).

There is also evidence that conditions of severe scarcity can lead individuals to engage in short-term opportunism, where one becomes more alert to readily accessible resources in their immediate environment (Griskevicius et al., 2013). Scarcity forces those in poverty to be frugal with resources, but also more creative or unorthodox in finding ways to meet needs (McCubbin et al., 1997; Muradian, 2019), which some have referred to as "hustling" (Fisher et al., 2020). Others have argued that poverty can induce a drive for success (John & Poisner, 2016) while also fostering a positive self-concept as well as social and problem-solving skills (Garmezy, 1991; Rouse, 1998; Wolin & Wolin, 1993).

Resiliency, short-term opportunism, hustle, frugality, creatively meeting needs, and a drive for success would seem consistent with elements of the entrepreneurial mindset. These poverty outcomes can help prepare the individual for the demands of venture creation. The challenge is to learn how to transfer these life survival skills to the business context.

RETHINKING THE ENTREPRENEURIAL MINDSET IN A POVERTY CONTEXT

Conditions of poverty suggest that the entrepreneurial mindset might mean something different in this context. If we return to the conceptualization of the entrepreneurial mindset captured in Figure 7.1, certain elements may be relatively less important when a person in poverty tries to build a successful business.

As with all entrepreneurs, for those in poverty the entrepreneurial mindset consists of cognitive, affective, and behavioral orientation elements, as illustrated in Figure 7.1. However, the relative significance of particular elements might be expected to vary in a poverty context. This perspective is reflected in the research of Nelson, Santana, and Wood (2016), where they examine entrepreneurs in a small Brazilian community. While they found some common orientations among all the entrepreneurs, they distinguish those whose mindset prioritizes profit, growth, and change from those with a more people-centric and community-oriented mindset that is oriented towards self-development.

Discussions of the entrepreneurial mindset tend to prioritize the central role of bold, innovative thinking that transforms industries through disruptive and scalable ventures (Ireland, Hitt, & Sirmon, 2003; McGrath & MacMillan, 2000). Hence, innovation, challenging the status quo, and aggressive growth are core elements of the mindset. However, in a poverty context, the concern is more with overcoming the odds in order to produce a venture that can generate stable profits and improve the entrepreneur's economic circumstances. As a result, when the low income or disadvantaged attempt to launch and develop a business, we might expect that innovation, a strong growth orientation, and the constant seeking of bold, new opportunities will be less salient elements of the entrepreneurial mindset (Amorós & Cristi, 2011; Webb et al., 2013). This is not to suggest that they do not innovate or seek growth, but these elements are not key to their initial entrepreneurial success.

Alternatively, elements of the mindset that center on leveraging the resources, creative problem-solving, and resilience would seem especially salient. A severe lack of resources, limited access to conventional sources of money, and inadequate network require a mindset that enables the entrepreneur to tap resources without owning or controlling them and find work-around solutions to a continuous stream of setbacks and obstacles. Further, the tendency of these entrepreneurs to operate in highly competitive circumstances where they must find ways to escape the commodity trap (see Chapter 8) highlights the essential need for these mindset elements.

Beyond this, the realities of literacy gaps, significant non-business distractions, and a scarcity mindset suggest that both self-efficacy, or the sense that one has the capacity to succeed at entrepreneurial tasks, and optimism, or confidence in the future, are particularly vital with poverty entrepreneurs. Moreover, with a limited opportunity horizon (see Chapter 6) the initial business concepts tend to have very limited profit potential, suggesting that perseverance, ongoing adaptation, and learning from trial and error must be prominent facets of the entrepreneurial mindset.

Our experience is that, for the poor, the entrepreneurial journey is less about disrupting industries and creating huge wealth, and more about human development, an improved standard of living, and contributing to one's community. The disadvantaged entrepreneur attempts to address the liabilities of poorness while also striving to deal with the problems all entrepreneurs confront, such as those reflected in the liabilities of newness and smallness (Hannan & Freeman, 1984; Stinchcombe, 1965). The primary challenges concern their abilities to adapt their venture concept and their behaviors, creatively overcome both the lack of resources and access to conventional sources of finance, be resilient in dealing with setbacks, and trust in their ability to succeed (Amorós & Cristi, 2011; Bruton, Ketchen, & Ireland, 2013). The entrepreneurial mindset can enable them to translate marginal ventures into businesses that produce sustainable profits. It can be instrumental in their ability to find and fill viable market niches, identify sources of differentiation in the face of ample competition, and build efficiencies while expanding capacity— ultimately producing an enterprise that provides a pathway out of poverty (McMullen, 2011; Santos, Costa, & Morris, 2022).

CONCLUSION

This chapter has argued that context matters when we consider the entrepreneurial mindset. We have suggested that this mindset is a powerful means for enabling an individual to build a business that achieves both profitability and sustainability. Yet, the nature of the poverty experience, and particularly, the liabilities of poorness, can produce an orientation or approach to venture creation that directly conflicts with key elements of the mindset. At the same time, the poverty experience may contain aspects that can help bridge the gap between surviving poverty and successfully launching a venture. The potentially positive and negative effects of poverty conditions on the mindset are captured in Figure 7.2, which also suggests a stronger mindset will lead to a higher rate of venture creation, a tendency to create more lifestyle and managed growth businesses, and businesses that are more profitable.

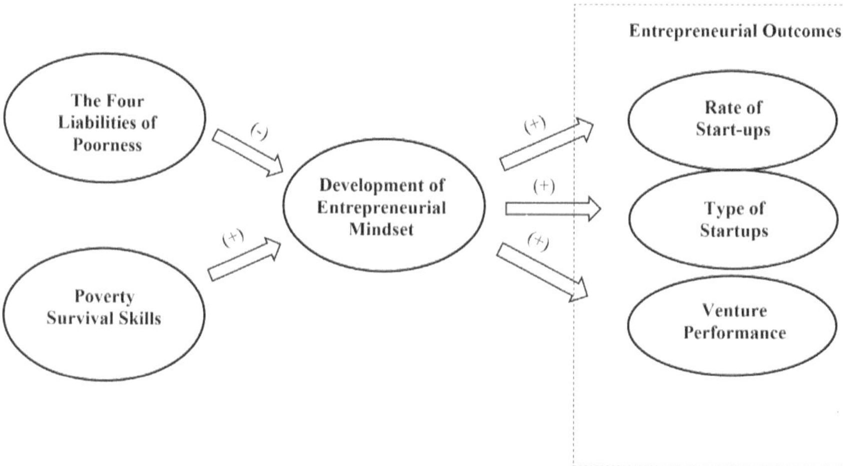

Figure 7.2. The Entrepreneurial Mindset as Mediator between Poverty and Venture Outcomes.
Created by Authors

For the person in poverty, the entrepreneurial mindset can be a game changer. It helps compensate for the entrepreneur's shortcomings and can turn disadvantage into advantage. It does not eliminate literacy problems or the lack of financial slack, but it promotes ways of thinking and acting that can lessen the extent to which these liabilities hold the individual back. Arguably, the greater the liabilities of poverty, as reflected in severe literacy gaps, a scarcity mentality, an inability to focus due to intense outside pressures, and a lack of a safety net, the stronger the mindset needed to build a sustainable enterprise. Further, the strength of the mindset will vary depending on the ambitiousness of the entrepreneur, and particularly depending upon whether they are attempting to build a survival, lifestyle, managed growth, or aggressive growth venture (see Chapter 3).

There are many elements that can contribute to the ability of an individual to think and act entrepreneurially, and the mindset is meant to capture all of them. In a poverty context, we have argued that certain of these elements play a more paramount role. Of priority concern is the need to develop the following elements:

- resource leveraging,
- creative problem-solving,
- self-efficacy,
- optimism,
- learning from trial and error,
- adaptation, and

- resiliency.

Such a nuanced view suggests that the entrepreneurial mindset takes on different meanings depending on context while always representing a vehicle for better navigating the venture creation process.

The key to the mindset is the extent to which it can be cultivated or nurtured. This is a widely accepted assumption, but one with little empirical evidence regarding how and over what sort of time period the mindset can be developed. With those in poverty, it is not enough to simply encourage them to think in entrepreneurial ways. Cultivation of the mindset must be accomplished in the presence of poverty characteristics (e.g., a short-term orientation, non-business distractions) that conflict with or potentially work against some of its underlying components. Yet, with the poor, there may be a foundation to build upon. Surviving the poverty experience can cultivate resilience, creative approaches to dealing with a lack of resources, and other elements of the mindset.

Progress in developing the mindset among disadvantaged populations must be tied to an emphasis on entrepreneurial competency development. For example, a person in poverty may understand the importance of risk mitigation, especially given their lack of a safety net when confronting adverse developments. Yet, these entrepreneurs may know little regarding techniques that can be employed to mitigate risks. For example, gaps in the five literacies (see Chapters 4 and 5) can be an especially significant challenge when encouraging the entrepreneur to employ such risk mitigation tactics as lessening fixed costs, carrying inventory on consignment, or outsourcing certain business functions.

One's environment also matters when developing the mindset. The poor often lack entrepreneurial role models and exposure to successful small business operations (Fairlie & Robb, 2007; Morris, Santos, & Neumeyer, 2018). Local entrepreneurial ecosystems can be an important conduit for nurturing entrepreneurial thinking and acting by people experiencing poverty (see Chapter 12). Unfortunately, the poor are frequently not well served by the community-level entrepreneurial support organizations that comprise local ecosystems. Yet, these ecosystems offer rich opportunities to expand the networks of these entrepreneurs and give them access to training, while also exposing them to the entrepreneurial mindset in practice. While some ecosystems provide tailored programs to the disadvantaged, such as with inner city incubators and microcredit programs, more is needed that explicitly introduces the mindset. Examples include mentor-protégé programs that assign successful entrepreneurs to people from poverty backgrounds, internships within entrepreneurial companies for disadvantaged entrepreneurs, or community forums in impoverished neighborhoods that feature prominent entrepreneurs who overcame adversity. Additionally, it becomes important to adopt a broader conceptualization of local ecosystems beyond accelerators, venture capitalists, universities, research parks, and other entities they are conventionally associated with. We must consider the potential roles of schools, churches, libraries, neighborhood associations, community action groups, and others in exposing those in poverty to entrepreneurial ways of thinking and acting. A supportive environment creates more opportunities for victims of poverty, encourages greater self-confidence, provides more resources that can be leveraged, and rewards perseverance. Entrepreneurship becomes more of a norm than an exception.

Finally, as a caveat, a very strong mindset can also result in behaviors that may penalize or undermine the progress of the poverty entrepreneur. The potential for creative actions that serve the immediate needs of the venture but have negative long-term consequences for the venture is great with poverty entrepreneurs. Their limited social networks and the absence of entrepreneurial role models, together with a lack of familiarity with stakeholder expectations and roles within the venture (Fairlie & Robb, 2007; Payne, DeVol, & Smith, 2006), can serve to limit the entrepreneur's appreciation for the inappropriateness of certain creative or risky behaviors.

REFERENCES

Accion (2020). Entrepreneurial mindset: Five characteristics to cultivate. https://us.accion.org/resource/entrepreneurial-mindset-5-characteristics-to-cultivate/

Ahmed, M. (2011). Defining and measuring literacy: Facing the reality. *International Review of Education, 57*(1), 179–95.

Alvarez, S. A., & Barney, J. B. (2014). Entrepreneurial opportunities and poverty alleviation. *Entrepreneurship Theory and Practice*, *38*(1), 159–184.

Amabile, T. M., Hadley, C. N., & Kramer, S. J. (2002). Creativity under the gun. *Harvard Business Review*, *80*, 52–63.

Amato, C., Baron, R. A., Barbieri, B., Belanger, J. J., & Pierro, A. (2017). Regulatory modes and entrepreneurship: The mediational role of alertness in small business success. *Journal of Small Business Management*, *55*(S1), 27–42.

Amorós, J. E., & Cristi, O. (2011). Poverty, human development and entrepreneurship. In Minniti, M. (Ed.), *Dynamics of entrepreneurship*. London: Oxford University Press.

Baker, T., & Nelson, R. E. (2005). Creating something from nothing: Resource construction through entrepreneurial bricolage. *Administrative Science Quarterly*, *50*(3), 329–366.

Barr, M., & Blank, R. (Eds.) (2009). Savings, assets, credit, and banking among low-income households: Introduction and overview. In R. Bland and M. Barr

(Eds.), *Insufficient funds: Savings, assets, credit, and banking among low-income households* (pp. 1–22). New York: Russell Sage Foundation.

Bene, C., Newsham, A., Davies, M., Ulrichs, M., & Godfrey-Wood, R. (2014). Review article: Resilience, poverty and development. *Journal of International Development, 26*, 598–623.

Boermans, M. A., & Willebrands, D. (2017). Entrepreneurship, risk perception and firm performance. *International Journal of Entrepreneurship and Small Business, 31*(4), 557–569.

Bosman, L., & Fernhaber, S. (Online service). (2018). *Teaching the entrepreneurial mindset to engineers*. Switzerland: Springer International Publishing.

Bruton, G. D., Ketchen, D. J., & Ireland, R. D. (2013). Entrepreneurship as a solution to poverty. *Journal of Business Venturing, 28*(6), 683–689.

Castaldi, L., Sepe, E., Turi, C., & Iscaro, V. (2020). An experiential learning program for entrepreneurship education. *Global Business and Economics Review, 22*(1–2), 178–197.

Clark, D. A. (2007). Adaptation, poverty and well-being: Some issues and observations with special reference to the capability approach and development studies. *Working paper GPRG-WPS-081* Global Poverty Research Group, University of Manchester, UK.

Cohen, J. R., & Ferrari, J. R. (2010). Take some time to think this over: The relation between rumination, indecision, and creativity. *Creativity Research Journal, 22*(1), 68–73.

Corbett, A. C. (2005). Experiential learning within the process of opportunity identification and exploitation. *Entrepreneurship Theory and Practice, 29*(4), 473–491.

Davis, M. H., Hall, J. A., & Mayer, P. S. (2016). Developing a new measure of entrepreneurial mindset: Reliability, validity, and implications for practitioners. *Consulting Psychology Journal: Practice and Research, 68*(1), 21–48.

Dawson, C. (2017). Financial optimism and entrepreneurial satisfaction. *Strategic Entrepreneurship Journal, 11*(2), 171–194.

Desai, V. M. (2008). Constrained growth: How experience, legitimacy, and age influence risk taking in organizations. *Organization Science, 19*(4), 594–608.

Dercon, S., & Christiaensen, L. (2011). Consumption risk, technology adoption and poverty traps: Evidence from Ethiopia. *Journal of Development Economics, 96*(2), 159–173.

Dyer, J. H., Gregersen, H. B., & Christensen, C. (2008). Entrepreneur behaviors, opportunity recognition, and the origins of innovative ventures. *Strategic Entrepreneurship Journal, 2*(4), 317–338.

Dweck, C. S. (2006). *Mindset: The new psychology of success*. Random House.

Fafchamps, M. (2003). *Rural poverty, risk and development* (Vol. 144). Cheltenham, UK: Edward Elgar Publishing.

Fairlie, R. W., & Robb, A. M. (2007). Why are black-owned businesses less successful than white-owned businesses? The role of families, inheritances, and business human capital. *Journal of Labor Economics, 25*(2), 289–323.

Fisher, G., Stevenson, R., Neubert, E., Burnell, D., & Kuratko, D. F. (2020). Entrepreneurial hustle: Navigating uncertainty and enrolling venture stakeholders through urgent and unorthodox action. *Journal of Management Studies, 57*(5), 1002–1036.

Franzén, R., Heljakka, K., & Nieminen, L. (2020). Playful approaches to entrepreneurial competencies in university teaching: Introducing the 4Cs model. In *Advances in Creativity, Innovation, Entrepreneurship and Communication of Design: Proceedings of the AHFE 2020 Virtual Conferences on Creativity, Innovation and Entrepreneurship, and Human Factors in Communication of Design, July 16–20, 2020, USA* (pp. 105–112). Springer International Publishing.

Garmezy, N. (1991). Resiliency and vulnerability to adverse developmental outcomes associated with poverty. *American Behavioral Scientist, 34*(4), 416–430.

Gibb, A. A. (1997). Small firms' training and competitiveness: Building on the small business as a learning organization. *International Small Business Journal, 15*(3), 13–29.

Goss, D. (2005). Schumpeter's legacy? Interaction and emotions in the sociology of entrepreneurship. *Entrepreneurship Theory and Practice, 29*(2), 205–218.

Griskevicius, V., Ackerman, J. M., Cantú, S. M., Delton, A. W., Robertson, T. E., Simpson, J. A., & Tybur, J. M. (2013). When the economy falters, do people spend or save? Responses to resource scarcity depend on childhood environments. *Psychological Science, 24*(2), 197–205.

Gupta, A. K., & Govindarajan, V. (2002). Cultivating a global mindset. *Academy of Management Perspectives, 16*(1), 116–126.

Hampton, J. J. (2009). *Fundamentals of enterprise risk management: How top companies assess risk, manage exposure, and seize opportunity*. New York: AMACOM

Hannan, M. T., & Freeman, J. (1984). Structural inertia and organizational change. *American Sociological Review, 49*, 149–164.

Haushofer, J., & Fehr, E. (2014). On the psychology of poverty. *Science, 344*(6186), 862–867.

Haynie, M., & Shepherd, D. A. (2007). Exploring the entrepreneurial mindset: Feedback and adaptive decision-making. *Frontiers of Entrepreneurship Research.* Wellesley, MA: Babson College.

Haynie, J. M., Shepherd, D., Mosakowski, E., & Earley, P.C. (2010). A situated metacognitive model of the entrepreneurial mindset. *Journal of Business Venturing, 25*(2), 217–229.

Hernandez, D. J. (2011). *Double jeopardy: How third-grade reading skills and poverty influence high school graduation.* ERIC, April. Baltimore, MD: Annie E. Casey Foundation.

Ireland, R. D., Hitt, M. A., & Sirmon, D. G. (2003). A model of strategic entrepreneurship: The construct and its dimensions. *Journal of Management, 29*(6), 963–989.

Ireland, R. D., & Webb, J. W. (2009). Crossing the great divide of strategic entrepreneurship: Transitioning between exploration and exploitation. *Business Horizons, 52*(5), 469–479

John, D. & Poisner, D. (2016). *The power of broke*. New York: Currency Publishing.

Kuratko, D. F., Fisher, G., & Audretsch, D. B. (2020). Unraveling the entrepreneurial mindset. *Small Business Economics*, 1–11. https://doi.org/10.1007/s11187-020-00372-6

Li, J. J., Chen, X. P., Kotha, S., & Fisher, G. (2017). Catching fire and spreading it: A glimpse into displayed entrepreneurial passion in crowdfunding campaigns. *Journal of Applied Psychology, 102*(7), 1075–1090.

Lichtenstein, B. B. (2014). *Generative emergence: A new discipline of organizational, entrepreneurial and social innovation*. New York: Oxford University Press.

Lichtenstein, B. B., Dooley, K. J., & Lumpkin, G. T. (2006). Measuring emergence in the dynamics of new venture creation. *Journal of Business Venturing, 21*(2), 153–175.

Livingston, L. (2010). Teaching creativity in higher education. *Arts Education Policy Review, 111*(2), 59–62.

Mani, A., Mullainathan, S., Shafir, E. & Zhao, J. (2013). Poverty impedes cognitive function. *Science, 341*(6149), 976–980.

Manso, G. (2016). Experimentation and the returns to entrepreneurship. *The Review of Financial Studies, 29*(9), 2319–2340.

Marín-García, J. A., Pérez-Peñalver, M. J., & Watts, F. (2013). How to assess innovation competence in services: The case of university students. *Dirección y Organización, 50*(51), 48–52. DOI: 10.37610/dyo.v0i50.431

Markman, G. D., Baron, R. A., & Balkin, D. B. (2005). Are perseverance and self-efficacy costless? Assessing entrepreneurs' regretful thinking. *Journal of Organizational Behavior, 26*(1), 1–19.

Masten, A. S., & Reed, M. G. J. (2002). Resilience in development. *Handbook of Positive Psychology, 74*, 88.

Mathisen, J. E., & Arnulf, J. K. (2013). Competing mindsets in entrepreneurship: The cost of doubt. *The International Journal of Management Education, 11*(3), 132–141.

Mauer, R., Neergaard, H., & Linstad, A. K. (2017). Self-efficacy: Conditioning the entrepreneurial mindset. In *Revisiting the entrepreneurial mind* (pp. 293–317). Springer, Cham.

McGrath, R. G., & MacMillan, I. C. (2000). *The entrepreneurial mindset: Strategies for continuously creating opportunity in an age of uncertainty*. Boston: Harvard Business Press.

McCubbin, H. I., McCubbin, M. A., Thompson, A. I., Sae-Young, H., & Allen, C. T. (1997). Families under stress: What makes them resilient. *Journal of Family and Consumer Sciences, 89*(3), 2–11.

McMullen, J. (2011). Delineating the domain of development entrepreneurship: A market-based approach. *Entrepreneurship Theory and Practice, 35*(1), 185–193.

McMullen, J. S., & Kier, A. S. (2016). Trapped by the entrepreneurial mindset: Opportunity seeking and escalation of commitment in the Mount Everest disaster. *Journal of Business Venturing, 31*(6), 663–686.

Mercer, S., & Ryan, S. (2010). A mindset for EFL: Learners' beliefs about the role of natural talent. *ELT Journal, 64*(4), 436–444.

Morris, M. H., & Kuratko, D. F. (2020). *What do entrepreneurs create?: Understanding four types of ventures*. Cheltenham, UK: Edward Elgar Publishing.

Morris, M. H., Kuratko, D. F., Schindehutte, M., & Spivack, A. J. (2012). Framing the entrepreneurial experience. *Entrepreneurship Theory and Practice, 36*(1), 11–40.

Morris, M. H., Kuratko, D. F., & Cornwall, J. R. (2013). *Entrepreneurship programs and the modern university*. Edward Elgar Publishing.

Morris, M. H., Neumeyer, X., & Kuratko, D. F. (2015). A portfolio perspective on entrepreneurship and economic development. *Small Business Economics*, *45*(4), 713–728.

Morris, M. H., Santos, S. C., & Neumeyer, X. (2018). *Poverty and entrepreneurship in developed economies*. Edward Elgar Publishing.

Morris, M. H., Santos, S. C., & Neumeyer, X. (2020). Entrepreneurship as a solution to poverty in developed economies. *Business Horizons*, *63*(3), 377–390.

Morris, M. H., & Tucker, R. (2023). The entrepreneurial mindset and poverty. *Journal of Small Business Management, 61*(1), 102–13

Muradian, R. (2019). Frugality as a choice vs. frugality as a social condition. Is de-growth doomed to be a Eurocentric project? *Ecological Economics*, *161*, 257–260.

Nelson, R. E., Santana, A., & Wood, M. S. (2016). Sociocultural context, entrepreneur types, mindsets and entrepreneurial action in Tiradentes, Brazil. In Katz, J. A., & Corbett, A. C. (Eds.), *Models of start-up thinking and action: Theoretical, empirical and pedagogical approaches* (pp. 33–74). West Yorkshire, UK: Emerald Group Publishing.

Nussbaum, M. C., & Sen, A. (1993). *Quality of life*. Clarenden Press: Oxford.

Payne, R. K., DeVol, P. E., & Smith, T. D. (2006). *Bridges out of poverty*. New York: Aha.

Pittaway, L., & Cope, J. (2007). Simulating entrepreneurial learning: Integrating experiential and collaborative approaches to learning. *Management Learning*, *38*(2), 211–233.

Politis, D. (2005). *Entrepreneurship, career experience and learning-developing our understanding of entrepreneurship as an experiential learning process*. Lund University.

Radel, R., & Clement-Guillotin, C. (2012). Evidence of motivational influences in early visual perception: Hunger modulates conscious access. *Psychological Science*, *23*, 232–234.

Rhinesmith, S. H. (1992). Global mindsets for global managers. *Training & Development, 46*(10), 63–69.

Rouse, K. A. G. (1998). Resilience from poverty and stress. *Human Development and Family Life Bulletin*, *4*(1), 1–10.

Santos, S. C., Costa, S., & Morris, M. H. (2022). Entrepreneurship as a pathway into and out of poverty: A configuration perspective. *Entrepreneurship & Regional Development*, *34*(1–2), 82–109.

Schumpeter, E. B. (1938). English prices and public finance, 1660–1822. *The Review of Economics and Statistics, 20*(1), 21–37.

Secundo, G., Vecchio, P. D., & Passiante, G. (2015). Creating innovative entrepreneurial mindsets as a lever for knowledge-based regional development. *International Journal of Knowledge-Based Development*, *6*(4), 276–298.

Shah, A. K., Shafir, E., & Mullainathan, S. (2015). Scarcity frames value. *Psychological Science*, *26*(4), 402–412.

Shepherd, D. A., & Patzelt, H. (2018). *Entrepreneurial cognition: Exploring the mindset of entrepreneurs*. Springer Nature.

Sinclair, A. J., Doelle, M., & Duinker, P. N. (2017). Looking up, down, and sideways: Reconceiving cumulative effects assessment as a mindset. *Environmental Impact Assessment Review*, *62*, 183–194.

Stenros, J. (2015). *Playfulness, play, and games: A constructionist ludology approach*. Tampere, Finland: Tampere University Press.

Stinchcombe, A. L. (1965). *Social structure and organizations*. In J. G. March (Ed.), *Handbook of organizations* (pp. 142–193). Rand McNally: Chicago.

Stinchfield, B. T., Nelson, R. E., & Wood, M. S. (2013). Learning from Levi-Strauss' legacy: Art, craft, engineering, bricolage, and brokerage in entrepreneurship. *Entrepreneurship Theory and Practice*, *37*(4), 889–921.

Sun, D., Li, S., & Xu, X. (2020). Analysis of reform and development strategies of China's Internet innovation and entrepreneurship education. *Entrepreneurship Education, 3*, 77–93.

Sun, H., Wong, S. Y., Zhao, Y., & Yam, R. (2012). A systematic model for assessing innovation competence of Hong Kong/China manufacturing companies: A case study. *Journal of Engineering and Technology Management, 29*(4), 546–565.

Turner, M .L. (2015). Twelve signs you have an entrepreneurial mindset. *Entrepreneur Magazine*. https://www.entrepreneur.com/article/243054.

Uy, M. A., Chan, K-Y., Sam, Y. L., Ho, M-h. R., & Chernyshenko, O. S. (2015). Proactivity, adaptability and boundaryless career attitudes: The mediating role of entrepreneurial alertness. *Journal of Vocational Behavior*, *86*, 115–123.

Van Vuuren, J. J., & Dhliwayo, S. (2007). The strategic entrepreneurial thinking imperative. *Professional Accountant*, *7*(1), 123–134.

Voss, G. B., Sirdeshmukh, D., & Voss, Z. G. (2008). The effects of slack resources and environmental threat on product exploration and exploitation. *Academy of Management Journal, 51(*1), 147–164.

Walsh, F. (1998). *Strengthening family resilience*. New York: Guilford Press.

Webb, J., Bruton, G., Tihanyi, L., & Ireland, R. D. (2013). Research on entrepreneurship in the informal economy: Framing a research agenda. *Journal of Business Venturing*, *28*(5), 598–614.

Wolin, S. J., & Wolin, S. (1993). *The resilient self: How survivors of troubled families overcome adversity.* New York: Villard Books.

Zupan, B., Cankar, F., & Setnikar Cankar, S. (2018). The development of an entrepreneurial mindset in primary education. *European Journal of Education*, *53*(3), 427–439.

PART III

From Fragility to Sustainability

Chapter Eight

Escaping the Commodity Trap

Entrepreneurship can be a relevant and meaningful vehicle for helping those in poverty develop capabilities and create better life prospects. However, the journey to the creation of a sustainable venture is not linear, controllable, or predictable. It is a challenging journey for any entrepreneur and becomes even more difficult for those in adverse circumstances. Due to the constraints captured in the liabilities of poorness (Chapter 5), people experiencing poverty tend to create survival and lifestyle ventures, both of which have unique characteristics that may limit their potential, as discussed in Chapter 3.

Yet, it is possible even for survival and lifestyle ventures to make money and improve an entrepreneur's economic well-being. The fact that they often fail to do so can be tied to fatal flaws in the underlying business models and managerial approaches involved when the poor launch ventures (Morris, Soleimanof, & Tucker, 2023). These flaws are captured in a concept we call the "commodity trap." It comprises a set of elements that, when combined, severely limit the potential of a start-up venture. These elements center around providing a relatively homogeneous offering to customers, one that is not perceived to differ meaningfully from those of competitors. They are traceable to the kinds of business opportunities recognized by those in poverty, a severe lack of resources available to pursue these opportunities, shortcomings in the skills, capabilities, perceptions, and beliefs of the entrepreneurs who launch these ventures, and lack of support from entrepreneurial ecosystems (Alvarez & Barney, 2014: Morris & Tucker, 2021).

This chapter delves into the problematic nature of many ventures launched by low-income and disadvantaged entrepreneurs. Using the commodity trap as our central vehicle for capturing the struggles of these businesses, we examine its underlying elements and how they interact to undermine business viability. Arguing the commodity trap can be avoided or overcome, we first explore the core importance of differentiating the business in ways that are meaningful to targeted customer segments and identify a number of ways in which such differentiation can be achieved. Different pathways for escaping the commodity trap are then introduced. Ongoing challenges in terms of market and competitive dynamics are addressed. The chapter closes with a reflection on the implications of the commodity trap for human development and enhanced well-being on the part of poverty entrepreneurs.

THE COMMODITY TRAP

When someone who comes from disadvantaged circumstances starts a cleaning company, a business that sells baked goods, a local transport business, or a hair salon, they struggle to make money. These entrepreneurs often create ventures that suffer to varying degrees from a phenomenon we call the "commodity trap." This trap is created by eight interacting elements, each of which can be experienced to greater or lesser degrees, but all of which tend to be present (see Figure 8.1). They include:

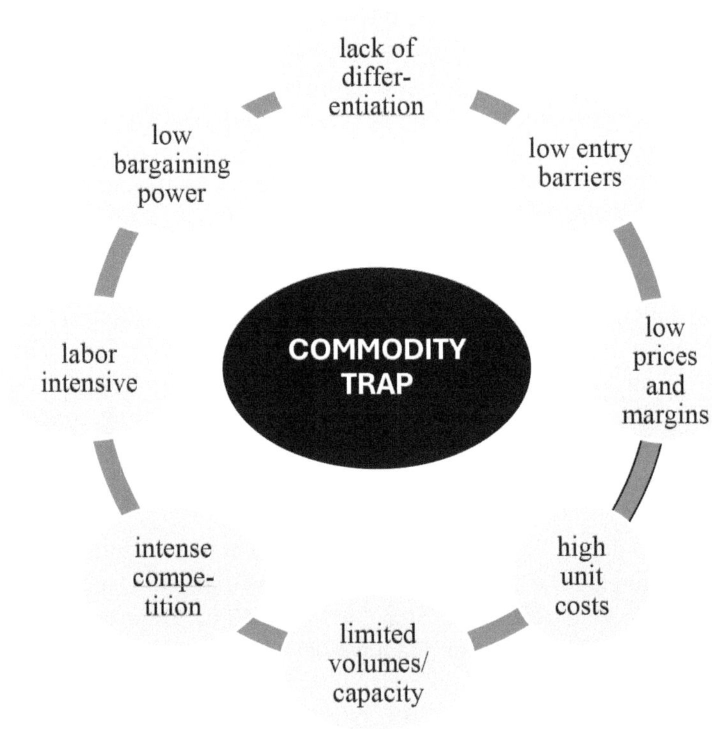

Figure 8.1. The Commodity Trap Experienced by Poverty Entrepreneurs.
Created by Authors

a. *Lack of differentiation:* Customers perceive little to no difference among the offerings of the various competitors in the marketplace. In effect, the product or service has become commoditized. As a result, they tend to be price sensitive and demonstrate little brand loyalty.
b. *Intense competition:* Entry barriers tend to be very low for these types of businesses, meaning there are numerous competitors for customers to select from.
c. *Under-pricing:* Out of a concern that the only way to generate sales is to price low, or based on a tendency to undervalue their product or service, or because they are targeting customers who have low incomes, the entrepreneur tends to price too low.
d. *Labor-intensive operations:* Production of the product or service tends to be fairly labor-intensive, with the entrepreneur providing most of the labor.
e. *Lack of equipment and technology:* Limited resources combined with literacy gaps find the entrepreneur unable to employ the kinds of equipment or technology that could increase production levels and create efficiencies.
f. *Limited capacity and low volumes:* Labor-intensive operations, an inability to afford raw materials, and a lack of space, equipment, and technology combine to limit the production capacity of the business, suggesting the entrepreneur is only able to produce and sell relatively low volumes of products or services.
g. *Lack of bargaining power:* Lack of money and limited capacity put the entrepreneur in a position where only small quantities of ingredients, materials, or inventories can be purchased at a time from suppliers. Small purchase quantities mean the entrepreneur has no bargaining power with suppliers, cannot negotiate procurement terms, and may be forced to buy at retail rather than wholesale.
h. *No production economies:* The scale of operations is severely limited by labor intensity, lack of equipment, absence of technology, and limited space. Small scale combined with higher procurement costs suggests the business struggles to be cost competitive with incumbent firms.

The end result of the interaction of these factors is a business that experiences low volumes of sales and low margins on each sale. Such a combination means these entrepreneurs cannot make money and potentially may find the venture makes them financially worse off.

A simple example of the commodity trap at work can be seen with a home-based business involved in making and selling baby bibs (described in Chapter 3). Capacity constraints based on a single laborer (the entrepreneur, who must do the the sewing, procurement, inventory management, order taking, marketing, and bookkeeping), and very basic machinery (a few sewing machines, snap fastener tools, etc.), find the business able to produce no more than ten bibs per day. This output would require her to do nothing but make bibs for eight hours, five days per week. While her products are much nicer than those sold at large retail chains, the stores are able to charge a price that is lower than her cost of making a bib. She buys her materials in small quantities from local retailers. She has no money for marketing and finds most of her sales are to her network of friends and acquaintances. Relatively low sales and competition from low-cost retailers make her hesitant to raise prices. Profit margins of about $5 per bib suggest that, even if she sells everything she makes, total monthly profit would amount to $1,000. She is caught in a trap, needing more sales to allow her to hire people and increase production (which would also enable her to purchase materials at wholesale), but without the money to do the marketing necessary to create brand awareness and differentiate her bibs, and afraid to raise prices to reflect the real value she is creating.

WHAT PUSHES THE POVERTY ENTREPRENEUR INTO THE COMMODITY TRAP?

The tendency for low-income and disadvantaged entrepreneurs to fall into the commodity trap can be traced to entrepreneur-related, market-related, and ecosystem-related considerations. It starts with the entrepreneur. Poverty conditions can constrain the set of opportunities a person is able to recognize (see Chapter 6), resulting in copycat businesses in well-established markets (Sutter, Bruton, & Chen, 2019). They lead the entrepreneur to pursue businesses having low start-up costs, limited fixed cost commitments, no employees, and little intellectual property. The result is low-capacity ventures struggling to take business away from existing competitors. Further, as we saw in Chapter 5, literacy gaps, a scarcity mindset, an inability to focus, and a lack of any safety net can lead to a short-term, reactive approach to management.

When it comes to the markets being reached, the poor tend to sell to the poor, meaning customers with less purchasing power and greater price-sensitivity. For a number of reasons, they struggle to penetrate mainstream markets and enter established distribution channels. The market is often loosely defined, and there is little market segmentation, targeting, and positioning. By trying to serve anybody and everybody, it becomes difficult to differentiate the business in the minds of particular target audiences (Dickson & Ginter, 1987).

The entrepreneur is overly dependent on word of mouth and passers-by to generate business.

Finally, there are ecosystem-related factors that drive the commodity trap. As we will explore further in Chapter 12, local ecosystems tend to ignore or under-serve the ventures of the poor. It is difficult for these entrepreneurs to tap into networks that can open doors, provide advice, assist them in developing capabilities and accessing key resources, and overcome institutional barriers. Little in the way of microcredit is available. Many of these businesses end up operating in the informal economy and have difficulties with regulatory compliance and understanding the explicit and implicit rules of the game. They are forced to keep things simple and limit complexity in operations.

The long-term implication of the commodity trap is the creation of a marginal and highly fragile businesses (Morris et al., 2023). However, this need not be the destiny of the poverty entrepreneur. A sizeable but unknown percentage of these businesses achieve stable and meaningful profit levels, and some go on to build significant wealth. In terms of the latter, Daymond John (FUBU), Janice Bryant Howroyd (ActOne Group), Do Won Chang (Forever 21), Howard Schultz (Starbucks), Jan Koum (WhatsApp), Lakshmi Mittal (ArcelorMittal) are but a few examples. The beginning point is the creation of a venture that lends itself to building a brand that can be differentiated in the minds of customers, a subject to which we now turn.

THE CENTRAL CHALLENGE OF DIFFERENTIATION

At the heart of the commodity trap is a lack of differentiation in the offerings of the business. Regardless of how unique the entrepreneur believes the business to be, if customers do not perceive meaningful differences, then effectively there are no differences. The word commodity has traditionally been used to describe things like oil, copper, grain, or chicken where the market treats the good as similar regardless of who produces it. The goods or services are seen as relatively standardized and interchangeable, and customers typically base their purchasing decisions on price, availability, and convenience rather than brand loyalty or specific attributes of the product or business. Their loyalty to any one competitor, and switching costs between competitors, are low.

In a practical sense, many everyday products and services are effectively viewed by customers as commodities or have become commoditized. As examples, it is common for customers to perceive a painting contractor, screenprinting business, or delivery company as an undifferentiated commodity. Each may strive to provide better quality or faster service, but other firms are trying (or claiming) to do the same thing. Lack of differentiation between the offerings of different firms forces the entrepreneur to compete on price, which is a no-win proposition. On the one hand, the entrepreneur cannot out-price firms that enjoy scale economies. On the other hand, there are always other small firms willing to offer even lower prices. The better pathway is to compete on something other than price.

One approach to disentangle the commodity trap and finding ways to overcome the differentiation challenges faced by poverty entrepreneurs is by focusing on different types of offerings and how they are expressed in the context of poverty. If we consider both the viewpoint of the customer and the objective differentiation features of what is being sold, we can conceptualize a matrix with four types of offerings by the disadvantaged entrepreneur (see Figure 8.1). Based on the work of Enke et al. (2014), the matrix is based on two dimensions:

a. Features or attributes of the offering that drive the perception of difference—these are objective features and their presence is perceived to range from minimal and low to substantial and high; and
b. The perceived value of the offering for the customer—this is a subjective evaluation which ranges from being perceived as having no differences or differences that are relatively meaningless to having differences that are highly valued.

As such, these two dimensions capture both the characteristics of the offering itself as provided by the entrepreneur and how customers perceive the entrepreneur's offering. Their intersection results in four main types of goods:

- *Basic commodities*—this category includes products and services with a low level of objective differentiation, meaning the entrepreneur is not offering anything meaningfully different than competitors, and the products or services are perceived as undifferentiated or homogeneous by customers. This type of offering tends to have an undifferentiated customer segment.
- *Emerging commodities*—this category includes products and services that have some objective differentiating features and attributes. However, these differences are not perceived by customers, or they do not see them as especially meaningful differences. The entrepreneur is making an effort to provide something unique but the market does not recognize or value these differences all that much. Businesses in this category can also be ones that previously had a unique market positioning, but their competitive advantage becomes blurred and the competitive edge disappears over time.

- *Preferential commodities*—these are products and services that, from an objective standpoint, have little to no differences, yet the market perceives differences. The perception of difference is typically created and reinforced through marketing, advertising, and branding activities. Buyers develop a clear preference for a particular provider, but the entrepreneur faces an ongoing challenge in maintaining the perception of difference over time.
- *Unique value propositions*—in this category are products and services with objectively and substantial differentiating attributes that distinguish the offering from competitors. The offering has a unique competitive advantage that is difficult for competitors to imitate. For their part, customers also perceive products and services as different and place a high value on these differences. The result tends to be high customer loyalty, a willingness to pay a higher price, and high switching costs (Aaker, 1996).

As both the efforts of the entrepreneur and the perceptions of the market can change over time, competitors may be able to move from one cell to another, ascending and declining on one or both dimensions. Consider an entrepreneur who starts a business that is, in effect, offering a basic commodity. He or she then works on improving one or more attributes (e.g., quality, speed, selection) or adding a feature or benefit. However, these changes are either not recognized by customers, or they are not perceived as important. As

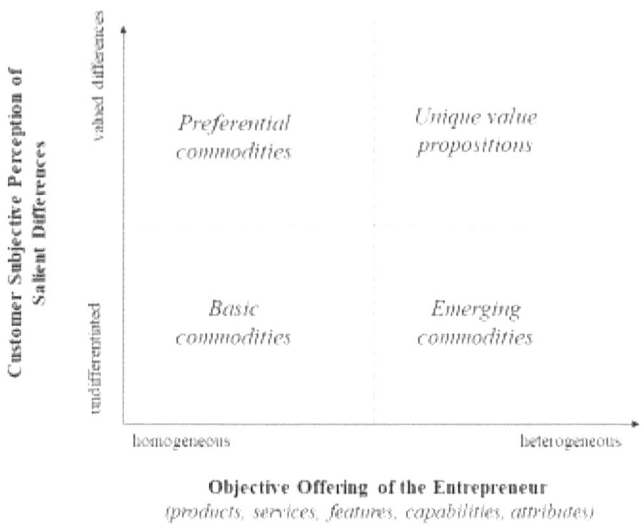

Figure 8.2. Types of Offerings by Disadvantaged Entrepreneurs.
Created by Authors

an emergent commodity, the entrepreneur may find that costs are higher, but revenue is not growing. The same entrepreneur may be able to engage in creative marketing efforts to create the veneer of meaningful difference among key target audiences. An example might be a business where the entrepreneur renames a product, has a compelling life story, or creates a clever slogan that resonates with customers. The challenge with this type of preferential commodity is the ability to maintain the perception of difference over time. Alternatively, the entrepreneur who begins as a basic commodity but learns from and communicates effectively with customers may be able to create real differences that the market recognizes and values, and that competitors struggle to mimic, in the process of establishing a unique value proposition.

Poverty entrepreneurs struggle to create unique value propositions. They are typically entering established markets where meaningful differentiation is hard to achieve and maintain. Their businesses lack the resources and capabilities needed to introduce significant innovations that would be difficult to replicate. Instead, they struggle to keep up with the novel efforts of competitors. They may add new products or services (sometimes completely unrelated to their core offering) based on the mistaken assumption that "if I have more things to sell I will make more money." Their marketing capabilities and resources are also constrained. Part of their challenge is having specific (higher potential) target markets in mind and understanding the potential sources of differentiation that would resonate with those customers, and the means by which such differentiation can be established.

FINDING WAYS TO DIFFERENTIATE

Every business, including those selling commodities, can pursue differentiation strategies to help them break out of the commodity trap (Brenes, Montoya, & Ciravegna, 2014; Morris, Santos, & Neumeyer, 2018). The goal is to create meaningful and sustainable differentiation, which means offering something unique that creates perceived meaningful value for enough customers (Porter, 1980). Below are examples of eight possible approaches that are especially relevant for low-income and disadvantaged entrepreneurs.

Differentiation Based on a Primary Benefit

All too often, the disadvantaged entrepreneur focuses on selling products or services without considering the underlying benefits the customer is actually seeking. Stated differently, customers are not buying products or services, they are buying benefits (Keller, 1993). Moreover, depending on the user, individuals can derive different benefits out of the same product or service.

A coat could be a source of warmth, a source of protection from the rain, or a source of enhanced self-image based on its style. The entrepreneur may be able to achieve differentiation by focusing on a unique benefit that competitors are not emphasizing. An example can be seen with a cleaning company that focuses on serving commercial clients. The entrepreneur, when trying to convince business owners and office managers of the superiority of her offering, emphasizes that "our cleaning services will make your employees more productive." Here, she is focused on a salient benefit on which the customers are likely to place a high value. Toward this end, she is concerned with providing not simply an office environment that appears to be clean, but one that is more sanitary and orderly.

Differentiation through Product and Service Characteristics

A wide range of options are available when it comes to the mix of products and/or services being sold. Examples include offering more selection of a given item (e.g., quality levels, sizes, styles, colors, flavors), a wider range of different items (e.g., being more of a one-stop provider), offering products with unique features or attributes not provided by competitors, bundling different items together, and packaging products in distinctive ways.

Differentiation through Customization

Rather than sell standardized products or services, the willingness of the entrepreneur to customize the offering to reflect individual client preferences represents another approach to differentiation. The approach can work when the poverty entrepreneur is willing and able to charge a higher price that reflects the additional time and expense involved with customization. As customization generally means the entrepreneur is able to produce fewer units or complete fewer jobs in a given amount of time, to compensate he or she must be able to realize higher margins on those units or jobs. As there are degrees of customization, it can sometimes be more effective to create the perception that the product is customized when only some of the more visible aspects are actually tailored to the client's requests.

Differentiation Before, During, and After the Sale

The creative entrepreneur can augment the sale of a product or service in a number of ways that create more value for customers. For instance, differentiation can result from being easier to order from or do business with. It can be created by offering better time-of-sale and after-sale support, no-cost delivery, more generous upgrade or returns policies, product installation and customer training, or a unique warranty or guarantee.

Differentiation through Creation of Experiences

Another source of differentiation finds the entrepreneur focusing less on selling products or services and more on creating customer experiences. Experience creation involves engaging customers in meaningful ways by addressing what they are meant to think, see, feel, and do when they interact with the business. Hence, a restaurant that provides Ethiopian cuisine strives to create an authentic Ethiopian experience through employee dress and communication, physical décor, music, dance, fun customer activities, and other stimuli.

Specializing in a Market Niche

For the disadvantaged entrepreneur, an especially valuable means of creating a difference is to focus on a specialty niche within the market. The business would then tailor its offerings to reflect the distinct needs of customers in that niche. Niches can be defined based on a large number of factors, ranging from customer demographics, personal characteristics, and lifestyles to behavioral preferences, price-sensitivity, and usage occasions. A cleaning company specializing in homes with pets, or a restaurant catering to deaf and blind customers would be examples.

Differentiation through Creative Communications

Marketing and brand building can also produce sources of differentiation. The entrepreneur may be able to use unique imagery or a distinctive tagline in their promotional efforts, or use marketing to create a personality around the business. In some cases, the founder of the business might have an especially compelling story that makes people want to support the business. Similarly, becoming certified as a woman-owned, minority-owned, or veteran-owned business can contribute to building a unique identity.

While they are promising, these differentiation strategies can represent a major challenge for someone who is poor, not only because of limited capabilities and resources, but also because differentiation requires customer insight, planning and discipline, and is a continuous effort. Yet, achieving differentiation is a critical step in escaping the commodity trap.

FINDING PATHWAYS OUT OF THE COMMODITY TRAP

There is no formula for escaping the commodity trap. However, there are pathways that can provide a way out. Simply differentiating the business from competitors is a start, but it is not enough (Khanna & Palepu, 2013). If we return to the entrepreneur who makes baby bibs, described earlier, the commodity trap is ultimately about a business that is selling low volumes at low margins.

So, let's assume our entrepreneur is able to differentiate her offering by producing bibs that have unique and artistic designs and are quite fashionable. The business is still trapped unless the owner is now willing to charge a higher price that reflects the enhanced value being provided to customers. With the additional profit generated, she may be able to hire assistants who can do much of the basic work in terms of cutting, pinning, trimming, topstitching, sewing in metal snaps, and so forth. This allows for an increase in the volume of bibs that can be produced. Higher volumes of production may enable the entrepreneur to begin buying materials at wholesale prices, reducing her costs and further enhancing her margins. The hiring of assistants frees up the entrepreneur to do more selling, and she can get some stores to start carrying her products.

Obviously, this pathway involves a number of leaps, and the ability to make these leaps is not straightforward. Beyond finding a source of differentiation or uniqueness, a major obstacle concerns pricing. People in poverty circumstances tend to underprice when they launch businesses. This tendency is traceable to a number of considerations. These entrepreneurs can think that the only way to generate sales is to offer a low price. In addition, they often find themselves selling to others in poverty who are quite price sensitive. An especially important consideration is the method used to determine price. Rather than price based on the value a customer is receiving (e.g., as airlines do with their flights), low-income entrepreneurs tend to focus on covering their costs and adding a markup. Even here, though, they underestimate unit costs by leaving out the costs of their own labor (which tends to be the primary source of labor), and the markup is too small. The pathway out of the commodity trap requires that the entrepreneur not look at price as their source of competitive advantage and instead compete based on other sources of differentiation.

Let's consider an example of a well-known business mainly selling coffee, tea, bite-sized pastries, and savory products, among other offerings. As just another coffee shop, this type of business could easily fall into the commodity trap and the pricing of the products could be based on production costs. However, this is the story of Howard Schulz, who went from poverty to create the global success story of Starbucks and took the concept of value as a core element of the differentiation strategy of the business. Because Schulz defined the company's core benefit not just around selling coffee but around creating a lifestyle experience, the value perceived by customers was higher, unique, and distinctive, allowing for pricing at a much higher level than any other competitors.

Another important aspect that influences pricing based on value is the self-perception of one's self-worth. As we will discuss in the next chapter, poverty entrepreneurs frequently question their abilities to grow successful businesses, which can lead to paralyzing behaviors that undermine growth. This insecurity in one's ability to create a valuable and distinctive business may lead the entrepreneur to undervalue the product/service, its growth potential, and how it should be positioned in the marketplace. Importantly, setting the price is also a signal of the perceived value of the offering and gives customers an expectation of the quality and features of the product/service. As such, customers will always perceive a decrease in the price more positively rather than an increase, suggesting that if the original price is low, it is hard to raise it later. So, pricing at the mid-range or higher end tends to convey the product'svalue positioning more favorably (McMullen & Bergman, 2018), is more advantageous, and gives the entrepreneur the opportunity to always temporarily reduce prices to stimulate sales without permanently cutting prices.

Creativity and flexibility in pricing are also important. Low-income entrepreneurs may be stuck on the idea that all customers should pay the same price, thinking this is only fair. Price is perceived differently based on the market being targeted (Monroe, 1973). As such, the same product or service can have different prices based on the characteristics of the customer and their perceived value. For example, a poverty entrepreneur can charge a fixed price for a lawn and landscaping service to a customer in their own neighborhood, but if the customer is in another part of town (where the purchasing power of the customer is higher), the entrepreneur can mark up the price for the same service because the value perception is different (Raghubir, 2006). Another example is when customers require last-minute services. The convenience and availability of the service are perceived as more valuable, and thus, the price can be higher.

The core dilemma produced by the commodity trap is that it results in a business with low volumes of goods sold and low profit margins on the items being sold. An entrepreneur can make money with low volumes and high margins (like a jewelry store), high volumes and low margins (like a grocery store), medium volumes and medium margins (like some restaurants). They can make a lot of money with high volumes and high margins (like Apple with its iPhone). But a business cannot survive with consistently low volumes and low margins, as there is no real profit. So, the challenge is to increase margins, volumes, or both.

On the margin side, the focus is on unit cost and unit price. The operations of the poverty entrepreneur tend to be quite lean, leaving not a lot of room to lower unit costs. The keys here are either to invest in machinery and technology that allow for more scale in production, or buy in larger quantities and obtain wholesale discounts. Absent this, the key is to increase profits by (a) raising prices to generate higher margins; or (b) selling more of the products that have higher (versus lower) margins. The latter requires a good understanding of the margins being earned on each product and service being sold—something the poverty entrepreneur may not know due to poor bookkeeping and a lack of financial literacy.

On the volume side, the struggle is not just with generating more sales, it also concerns the ability to produce more units or complete more jobs. When it comes to growing sales, marketing is a critical area where disadvantaged entrepreneurs require more assistance, and particularly how to properly segment markets, prioritize target markets, penetrate distribution channels, engage in low-cost but effective guerrilla tactics, and build customer relationships.

Growing production volumes can be more complicated. A kind of catch-22 is involved, in that the entrepreneur needs more sales to generate the cash flow to produce more, but needs more production volume so that there is something to sell. Increased production requires more raw materials, labor, equipment, and technology, and each costs money. Labor tends to be cheaper than equipment and technology, and so tends to be the first pathway selected, but both are needed if the entrepreneur is going to meaningfully increase volumes.

CONCLUSION

The commodity trap illustrates the critical role of enhanced capabilities in determining whether entrepreneurship is a viable solution to poverty. As this discussion has illustrated, it begins with capabilities in terms of opportunity identification (Tang, Kacmar, & Busenitz, 2012) but also includes capabilities at identifying and delivering sources of differentiation, setting value-based prices, addressing capacity constraints, hiring and managing employees, negotiating with suppliers, deciphering markets and engaging in targeted marketing, networking, and understanding and deploying technology. Each of these capabilities includes a knowledge component, a component that involves attitudes and beliefs, and a skill component.

For the person in poverty circumstances, the question becomes one of determining how such capabilities can be developed. Little in the life experiences of the low-income or disadvantaged person, including their work experiences, necessarily prepares them to avoid or escape the commodity trap. For the most part, the entrepreneur is expected to develop these capabilities in real-time as they develop the business. While some are able to learn from their venture experiences as they happen, many are not. The other liabilities of poorness (see Chapter 5), such as literacy gaps and non-business distractions, create significant roadblocks to capability mastery.

Again, we see how a lack of capabilities translates into a lack of freedom (see Chapter 2). The commodity trap can ensure that the entrepreneur's venture provides no more than a subsistence existence to the entrepreneur and his/her family, keeping them in poverty. The potential of entrepreneurship to foster the holistic development (e.g., material, social, psychological, cultural, and spiritual) of the individual is never realized (das Neves, 2009). In this sense, venture creation may only serve to restrict the individual and undermine his or her dignity (Mongelli et al., 2018).

In the final analysis, the commodity trap phenomenon and its tie-in to particular capabilities are not well-understood by those who could potentially intervene with or assist these entrepreneurs Both elements are critical if we are to change the status quo. The natural tendency for these entrepreneurs to fall into the commodity trap must be recognized as the focal challenge. Then, understanding the particular kinds of capabilities that enable one to address this trap must be a centerpiece of training, coaching, mentoring, and other intervention mechanisms. Simply providing financial investments to these businesses can address certain components of the commodity trap but not others. For instance, such investments can enable a person to hire people, buy equipment, and purchase in larger quantities. But they cannot ensure the business owner is able to differentiate, set appropriate prices, negotiate with suppliers, and grow their sales volumes. As such, it becomes even more critical to make human capital investments. It is enhanced human capital in the form of capabilities that will enable these entrepreneurs to build profitable and sustainable enterprises.

REFERENCES

Aaker, D. A. (1996). Measuring brand equity across products and markets. *California Management Review*, *38*(3), 102–120.

Alvarez, S. A., & Barney, J. B. (2014). Entrepreneurial opportunities and poverty alleviation. *Entrepreneurship Theory and Practice*, *38*(1), 159–184.

Brenes, E. R., Montoya, D., & Ciravegna, L. (2014). Differentiation strategies in emerging markets: The case of Latin American agribusiness. *Journal of Business Research, 67*(5), 847–855. https://doi.org/10.1016/j.jbusres.2013.07.003

das Neves, J. C. (2009). *Introdução à ética empresarial*. Cascais, Portugal: Principia Editora Lda.

Dickson, P. R., & Ginter, J. L. (1987). Market segmentation, product differentiation, and marketing strategy. *Journal of Marketing, 51*(2), 1–10.

Enke, M., Geigenmüller, A., & Leischnig, A. (2014). Commodity marketing—Eine Einführung. In M. Enke, A. Geigenmüller, & A. Leischnig (Eds.), *Commodity Marketing*. Wiesbaden: Springer Gabler. https://doi.org/10.1007/978-3-030-90657-3_1

Keller, K. L. (1993). Conceptualizing, measuring, and managing customer-based brand equity. *Journal of Marketing, 57*(1), 1–22.

Khanna, T., & Palepu, K. G. (2013). *Winning in emerging markets: A road map for strategy and execution*. Boston: Harvard Business Press.

McMullen, J. S., & Bergman Jr., B. J. (2018). The promise and problems of price subsidization in social entrepreneurship. *Business Horizons, 61*(4), 609–621.

Mongelli, L., Versari, P., Rullani, F., & Vaccaro, A. (2018). Made in carcere: Integral human development in extreme conditions. *Journal of Business Ethics, 152*, 977–995.

Monroe, K. B. (1973). Buyers' subjective perceptions of price. *Journal of Marketing Research, 10*(1), 70–80.

Morris, M. H., Santos, S. C., & Neumeyer, X. (2018). *Poverty and entrepreneurship in developed economies*. Edward Elgar Publishing.

Morris, M. H., Soleimanof, S., & Tucker, R. (2023). Drivers of fragility in the ventures of poverty entrepreneurs. *Small Business Economics, 61*(1), 305–323.

Morris, M. H., & Tucker, R. (2021). Poverty and entrepreneurship in developed economies: Re-assessing the roles of policy and community action. *Journal of Poverty*, *25*(2), 97–118.

Porter, M. E. (1980). *Competitive strategy*. New York: Free Press.

Raghubir, P. (2006). An information processing review of the subjective value of money and prices. *Journal of Business Research*, *59*(10–11), 1053–1062.

Sutter, C., Bruton, G. D., & Chen, J. (2019). Entrepreneurship as a solution to extreme poverty: A review and future research directions. *Journal of Business Venturing*, *34*(1), 197–214.

Tang, J., Kacmar, K. M. M., & Busenitz, L. (2012). Entrepreneurial alertness in the pursuit of new opportunities. *Journal of Business Venturing, 27*(1), 77–94.

Chapter Nine

Identity, Fear of Failure, and Fear of Success

The activities involved in starting a venture represent a continually changing emotional experience (Delgado García et al., 2015). The founder may be exhilarated one day and depressed the next. The ongoing parade of emotional and affective states influences entrepreneurial behavior in many ways. The strong interplay between emotion and basic cognitive processes (e.g., perceptions, judgments, decisions, memory, and creativity) has important implications for key aspects of the venture creation process, such as the ability to recognize opportunities, acquire and leverage resources, develop social networks, and cope with high levels of uncertainty (Baron, 2008; Morris et al., 2012).

Much less understood are the entrepreneurial experiences of low-income and disadvantaged individuals. The growing interest in entrepreneurship as a solution to poverty emphasizes its potential as a means of income generation but also as a source of enhanced self-efficacy, skills development, self-identity, pride, dignity, and ability to give back to the community (Shantz, Kistruck, & Zietsma, 2018; Sutter, Bruton, & Chen, 2019). Yet, poverty is a complex, multi-dimensional phenomenon. Beyond a lack of income, poverty entrepreneurs must overcome substandard literacy levels, lack of employment opportunities, poor housing conditions, undernutrition and food insecurity, chronic medical conditions, single parenthood, lack of dependable transportation, constant fatigue, physical insecurity and limited social networks (see Chapter 2). The complex mosaic of poverty suggests that these individuals confront unique obstacles beyond those encountered by most entrepreneurs (Morris et al., 2022). The additional obstacles, when combined with the risky, unscripted and uncertain conditions surrounding new venture creation, can contribute significantly to the range of emotions affecting decision-making.

A particularly potent emotion is fear. Fear is an unpleasant affective state triggered by the perception of threatening stimuli (Rogers, 1983). It can give rise to an immediate, concrete, and overwhelming sense of potential loss to the individual that is associated with feelings of anxiety and concerns about goal attainment (Lazarus, 1991). As a negative affective state, fear can be detrimental to entrepreneurial performance, as it triggers counterproductive behaviors, hinders motivation, and harms creativity, resulting in the pursuit of fewer business opportunities (Doern & Goss, 2014; Fodor & Pintea, 2017).

In this chapter, we explore the role of fear as an obstacle in the entrepreneurial pursuits of the poor. Two primary fears are examined. The first of these, fear of failure, has been examined extensively by scholars (Cacciotti et al., 2020). It is generally assumed to be a barrier or inhibitor when it comes to entrepreneurial behavior, although some observers suggest it can also motivate the individual (Cacciotti et al., 2016). Alternatively, when it comes to entrepreneurs in poverty, fear of failure has received scant attention and is not well-understood.

Our second focus is on fear of success, which has received much less emphasis, particularly within the competitive context of entrepreneurship. It is a seemingly paradoxical notion that individuals can perceive negative consequences from what is otherwise a successful outcome (Tresemer, 2012). It is a phenomenon that has been identified in such diverse contexts as sports (Taylor, Eklund, & Arthur, 2021), academic performance (Ishiyama & Chabassol, 1984), performing arts (Nagel, 1990), and the workplace (Prentice, 2022). For a person in poverty circumstances, success may be elusive in general, much less when trying to start a business. It can represent an intimidating outcome with a number of associated costs.

We examine the dualistic roles of both types of fears in the entrepreneurial journeys of disadvantaged entrepreneurs. It is argued that the relative impact of these two fears changes as a venture is established and becomes stabilized, with fear of failure playing an especially prominent role prior to start-up and in the very early days of the venture. Alternatively, fear of success becomes increasingly important as the business begins to take root and a viable pathway toward success is recognized.

UNDERSTANDING THE FEAR OF FAILURE

Fear of failure refers to negative feelings or emotions caused by the perceived threatening and aversive consequences of not achieving goals (Birney, Burdick, & Teevan, 1969). These consequences involve financial and non-financial costs to the individual (Conroy, Willow, & Metzler, 2002). It could be a fear not just of loss but of inequality and instability (An, 2021).

Based on how significant the individual believes these costs to be, the fear can undermine the willingness to act, and can lead to procrastination when it comes to critical tasks associated with a course of action (Parlade & Karayigit, 2022).

Fear of failure tends to be especially prevalent when someone is in achievement settings, such as with athletics, academics, or, in the present case, starting a new business. With the latter, performance is necessary to pay the bills and have enough left to support one's family. It is reflected in financial results, how much the entrepreneur can pay herself, and the ability to cover costs, meet payroll, and invest in equipment, among other indicators. It is also a context where successful results can take some time to achieve. The uncertain, ambiguous, unpredictable, and chaotic nature of the venture creation experience can make it difficult to interpret one's progress as the journey unfolds.

Researchers studying fear of failure when starting a business increasingly approach it as a multi-dimensional construct involving a combination of cognitive, affective, and behavioral elements (Cacciotti et al., 2016). From a cognitive vantage point, the individual is making an appraisal of the potential for failure based on:

a. his or her own ability to perform key tasks (e.g., create a product or service people will want, acquire and manage inventory, price correctly, maintain adequate quality, produce sufficient volumes, make sales happen, manage cash flow, address customer complaints), and,
b. factors that may be beyond their direct control (e.g., competitor actions, changing customer needs and preferences, downturns in the economy, technological changes, supply chain issues, regulatory requirements, and luck).

This cognitive appraisal can heighten the individual's sense of the likelihood of failure and, hence, their understanding of the relevancy of such an outcome for themselves. A negative appraisal can result in emotional reactions (e.g., stress, anxiety) and even physiological responses (e.g., sleeplessness, weight loss). The key to these reactions is how the entrepreneur perceives the various costs of failure. The more that it is perceived that an unsuccessful venture will result in financial loss, shame and embarrassment, devaluation of one's self-worth, career-related opportunity costs, an uncertain future, loss of interest from important others, and/or upsetting important others, the stronger the likely emotional and physiological reactions are likely to be (Kollmann, Stöckmann, & Kensbock, 2017).

The behavioral reaction to this cognitive and affective processing is socially situated, with poverty representing a unique social context (Mitchell et al., 2014). The evidence suggests that fear of failure can serve as both an inhibitor and motivator of behavior, depending upon the context (Minniti & Nardone, 2007; Welpe et al., 2012). It can undermine the incentive to start a business, negatively influencing judgments about the value of the new venture relative to the costs (Morgan & Sisak, 2016). However, it can also push the individual once a venture is underway to work harder and persevere in spite of negative outcomes. Further, it can lead to behaviors that are perceived to lessen the costs of failure, such as keeping one's job while starting a business or running the business from home rather than renting premises.

Entrepreneurship is an idiosyncratic experience where the individual encounters a stream of novel events as the venture emerges (Morris et al., 2012). The events range from rejection by a bank or customer to getting a store to carry one's product, having a successful grand opening, and acquiring a new piece of equipment. The context within which the entrepreneur is embedded can significantly impact how these events are interpreted and responded to. As such, poverty conditions might be expected to impact how the individual responds to events that increase or reinforce the prospect of failure.

POVERTY AND THE FEAR OF FAILURE

All entrepreneurs face obstacles when they launch a business. These obstacles have been captured in the so-called liabilities of newness and smallness (Hannan & Freeman, 1984). Here, newness and/or smallness result in a lack of legitimacy, inadequate resources and capabilities, misunderstood roles and unclear role definitions, few established routines and procedures, an unclear identity, and little bargaining power in early-stage ventures. As a result, the entrepreneur is at a relative disadvantage, especially relative to incumbent organizations.

With low-income entrepreneurs, the multidimensional nature of poverty poses the additional set of obstacles that we have described as the liabilities of poorness (see Chapter 5). These liabilities are imposed a priori, suggesting the poverty entrepreneur starts from a position of significant disadvantage compared to others. When combined, they often produce ventures that struggle to generate meaningful profits. Many of them fall into what we have labeled the "commodity trap" (see Chapter 8), where the business is largely undifferentiated from competitors, labor intensive, with limited capacity and little bargaining power with suppliers or customers. Combined with a severe lack of resources, the result can be a highly fragile business, where the probability of failure is higher.

What are the implications of this set of circumstances for fear of failure? Unfortunately, little research has been done in this area. If we consider conditions of adversity in general, one study found that women who are in abusive relationships and suffer domestic violence have lower entrepreneurial self-efficacy and increased fear of failure, and both of these hinder the willingness to start a business (Shahriar & Shepherd, 2019). However, with the poor, the dynamics of fear of failure may work differently. A number of factors might be at work here.

Those in poverty are likely aware of the high potential for failure. Literacy gaps, lack of training, and little previous exposure to successful ventures may cause the poverty entrepreneur to question their personal abilities when it comes to building a viable start-up (e.g., ability to raise funds, attract customers, manage cash flow, etc.). They are starting ventures with products or services that are generally proven in the marketplace (e.g., cleaning services, hair salons, transport businesses), but may be less aware of the competitive intensity and challenges in generating adequate profit margins. Because their businesses tend to be strongly embedded in the community, these entrepreneurs may over-estimate the support they will get from community members.

When it comes to the perceived costs of failure, two alternative forces are at work. On the one hand, the individual may have tied up their hopes and dreams in the creation of a successful venture. To the extent that the business was viewed as a vehicle for escaping poverty, and their scant resources were invested in the business, failure might represent a threatening and frightening outcome. It might reinforce that poverty is inescapable. There is also some sentiment that failure will reflect negatively on the community they come from. The entrepreneur believes they have an obligation, and letting the community down is a real cost of failure.

On the other hand, the ventures in question are often started with very little money, funded solely by the entrepreneur together with family and friends (who themselves tend to be poor). Little or no debt is incurred. As a result, the financial loss from failure may be limited, even in relative terms. Having been in a fragile financial position for much or all of their life, monetary loss and even bankruptcy may be perceived as just one additional financial consequence the individual will have to bear. Similarly, perceptions of such non-financial costs as shame, embarrassment, and devaluation of one's self-worth may be lower given that personal setbacks, disappointments, and unfulfilled ambitions are more commonplace in a poverty context. Further, the career-related opportunity costs and uncertain future that could result from failure are lessened when one has less access to attractive opportunities and the future is inherently uncertain.

On balance, then, we might expect that fear of failure is less about financial loss, although this certainly matters, and more about community obligation.

This might produce a higher tolerance threshold before fear of failure inhibits action or adversely affects judgments and decisions. Instead, fear of failure is more likely to have more of a motivating impact. It drives the entrepreneur to build a venture that can improve their well-being, enable them to become self-sufficient, and contribute to their community.

Where their fear of failure is lower, individuals are more likely to act. We know surprisingly little about the start-up rates of the poor, but anecdotal evidence suggests these rates are high (Morris, Santos, & Neumeyer, 2020), particularly if we include informal sector businesses and ventures started on a part-time basis or on the side (see Chapter 4). Once the business is started, the entrepreneur may lessen the potential costs of failure by maintaining some sort of job, avoiding debt, and minimizing capital purchases. However, as the business begins to earn profits and achieve a level of stability, a different fear may begin to influence behavior, and it concerns the implications of success.

FEAR OF SUCCESS

When someone succeeds, the outcomes are not all positive. Success, like failure, has costs associated with it. Although the tendency might be to assume the entrepreneur wants to do as well as possible, this may not always be the case. As a reflection of this possibility, over fifty years ago psychologists introduced a concept they label fear of success. It captures "the fear that success in competitive situations will lead to negative consequences" (Horner, 1969, p. 38). This concept suggests that success brings with it potentially threatening aspects, such as loss of friendships, alienation, and isolation. The individual tends to focus more on the sacrifices and costs involved in achieving success than on any rewards to be gained from succeeding (Widiyansa et al., 2021).

Work on fear of success initially emerged as researchers attempted to explain gender differences in achievement behavior, as females showed a disposition to feel anxious about their successes due to anticipated negative social consequences (Horner, 1972). This fear among women was explained by sex role socialization processes and stereotype bias (Horner, 1969, 1972). According to the prescribed social norms, women's success in particular contexts (school, work) represented a deviance from social expectations and thus resulted in social criticism, and thereby, negative consequences such as a loss of femininity and acceptance (Zuckerman & Allison, 1976).

Subsequent inconsistencies in the findings related to gender led researchers to seek alternative explanations for fear of success, moving the focus from motivation to the cognitive processes underlying this fear. One alternative approach adopts a social psychological lens that conceives fear of success as a reaction to a specific context (e.g., raising children, athletics) (Tresemer, 2012) and a set of beliefs grounded in cultural and socialization processes (Feather & Raphelson, 1974). Individuals may experience situational fear of success depending on the context or role in which they find themselves. This fear is a learned response to particular situational influences.

Approached in this manner, fear of success has four components or underlying dimensions. These include perceived social outcomes of success, internal anxiety about success, and the tendencies to both negate success and avoid success (Metzler & Conroy, 2004; Yilmaz, 2018). Social outcomes can include a variety of perceived costs, such as being conspicuous, guilt over excessive good fortune, alienation from significant others, new role responsibilities and pressures, loss of identity, and social rejection. The anxiety component concerns a disposition to become anxious about achieving success because of the aversive consequences. Negating success captures the tendency to downplay the importance or value of success. Finally, the avoidance of success is reflected in behaviors that effectively compromise the level of success one is able to achieve.

A number of research findings have highlighted the role of fear of success in different contexts. Examples include Gore et al. (2016), who demonstrate how less parental support and school connectedness contributed to fear of success among both high school and university students. Stanculescu (2013) found that, in an educational context, fear of success was positively associated with an individual's search for meaning and negatively related to optimism, self-esteem, and self-efficacy. Yilmaz (2018) shows how a higher fear of success is related to lower self-efficacy and lower life satisfaction among recent college graduates. Alternatively, in the context of competitive sports, André and Metzler (2011) report a relationship between this fear and concentration disruption, somatic anxiety, and a disposition to pursue mastery-avoidance goals. In a work setting, Sari (2018) found that fear of success negatively impacted career development but had no impact on organizational commitment.

The widely known concept of imposter syndrome represents a different, but related, phenomenon. Imposter syndrome refers to a situation where a person feels like a fraud and does not experience success internally despite performing at a high level. Researchers have provided evidence that fear of success is a predictor of the imposter syndrome (Zeinivand, Javid, & Morad, 2015). Separately, Ladge, Eddleston, and Sugiyama (2019) demonstrate how this syndrome hinders the success of women entrepreneurs.

Implications of Poverty for Fear of Success

Fear of success has not been investigated in the contexts of either poverty or entrepreneurship. Yet, both would seem to be circumstances where success is critical. Successful venture creation represents a pathway out of poverty, and successful performance is necessary for venture sustainability and impact. They are also both contexts where fear of success might seem counterintuitive. Why would a person in poverty or an entrepreneur be afraid to succeed? Yet, with the poverty entrepreneur, we have found clear evidence that the perceived costs of success may exceed the benefits, and success becomes less desirable than its alternatives.

As we shall further explore, it is our contention that fear of failure plays a more prominent role than fear of success in discouraging the poor from starting businesses. Success is a more amorphous concept when one is considering starting a business or a business idea is being conceptualized. For its part, fear of success is more likely to affect how the development of a new business is actually approached.

However, we first must address the question of how success is defined. For many entrepreneurial ventures, success refers to the achievement of high-level goals related to the venture (e.g., a targeted sales threshold, a high rate of return on investment, a sizeable customer base, a large number of employees) and the individual (e.g., accumulated wealth, recognition from the peers, social prestige). Further, this definition is not a static notion and instead tends to evolve. With high growth, scalable ventures, success metrics are often defined by external stakeholders, and especially investors. However, with poverty entrepreneurs, who rarely qualify for debt or equity investments, the measures of success tend to be more subjective.

As examples, success could be getting the business established and making sales, earning a profit, achieving enough profit to change the entrepreneur's economic circumstances, hiring employees, or expanding to new locations. It could be the ability to keep the business going for some specified number of years, or the ability to give back to the community.

Success ultimately implies achievement, winning, and rewards. For poor individuals, experiencing success might be less common and expected than failing. The prescriptive norm is that goals are harder to attain in disadvantaged contexts and that, when positive outcomes come along, they may be ascribed to external and uncontrollable causes, such as luck, chance, faith, or external support. Succeeding can represent the unknown and introduce a wide range of potential costs which, for a person in poverty, may be quite threatening. As a result, where fear of success is higher, the entrepreneur may tend to set lower standards in terms of what constitutes success. While he or she may dream of something bigger or more expansive, the standard for seeing the venture as successful might be established more conservatively.

Negative Outcomes of Success

What exactly is the poverty entrepreneur afraid of when demonstrating a high fear of success? It is not that success is unimportant or unvalued, but it represents the unknown for many people in poverty, and it comes with perceived costs. These costs can be considerably greater than they would be for someone who sees success as a more normal part of their life, or as a more realistically achievable thing. The poverty experience could contribute to a person fearing at least seven factors that they tend to associate with success. These include:

a. *Loss of self-identity*: Breaking out of poverty is not just about gaining income and wealth but also transforming one's identity and mindset. The entrepreneur's identity can be deeply rooted in their current socioeconomic status, struggles, lifestyle, and social standing. Entrepreneurial success can represent changes that challenge the individual's values, norms, and what they stand for. It might drive outcomes they believe are inconsistent with their identity or sense of self.
b. *Compromised relationships with family and friends*: Success can undermine relationships with the entrepreneur's immediate network. It can lead to resentment of new demands from others in the relatively dense personal networks of the poverty entrepreneur. It can take time away from relationships. Additionally, success can mean less reliance on family and friends as operations are formalized and relationships professionalized. A strong sense of social embeddedness can be undermined as one becomes part of new networks.
c. *Ostracism from one's place in the community*: When poverty entrepreneurs break social norms and stereotypes, they attract criticism. Such feedback can increase the self-perception of being undeserving and produce anxiety about pursuing ambitious goals. They can fear being ostracized by the community. Normative community sabotage is also a form of social criticism. Legitimacy concerns can intensify feelings of guilt, distrust regarding success, and internalization of unpleasant feelings about growth.
d. *Taking steps backward*: In the effort to achieve greater success, the entrepreneur could fear that the progress they have made thus far could be erased. Particularly when attempting to climb out of poverty, the entrepreneur may be more concerned with solidifying progress made

(e.g., an operating business, reasonably steady sales, marginal profits) than doing the things necessary to become highly successful.

e. *The journey to success is more demanding*: The individual may perceive that achieving success will require much more work than it should because they are poor. Meeting these demands will only increase the stress and fatigue the entrepreneur is already experiencing due to poverty's liabilities.

f. *Achieving success introduces new roles and responsibilities*: When one has not known business success, they may fear the unfamiliar. If successful, the entrepreneur anticipates that new burdens and responsibilities will be imposed that they are not ready or able to take on. Expectations from community members can introduce new, unfamiliar roles (e.g., spokesperson, advocate, representative, role model, resource provider) for the entrepreneur to fill.

g. *The individual does not feel worthy or belong*: Too much achievement and success might expose them as a fraud, as the entrepreneur can feel like an imposter and struggle to achieve legitimacy. Once successful, the individual can fear they will not be accepted or fit in with other successful people.

These are costs that can be tied to the needs of the individual (identity, relationships, acceptance, belonging, balance, being worthy); the requirements of a successful organization (resources, expanded capacity, professionalism, systems and structures, technology); as well as pressures from the social environment (judgments, demands, expectations of family, community, and other external stakeholders).

Behavioral Responses to the Fear of Success

This brings us to the question of how a poverty entrepreneur actually addresses fear of success. At tolerable levels, this fear is simply managed as one navigates the pathway to success. However, beyond some threshold, it is a fear that can lead to behavioral consequences and actions that make it more difficult to achieve success. There would appear to be three types of behavioral responses that emerge when the costs of success are perceived to exceed the likely benefits.

Procrastination and Avoidance. In an educational context, fear of success has been shown to lead individuals to delay or avoid studying, doing necessary research, and completing other academic tasks despite confidence that they could perform such activities, and despite knowing that it could be detrimental to their academic outcomes (Afzal & Jami, 2018; Rothblum, 1990). With poverty entrepreneurs, the threatening nature of success can lead the individual to procrastinate in addressing certain tasks, or avoid them altogether. They may purposely keep things relatively disorganized, which can further contribute to procrastination (Steel, 2007). For the poverty entrepreneur, such procrastination can take the form of not completing the business plan, getting a permit or license, following up on leads and making sales calls, and keeping proper records of sales and expenses, among many other examples.

Self-sabotage. In an exploration of women's ambivalence toward, and fear of, success, Ruderman (2006) associates this fear with not demonstrating ambition, aggression, or assertion in trying to advance oneself and one's self-identity. According to Pappo (1983), anxiety triggered by success cues can result in repeated patterns of self-sabotage. Sabotaging one's success can take various forms, from subverting one's talents and performing at a sub-par level to abandoning the activity (Post, 1988). In a poverty entrepreneurship context, examples of venture-related sabotage activities include not showing up for an important meeting, underperforming on quality because of a lack of attention to detail, not delivering a product or service on time, being inconsiderate with customers, and not paying a key invoice. At a personal level, self-sabotage can include neglecting health, avoiding opportunities to learn and develop literacy, and engaging in dangerous behaviors such as abusing drugs and getting involved in physical and emotional confrontations with others.

Failing to Pull the Trigger. In our experiences working with entrepreneurs in poverty conditions, we have noticed a number of individuals who achieve a level of stability in their operations, even if profits remain relatively low, but will not take an action that could clearly take the business to the next level. For instance, the entrepreneur can see a means by which he/she could purchase a key piece of equipment that would significantly reduce the labor intensity of production, expand capacity, and free up time for other activities in the business (e.g., marketing, bookkeeping). Potential funding is available and the equipment can be purchased at an acceptable price. However, he/she opts not to pursue the purchase. The entrepreneur is not procrastinating or engaging in self-sabotage, but instead, makes a deliberate decision not to pursue an opportunity that clearly could advance the business. The preference is to maintain the status quo.

For their part, the poverty entrepreneur may not be aware of why he or she is holding back the business. These behaviors, whether subtle or overt, serve to reinforce the status quo but may also contribute to the longer-term demise of the business. The idea that fear of success could ultimately result in failure suggests a need to further explore the relationship between the two types of fears.

RETHINKING THE SUCCESS-FAILURE PARADOX IN A POVERTY CONTEXT

The poverty entrepreneur can be simultaneously afraid to fail and succeed, which would seem paradoxical. An obvious way to address the fear of failure is to achieve success. However, failure does not necessarily represent the best way to address the fear of success. Further, engaging in behaviors that avoid success can increase the potential to fail. Both of these fears can produce conservative behaviors on the part of the entrepreneur, but one of them can also play a motivating role. Where fear of failure is high, the entrepreneur might behave more conservatively. Alternatively, the threat of failing can drive the entrepreneur to work harder and be more diligent. At the same time, conservativism and behaviors that work against venture progress can result from an excessive fear of success.

The relationship between these two fears within the context of poverty can be better understood if we consider venture creation as a process and the liabilities of poorness as constraints (Morris et al., 2022). A model to capture these relationships is presented in Figure 9.1. Here, new venture creation involves a non-linear, disjointed, chaotic, and emergent process as the entrepreneur moves from pre-launch to launch, adaptation of the business model and stabilization, and then growth. It is an emotional journey filled with positive and negative affect that reflects the ups and downs of business development (Morris et al., 2012). As the person in poverty navigates this process,

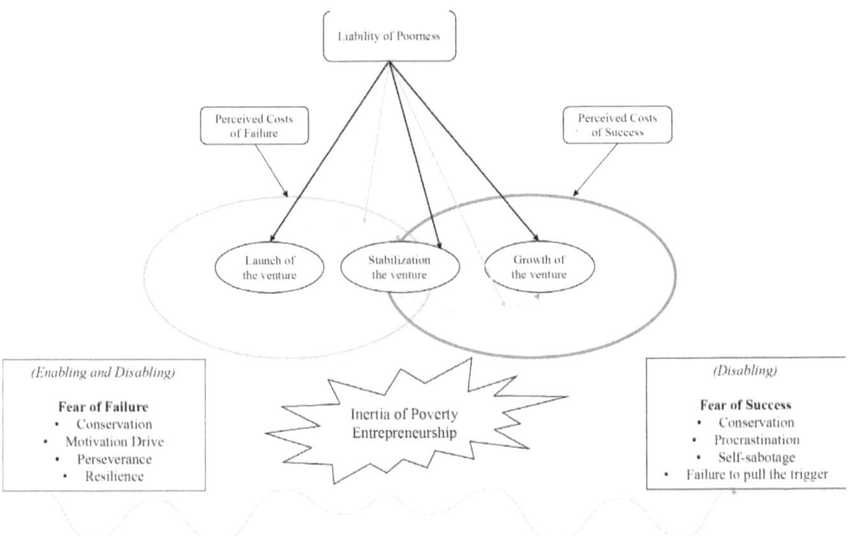

Figure 9.1. Fears of Success and Failure as the Venture Develops.
Created by Authors

the costs associated with the two fears will likely vary, changing the relative impact of each fear on behavior.

The liabilities of poorness significantly contribute to each of these two fears. For example, literacy gaps undermine the skills and capabilities of the entrepreneur, heightening their fear that the venture will fail while also making the changes that would result from success more threatening to take on. Similarly, both a scarcity mindset and an inability to focus have been associated with sub-optimal decision-making that produces a higher rate of failure and the avoidance of more challenging tasks (Banker, Bhanot, & Deshpande, 2020; Covington, 1985). With the lack of a safety net, fear of failure is greater because the entrepreneur knows resources are inadequate, particularly if unexpected negative developments arise, while fear of success has been associated with people who are under-resourced (Gore et al., 2016; Kuyatt, 2011).

If it does not prevent the person in poverty from starting a business, fear of failure plays a dual role in the earlier stages of the venture. On the one hand, it can lead the entrepreneur to approach the venture more conservatively, with limited commitments and a slower approach. Examples include keeping a full-time job while starting the business, working from home rather than investing in business premises, holding less inventory, buying less equipment, and the entrepreneur doing all the work instead of hiring employees. The individual behaves in ways that minimize the costs of failure, even at the cost of attaining success (Rothblum, 1990). On the other hand, fear of failure acts as an enabler. When a low-income individual has few attractive job opportunities, struggles to pay essential bills, and the venture represents the best alternative for lifting the family out of poverty, he or she is more driven, tenacious, and resilient. While there may be less to lose financially, the non-financial costs of failure serve to motivate the individual.

When the business starts to gain some traction in the marketplace, the possibility of success and what it will require becomes more apparent. As this occurs, fear of success begins to play a more prominent role. The perceived costs of success receive greater consideration, particularly where the path to success appears to be navigable, even if daunting. The entrepreneur becomes acutely aware of the possibility that actions related to pursuing more success can end up erasing any gains that have been made. They can also result in new role expectations, lost social connections, and other perceived costs. Where these costs are perceived to be sufficiently high, the behavioral response may be procrastination, avoidance, self-sabotage, and failure to pull the trigger on actions that would elevate the venture. Taken too far, such behaviors can actually increase the probability of failure.

The dynamic tension created between fear of failure as a driving force and fear of success as a force pushing back through avoidance behaviors can create a kind of inertia, where the poverty entrepreneur prioritizes the status quo and the definition of success itself is compromised. Attempting to escape the commodity trap and earn a living, while receiving little support from the entrepreneurial ecosystem, the entrepreneur is locked into a scenario where money is being made, but not enough to significantly change their economic circumstances. Growth and expansion are simply not realistic considerations.

APPROACHES TO THE PARADOX OF SUCCESS AND FAILURE

There are potential approaches to breaking down the paradox represented by these fears and helping poverty entrepreneurs build sustainable enterprises. We offer six specific suggestions for policymakers, economic developers, and entrepreneurial support organizations to consider.

Role Models. Having role models can positively influence poverty entrepreneurs by helping them recognize that success is both manageable and less threatening than perceived (Van Auken, Fry, & Stephens, 2006). They can reinforce the entrepreneur's sense of purpose. In an empirical study conducted over a six-year period, Kong, Zhao, and Tsai (2020), demonstrated that fear of failure does weaken the relationship between entrepreneurial intention and action. However, it was also shown that there was a moderating effect of business role models on both intention and behavior. Clifford (2019) reinforces the value of role models in successfully navigating the entrepreneurial process. Once a poverty entrepreneur has achieved some level of success, he/she can be a major influence in helping other aspiring poverty entrepreneurs to overcome their personal fears.

Teach Entrepreneurship Early. The value of entrepreneurship education has been substantiated by numerous scholars (e.g., Huber, Sloof, & Van Praag, 2014). There are different ways to teach the basic concepts at an early age (Jufri & Wirawan, 2018). The idea of inculcating entrepreneurial thinking into younger aged children can help children learn valuable skills that they can use to cope with stress and ongoing change, and expand their opportunity horizons (Al Uzaizi, 2019; Morris, Santos, & Neumeyer, 2018). Entrepreneurship education at all levels has achieved greater acceptance than ever before, and the disruptive future will demand even more emphasis here (Kuratko & Morris, 2018). This type of early education can certainly help potential entrepreneurs from disadvantaged circumstances learn basic skills and internalize the knowledge for later applications. However, it can also help normalize the concept of success and reduce the fear of failure and the perceived costs of becoming successful.

Provide Mentorship. Morris (2015) analyzed startup tech companies in New York from 2003–2013 in an attempt to determine why certain companies were successful. A key factor was whether the founders were being mentored by successful entrepreneurs. More recently, mentoring has become a key emphasis among entrepreneurial support organizations at the community level (Cohen et al., 2019). However, the process is much more likely to be successful when the entrepreneur working with the mentor is "coachable." Ciuchta et al. (2018, p. 868) defined coachability as "the degree to which an entrepreneur seeks, carefully considers, and integrates feedback to improve his or her venture's performance." In a study of 401 startup mentors and 695 founders, Kuratko, Neubert, and Marvel (2021) discovered that an entrepreneur's coachability was positively correlated to venture goal progress, firm performance, and whether or not the entrepreneur's mentorship expectations were met. For poverty entrepreneurs, this suggests the need for mentors to directly address the meaning of success and how it translates into achievable performance targets, as well as the need to increase these targets incrementally while helping the entrepreneur balance the perceived costs and benefits of success. Moreover, the ability of mentors to proactively change perceptions surrounding both failure and success can contribute to how coachable these entrepreneurs prove to be.

Position Entrepreneurship as an Option for Workforce Development. Traditional workforce development programs directed at the poor can cost in the realm of a few hundred to several thousand dollars per participant, where the end result may be the addition of one living wage employee. However, consider the impact of a qualified entrepreneurial support program being officially recognized at different government levels as a viable path for those seeking new jobs. At least one and possibly more new jobs are created while the self-efficacy and skill set of the poverty entrepreneur are being enhanced (Naquin, 2021). Such programs can also serve as vehicles for addressing the fears of both failure and success, putting both in context.

Develop More Flexible and Holistic Microfinance Programs. Concerns have been raised about the efficacy of microfinance in achieving its primary goal of assisting the poor (Garrity & Martin, 2018). A severe lack of access, inflexible funding criteria, and high interest rates leave the poor severely underserved. Moreover, the poor often fear debt, and this likely increases their fears of failure and success. Changing this situation requires that we approach early financing for poverty entrepreneurs more holistically, where funding is tied to the completion of integrated training and mentoring programs and to staged success metrics, where the entrepreneur and funder jointly establish these metrics. Such an approach can directly deal with fears of both failure and success. An example is found in the activity step model we use with the University of Notre Dame's *Urban Poverty and Business Initiative*, where investments are tied to the entrepreneur's progress (assisted by others in local ecosystems) in moving through eighty steps to a sustainable enterprise (Morris et al., 2024). This suggestion is consistent with the work of Armstrong, Ahsan, and Sundaramurthy (2018), who stress coordinated relationships between microfinance institutions and other players in a more broadly conceived ecosystem.

CONCLUSION

The concept of fear, whether of failure or success, is a major factor to be considered in trying to understand the venture creation experience of poverty entrepreneurs. In this chapter, we have described each of these fears and how they come into play when one comes from disadvantaged circumstances. Both fears are tied to a range of perceived costs and play differing roles as the entrepreneurial process unfolds. Both can produce counter-productive behaviors. The paradox of fearing both failure and success represents a critical behavioral roadblock that can prevent poverty entrepreneurs from effectively navigating the uncertain terrain involved when creating a new business.

While individuals are responsible for their choices, under conditions of inequality, the poor face meaningful challenges that constrain their freedom to make the kinds of decisions that can enable them to achieve success and achieve a better quality of life. These entrepreneurs have unique needs that reflect the complex influences of the poverty experience on the manner in which a new venture is approached. The implications of fearing both failure and success represent a case in point. Such fears and how they impact decision-making must be considered when designing training, mentoring, funding, or other forms of support. This highlights the critical need to rethink the nature and functioning of entrepreneurial ecosystems if we are to improve the potential for entrepreneurship to serve as a viable pathway out of poverty. This is a topic we shall investigate further in Chapters 12 and 13.

REFERENCES

Afzal, S., & Jami, H. (2018). Prevalence of academic procrastination and reasons for academic procrastination in university students. *Journal of Behavioural Sciences*, *28*(1), 51–69.

Al Uzaizi, H. (2019). Three reasons why it's good to teach entrepreneurial thinking at a young age. Entrepreneur, August 15. https://www.entrepreneur.com/en-ae/starting-a-business/three-reasons-why-its-good-to-teach-entrepreneurial/338141

An, W. (2021). Fear not scarcity but inequality, not poverty but instability. *Sociological Methods & Research*, *50*(3), 939–943.

André, N., & Metzler, J. N. (2011). Gender differences in fear of success: A preliminary validation of the Performance Success Threat Appraisal Inventory. *Psychology of Sport and Exercise*, *12*(4), 415–422.

Armstrong, K., Ahsan, M., & Sundaramurthy, C. (2018). Microfinance ecosystem: How connectors, interactors, and institutionalizers co-create value. *Business Horizons, 61*(6), 147–155.

Banker, S., Bhanot, S. P., & Deshpande, A. (2020). Poverty identity and preference for challenge: Evidence from the US and India. *Journal of Economic Psychology*, *76*, 102214.

Baron, R. A. (2008). The role of affect in the entrepreneurial process. *Academy of Management Review*, *33*(2), 328–340.

Birney, R. C., Burdick, H., & Teevan, R. C. (1969). *Fear of failure*. Van Nostrand-Reinhold Company.

Bruton, G. D., Ketchen Jr., D. J., & Ireland, R. D. (2013). Entrepreneurship as a solution to poverty. *Journal of Business Venturing*, 28(6), 683–689.

Cacciotti, G., Hayton, J. C., Mitchell, J. R., & Allen, D. G. (2020). Entrepreneurial fear of failure: Scale development and validation. *Journal of Business Venturing*, *35*(5), 106041.

Cacciotti, G., Hayton, J. C., Mitchell, J. R., & Giazitzoglu, A. (2016). A reconceptualization of fear of failure in entrepreneurship. *Journal of Business Venturing, 31*(3), 302–325.

Ciuchta, M. P., Letwin, C., Stevenson, R., McMahon, S., & Huvaj, M. N. (2018). Betting on the coachable entrepreneur: Signaling and social exchange in entrepreneurial pitches. *Entrepreneurship Theory and Practice, 42*(6), 860–885.

Clifford, M. (2019). Why this generation needs more relatable entrepreneurial role models. Fast Company, November 26. Accessed at https://www.fastcompany.com/90436097/the-importance-of-role-models-in-entrepreneurship

Cohen, S., Fehder, D. C., Hochberg, Y. V., & Murray, F. (2019). The design of startup accelerators. *Research Policy, 48*(7), 1781–1797.

Conroy, D. E., Willow, J. P., & Metzler, J. N. (2002). Multidimensional fear of failure measurement: The performance failure appraisal inventory. *Journal of Applied Sport Psychology*, *14*(2), 76–90.

Covington, M. V. (1985). Strategic thinking and the fear of failure. *Thinking and learning skills*, *1*, 389–416.

Delgado García, J. B., De Quevedo Puente, E., & Blanco Mazagatos, V. (2015). How affect relates to entrepreneurship: A systematic review of the literature and research agenda. *International Journal of Management Reviews*, *17*(2), 191–211.

Doern, R., & Goss, D. (2014). The role of negative emotions in the social processes of entrepreneurship: Power rituals and shame-related appeasement behaviors. *Entrepreneurship Theory and Practice, 38*(4), 863–890.

Feather, N. T., & Raphelson, A. C. (1974). Fear of success in Australian and American student groups: Motive or sex-role stereotype? *Journal of Personality, 42*(2), 190–201.

Fodor, O. C., & Pintea, S. (2017). The "emotional side" of entrepreneurship: A meta-analysis of the relation between positive and negative affect and entrepreneurial performance. *Frontiers in Psychology, 8*, 310. https://doi.org/10.3389/fpsyg.2017.00310

Garrity, P., & Martin, C. (2018). Developing a microfinance model to break the cycle of poverty. *Business Horizons, 61*(6), 937–947.

Gore, J. S., Thomas, J., Jones, S., Mahoney, L., Dukes, K., & Treadway, J. (2016). Social factors that predict fear of academic success. *Educational Review*, *68*(2), 155–170.

Hannan, M. T., & Freeman, J. (1984). Structural inertia and organizational change. *American Sociological Review, 49*(2), 149–164.

Hannan, M. T., & Freeman, J. (1984). Structural inertia and organizational change. *American Sociology Review, 49*, 149–164.

Horner, M. (1969). Fail-bright women. *Psychology Today, 3*(6), 36–39.

Horner, M. S. (1972). Toward an understanding of achievement-related conflicts in women. *Journal of Social Issues, 28*(2), 157–175.

Huber, L. R., Sloof, R., & Van Praag, M. (2014). The effect of early entrepreneurship education: Evidence from a field experiment. *European Economic Review, 72*, 76–97.

Ishiyama, F. I., & Chabassol, D. J. (1984). Fear of Success Consequence Scale: Measurement of fear of social consequences of academic success. *Psychological Reports*, *54*(2), 499–504.

Jufri, M., & Wirawan, H. (2018). Internalizing the spirit of entrepreneurship in early childhood education through traditional games. *Education + Training, 60*(7/8), 767–780.

Kollmann, T., Stöckmann, C., & Kensbock, J. M. (2017). Fear of failure as a mediator of the relationship between obstacles and nascent entrepreneurial activity—An experimental approach. *Journal of Business Venturing, 32*(3), 280–301.

Kong, F., Zhao, L., & Tsai, C. H. (2020). The relationship between entrepreneurial intention and action: The effects of fear of failure and role model. *Frontiers in Psychology, 11*, 229.

Kuratko, D. F., Neubert, E., & Marvel, M. R. (2021). Insights on the mentorship and coachability of entrepreneurs. *Business Horizons, 64*(2), 199–209.

Kuratko, D. F. & Morris, M. H. (2018). Examining the future trajectory of entrepreneurship. *Journal of Small Business Management*, *56*(1), 11–23.

Kuyatt, A. (2011). Managing for innovation: Reducing the fear of failure. *Journal of Strategic Leadership*, *3*(2), 31–40.

Ladge, J., Eddleston, K. A., & Sugiyama, K. (2019). Am I an entrepreneur? How imposter fears hinder women entrepreneurs' business growth. *Business Horizons, 62*(5), 615–624.

Lazarus, R. S. (1991). Progress on a cognitive-motivational-relational theory of emotion. *American Psychologist, 46*, 819–834.

Metzler, J. N., & Conroy, D. E. (2004). Structural validity of the Fear of Success Scale. *Measurement in Physical Education and Exercise Science*, *8*(2), 89–108.

Minniti, M., & Nardone, C. (2007). Being in someone else's shoes: The role of gender in nascent entrepreneurship. *Small Business Economics, 28*(2/3), 223–238.

Mitchell, J. R., Mitchell, R. K., & Randolph-Seng, B. (2014). *Handbook of entrepreneurial cognition*. Edward Elgar, London UK.

Morgan, J., & Sisak, D. (2016). Aspiring to succeed: A model of entrepreneurship and fear of failure. Journal of *Business Venturing, 31,* 1–21.

Morris, R. (2015). Mentors are the secret weapons of successful startups, March 22. Retrieved April 10, 2020, from https://techcrunch.com/2015/03/22/mentors-are-the-secret-weapons-of-successful-startups/

Morris, M. H., Becker, R., McDonald, S. and Snyder, P. (2024). *80 Steps to sustainable success: The UPBI handbook on building a business*, South Bend, IN: UPBI Press.

Morris, M. H., Kuratko, D. F., Schindehutte, M., & Spivack, A. (2012). Framing the entrepreneurial experience. *Entrepreneurship Theory & Practice*, 36(1), 11–40.

Morris, M. H., Kuratko, D. F., Audretsch, D. B. & Santos, S. C. (2022). Overcoming the liability of poorness: Disadvantage, fragility, and the poverty entrepreneur. *Small Business Economics*, *58*, 41–55.

Morris, M. H., Santos, S. C., & Neumeyer, X. (2018). *Poverty and entrepreneurship in developed economies*. Edward Elgar Publishing.

Morris, M. H., Santos, S. C., & Neumeyer, X. (2020). Entrepreneurship as a solution to poverty in developed economies. *Business Horizons*, *63*(3), 377–390.

Nagel, J. J. (1990). Performance anxiety and the performing musician: A fear of failure or a fear of success? *Medical Problems of Performing Artists*, *5*(1), 37–40.

Naquin, H. (2021, September 16). Entrepreneurship: The key to sustained workforce development. Science Center. https://sciencecenter.org/blog/entrepreneurship-the-key-to-sustained-workforce-development

Pappo, M. (1983). Fear of success: The construction and validation of a measuring instrument. *Journal of Personality Assessment*, *47*(1), 36–41.

Parlade, J., & Karayigit, C. (2022). Examining procrastination and fear of failure among college students. *Cognition, Brain, Behavior*, *26*(4), 199–213.

Post, R. (1988). Self-sabotage among successful women. *Psychotherapy in Private Practice*, *6*(3), 191–205.

Prentice, S. (2022). *The future of workplace fear*. Berkeley, CA: Springer Apress

Rogers, R. W. (1983). Cognitive and physiological processes in fear appeals and attitude change: A revised theory of protection motivation. In Cacioppo, J. T. & Petty, R. E. (Eds.), *Social psychophysiology: A sourcebook* (pp. 153–176). New York: Guilford Press.

Rothblum, E. D. (1990). Fear of failure: The psychodynamic, need achievement, fear of success, and procrastination models. *Handbook of Social and Evaluation Anxiety*, 497–537.

Ruderman, E. G. (2006). Nurturance and self-sabotage: Psychoanalytic perspectives on women's fear of success. In *International Forum of Psychoanalysis* (Vol. 15, No. 02, pp. 85–95). Taylor & Francis Group.

Sari, W. P. (2018). *Work family conflict, fear of success, and organizational commitment in working women. HIKARI Ltd*, *4*(2), 71–82.

Shahriar, A. Z. M., & Shepherd, D. A. (2019). Violence against women and new venture initiation with microcredit: Self-efficacy, fear of failure, and disaster experiences. *Journal of Business Venturing, 34*(6), 105945.

Shantz, A. S., Kistruck, G., & Zietsma, C. (2018). The opportunity not taken: The occupational identity of entrepreneurs in contexts of poverty. *Journal of Business Venturing*, *33*(4), 416–437.

Stanculescu, E. (2013). University students' fear of success from the perspective of positive psychology. *Procedia-Social and Behavioral Sciences*, *78*, 728–732.

Steel, P. (2007). The nature of procrastination: A meta-analytic and theoretical review of quintessential self-regulatory failure. *Psychological Bulletin*, *133*(1), 65–94.

Sutter, C., Bruton, G. D., & Chen, J. (2019). Entrepreneurship as a solution to extreme poverty: A review and future research directions. *Journal of Business Venturing, 34*(1), 197–214.

Taylor, S., Eklund, R., & Arthur, C. (2021). Fear of failure in sport, exercise, and physical activity: A scoping review. *International Review of Sport and Exercise Psy chology,* DOI: 10.1080/1750984X.2021.1901299

Tresemer, D. W. (2012). *Fear of success*. Springer Science & Business Media.

Van Auken, H., Fry, F., & Stephens, P. (2006). The influence of role models on entrepreneurial intentions. *Journal of Developmental Entrepreneurship, 11*(2), 157–167.

Welpe, I. M., Spörrle, M., Grichnik, D., Michl, T., & Audretsch, D. B. (2012). Emotions and opportunities: The interplay of opportunity evaluation, fear, joy, and anger as antecedent of entrepreneurial exploitation. *Entrepreneurship Theory and Practice, 36*(1), 69–96.

Widiyansa, A. R., Buana, A., & Martri, D. (2021). Fear of success is everywhere: Fake or real? *Technium Social Sciences Journal*, *15*, 427–436.

Yilmaz, H. (2018). Fear of success and life satisfaction in terms of self-efficacy. *Universal Journal of Educational Research*, *6*(6), 1278–1285.

Zeinivand, Z., Amini Javid, L., & Morad, A. (2015). A study on the relationship between fear of success, emotions of shame and guilt with imposter syndrome among female students. *Women's Studies Sociological and Psychological*, *13*(1), 161–180.

Zuckerman, M., & Allison, S. N. (1976). An objective measure of fear of success: Construction and validation. *Journal of Personality Assessment, 40*(4), 422–430.

Chapter Ten

The Role of Faith in Poverty Entrepreneurship

Values and belief systems strongly influence an individual's intentions and behaviors, shape social perceptions, and influence decision-making. They are the foundation of cultures and societies. Values act as a compass, guiding how one should behave and act in situations, how they perceive others in the environment, and how cultures work. They serve as both a guide and motivator for human behavior and are expressed at the individual, group, and societal levels.

At the individual level, values are "trans-situational goals, varying in importance, which serve as guiding principles in the life of a person or group" (Schwartz, 2017, p.52). Various perspectives highlight particular core values when attempting to explain human behavior. For instance, personal values theory identifies ten basic values: power, achievement, hedonism, stimulation, self-direction, universalism, benevolence, conformity, tradition, and security. Alternatively, at a group and social level, individuals come to internalize the "shared motives, values, beliefs, identities and interpretation or meaning of significant events that result from common experiences of members of collectivities that are transmitted across generations" (House & Javidan, 2004, p. 15). In this vein, Hofstede (1984) posits the existence of national value systems built around four cultural dimensions: individualism-collectivism, uncertainty avoidance, power distance (strength of social hierarchy), and masculinity-femininity. National cultural value systems are relatively stable over time and carried forward through generations (Hofstede & Usunier, 2003).

While a significant volume of research has explored these personal and cultural values and beliefs, less attention has been devoted to values related to faith, religion, and spirituality. Yet, faith is an important aspect of personal value structures (Dodd & Seaman, 1998), with diverse religious beliefs and practices commonly embedded in the everyday lives of millions of people. Around the world, religious groups (e.g., Christianity, Judaism, Islam, Buddhism, and Hinduism, among many others) are prevalent, but there are also many unaffiliated believers (Hackett et al., 2012). Berger (2001, p. 445) argues that the world "is as religious as it has ever been, and in some places is more religious than ever." Despite its prominence, we know relatively little about how faith and its different manifestations affect business organizations, especially when compared to other values (Tracey, 2012). Higher-impact academic journals have been especially remiss in tackling issues of faith (see Block, Fisch, & Rehan, 2020, for a bibliometric analysis). However, as Smith et al. (2019; 2021) have illustrated, faith holds much promise in explaining how and why many entrepreneurs behave the way they do.

In this chapter, we frame religion and faith broadly to include "both institutional religious expressions and personal religious expressions, such as feelings of spirituality, beliefs about the sacred, and religious practices" (Pargament, 2001, p. 4). Because we want to understand the experience of religion and faith when starting and developing a venture within the poverty context, we adopt a psychological lens to define religion as "a search for significance in ways related to the sacred" (Pargament, 2001, p. 32). This implies that our discussion centers on the role of a higher power, being, or realm understood by faith-based people to be at the core of their existence (Pargament et al., 2005).

Religion and faith-related beliefs have significant implications for poverty. They affect many aspects of daily life and have important consequences for the poverty experience. They can influence educational attainments, family and marital decisions and roles, belongingness and identification with social groups, involvement in certain types of activities and rituals, career and occupational choices, political influence, and wealth accumulation (Keister, 2011). One can reflect on the challenges that impoverished individuals face daily and how religion can both help to alleviate those conditions or, alternatively, perpetuate such adversity. For example, a religious family going through difficult times and unable to afford basic necessities may find a local church that provides a nutritious meal after Sunday services or clothing to get through a cold winter. Frequently, churches organize social functions, and households in poverty can find support there to help alleviate the hardships affecting their lives. The church serves as a refuge and source of spiritual guidance and fellowship. A very different example can be found in religious traditions where women's agency and freedoms are stifled, placing them under the authority of their fathers and husbands, and defining their social role as family caretakers. The implications of such traditions for limited self-development and constrained entrepreneurial behaviors can be dramatic. Further, the extant evidence indicates that some religious groups are much more likely to experience persistent poverty than others (Keister 2003, 2005), suggesting a correlation between religion and asset ownership. For example, conservative Protestants in the United States are overrepresented at the bottom of the wealth distribution (Keister 2003, 2005), and this religious affiliation indirectly affects wealth through educational attainment, fertility, and female labor force participation (Keister, 2008).

This chapter will explore interfaces between faith, religion, spirituality, poverty, and entrepreneurship. We reflect on how they are complementary and how religion can be reflected in several aspects of the poverty experience and entrepreneurial journeys of the poor. How much do individuals rely on prayer and faith when facing challenges and setbacks related to meeting basic needs? To what extent do those in poverty conditions tend to demonstrate stronger faith? How can religion serve as a resource or a barrier for poverty entrepreneurs? In what ways can religious and faith-based values shape the entrepreneurial experiences of those for whom faith plays a central role in their lives? To address such questions, we borrow from the sociology of religion lens (Beckford, 2003) and from identity, sense-making, and boundary theories.

ARE THE POOR MORE RELIGIOUS?

Strong religious or faith-based values can be found among all socio-economic groups in society but are especially strong among those in poverty and disadvantaged circumstances. In terms of more applied research, Pew Research (2018) finds that people in poorer nations are generally more religious than those in wealthier nations (see also Crabtree, 2010). Within a given nation, Stasna (2015) reports that people in the lowest income bracket are more religious than those in the highest bracket. Various observers have concluded that, over time, societies become more secular as incomes increase (e.g., Lozano, 2017; Wilson, 2016). Further, religious participation is generally associated with better socio-economic outcomes, and this relationship may be more marked among lower-skilled and marginalized groups, at least in societies that do not have a state religion (Lozano, 2017).

From a more scholarly perspective, a distinction is made between religious affiliation, or the tendency to join, associate or identify with a religious group, and religious identification, which is concerned with the strength of one's religious commitment (Stark, 1972). Deprivation has been associated with the latter, particularly among those already affiliated with a religion. This relationship has been identified across different nations, cultural contexts, and religious traditions (Hoverd, Bulbulia, & Sibley, 2013).

Experiencing sustained poverty has been associated with lower levels of individual control and higher levels of anxiety (Kay et al., 2010). Such conditions can lead one to turn to a higher power. Faith can serve to buffer those in poverty from the negative effects of trauma and anxiety. There is evidence that people tend to rely more heavily on prayer and faith in times of difficulty and crisis, and this is consistent across a wide range of personal challenges (Trevino et al., 2010). Hence, when one is exposed to suffering, uncertainties related to harm, and death or mortality, they are more apt to turn to faith (Hoverd et al., 2013). Sullivan (2012) finds that low-income women rely upon faith as a source of stress management, while Schwadel (2009) indicates faith can provide a means for building social capital and adaptive social responses to economic deprivation.

Divine control has been defined as "the extent to which an individual perceives that God exerts a commanding authority over the course and direction of his or her life" (Schieman et al., 2006, p. 27). Such perceptions could have important implications for the person in poverty who attempts to launch a business venture. For instance, research findings by Schieman (2010) suggest perceptions regarding divine control are greater among those in marginalized circumstances. Khenfer and colleagues (2017) demonstrate that, when people feel low self-efficacy such as that associated with poverty circumstances, belief in divine control can help individuals restore their goal commitment. Let us further explore the implications of faith for the pursuit of entrepreneurship by the poor.

RELIGIOUS AND FAITH-BASED VALUES IN POVERTY ENTREPRENEURSHIP

As we shall further explore in Chapter 11, our ability to ensure more people in poverty are able to develop sustainable enterprises requires that we focus on the development of both the venture and the entrepreneur. The ventures being created all too frequently are marginal performers that fall into the commodity trap (see Chapter 8). The entrepreneur must overcome the liabilities of poorness (Chapter 5) and a limited opportunity horizon (Chapter 6). For its part, faith represents an important mechanism for understanding ongoing developments related to the venture as well as how the poverty entrepreneur experiences and is affected by the venture development process. Figure 10.1 summarizes the potential effects of faith-based influences. To better understand these influences, let us first consider the underlying motives for launching a business venture, then the impacts once a venture is up and running, and finally, the ongoing impacts on the individual.

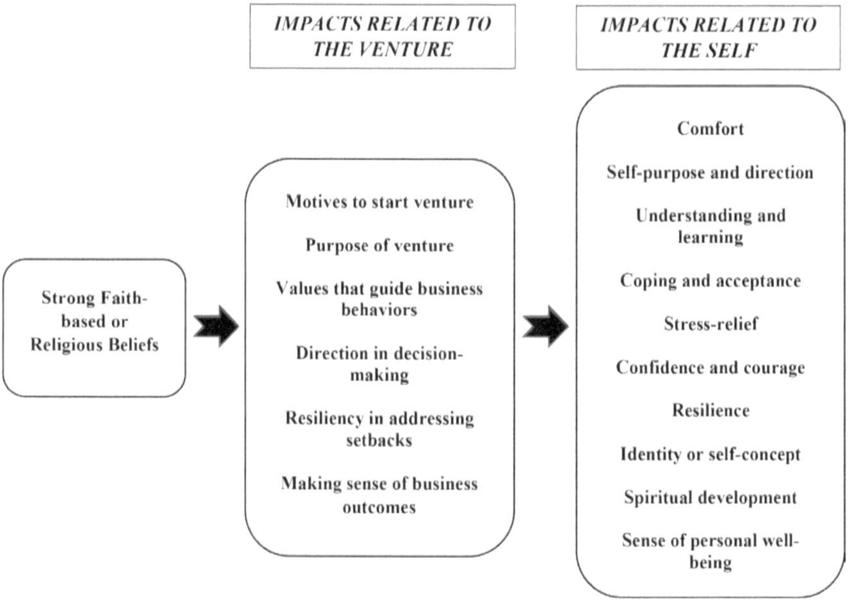

Figure 10.1. Potential Roles of Faith and Religion in Poverty Entrepreneurship.
Created by Authors

Religious Motivations as Drivers of Entrepreneurship in Poverty

Audretsch, Bönte, and Tamvada (2013) note how belonging to some religions, such as Hinduism, results in a lower propensity to be self-employed, while others, such as Islam and Jainism, are more encouraging of entrepreneurial behavior. Henley (2017) found a significant association between entrepreneurial activity and evangelical or Pentecostal Christian religious affiliation. Religions affect entrepreneurship by encouraging or discouraging certain kinds of behavior. For instance, where they encourage self-reliance, achievement, risk-sharing, or philanthropy, the general impact may be positive. However, starting a venture while facing significant hardships is difficult, and can be considered an act of courage. It requires self-motivation, and faith can play a role here as well.

A wide range of factors motivates entrepreneurial behavior, from income and wealth generation to independence and achievement (Morris et al., 2006). However, faith can be especially instrumental in motivating the poverty entrepreneur in two significant ways.

Ulterior Motives to Do Good and Contribute to the Community

For some, entrepreneurship is a "calling from God,[1]" particularly when the business opportunity involves serving the community. The concept of calling and vocation at work is related to meaningfulness and the personal significance of work (Rosso et al., 2010). Individuals try to find purpose in many facets of their lives, including work, answering the question "Why I am here?" (Pratt & Ashforth, 2003). When religious identity is very salient, individuals refer to a sense of purpose or direction tied to the significance of God or the divine, which they see as a calling. This calling can be defined as "a transcendent summons, experienced as originating beyond the self, to approach a particular life role in a manner oriented toward demonstrating or deriving a sense of purpose or meaningfulness and that holds other-oriented values and goals as primary sources of motivation" (Dik & Duffy, 2009, p. 427). For poverty entrepreneurs, the purpose and drive to start a venture can be perceived as "God's plans" for them and to fulfill the religious values of making good for others. Think about an entrepreneur in poverty who starts an at-home babysitting and child care service, which allows other women from the community to gain more flexibility in their lives, while providing a safe place for children to develop, and creating jobs for others in disadvantaged circumstances. From a religious standpoint, this business concept can be framed as a way to practice the good and serve others, as the outcome is aligned with the religious value of helping to relieve the burdens in others and serve a prosocial role.

Thus, the poverty entrepreneur may be moved to start a business based on the belief that the opportunity came their way as a divine sign. They may or may not have been thinking about entrepreneurship, but some development or set of developments in life is viewed as a sign that one is meant to start a business. It might be reinforced by prayer, the individual's personal relationship with the divine, and the words and prayers of others. There is a feeling and alignment and a sense that this is what I am supposed to do.

When spirituality is very salient, individuals may attribute the business's meaning and purpose to God. Individuals are moved by the faith that the venture will create better opportunities for their communities, such as alleviating social segregation, improving dignity in living conditions, creating jobs for others who are poor, and bringing new opportunities to the neighborhood. This is related to an extrinsic religious orientation of entrepreneurship (Balog et al., 2014).

Aspirational Hope for God's Blessing

In conditions of poverty where individuals feel desperate, God can be the only hope, and faith and religion are a source of motivation. Here we refer to hope as characterized by self-determination and optimism—that is, wishful and aspirational hope—rather than low agency and fatalism, which would portray a state of victimization (Lybbert & Wydick, 2018). This is to say that belief in the will of God and the influence of benevolence of a patron, combined with grit, constitutes a key element of resilience as a way to cope with adversity (Ong, Edwards, & Bergeman, 2006). A religious framing of both hardships and opportunities suggests that individual choices matter in tandem with the guidance and grace of a divine authority, and this forms the basis for hope that drives action and motivates the individual to pursue opportunities. Thus, as secular and theological views of hope evolved from a wishful to a proactive framing, faith in the divine may be interpreted as a sign that their entrepreneurial efforts will be blessed, which triggers agency and lessens the fear of failure. Hence, the person trusts that, by believing in and staying faithful to the Divine, while attempting to do one's best and remaining true to core values, the entrepreneur will be provided for.

This aspirational hope for God's blessing is also expressed through rationalizing hardships through faith. If God puts individuals in such adverse contexts and presents them with the challenge of overcoming adversity, He will now compensate their efforts and, through the divine force, influence things positively—and that can include the success of the venture. Individuals of faith may believe that their venture is a mission, or that their work is a partnership with God, and they adapt work-related decision-making and tasks to realize this fulfillment (Walker, 2013). In this case, poverty entrepreneurs are guided through intrinsic religious orientations in their ventures (Balog et al., 2014), and religious faith serves as a source for perseverance and personal initiative. Any success is attributed to God's fortune.

Whether the motivations to pursue entrepreneurship in poverty conditions are driven by religious values related to serving the community and making *good*, or compelled by the aspirational hope for God's blessing, these motives will lead to action and activity when coupled with the important psychological attributes that drive goal attainment, such as internal locus of control (Rotter, 1954), self-efficacy (Bandura, 1977), and resilience (Corner et al., 2017). Commitment to religious values and identity may serve to sanctify the individual goals one decides to pursue, and help raise one's self-efficacy and ability to self-regulate (McCullough & Willoughby, 2009). Lybbert and Wydick (2018) developed an economic model of hope based on these constructs from the psychology literature, helping to explain hope as a function of aspirations and agency which can produce pathways for transitioning out of poverty and generating wealth.

Faith-based Influences on Venture Development When in Poverty

Religion and faith also have important implications for how a venture started by someone in poverty circumstances develops. A business can be a place for religious practice, and strong faith-based views can inform different aspects of organizational and entrepreneurial practice. There are forms of religious organizing, such as activities, strategies, and processes by which individuals integrate their religion into the venture (Smith et al., 2019).

Meaningfulness and Purpose of the Business

Faith and religious values can guide the poor in how they approach a business, signaling that the purpose and meaningfulness of the venture matter in decision-making. Again, purpose and meaningfulness derive from providing for the family and aspiring to transition the household out of poverty and fulfilling one's purpose to giving back to the community and creating an opportunity to empower and lift one's peers. Accordingly, the goals of the business are strongly influenced by its purpose.

An extension of this purpose can find the poverty entrepreneur approaching the business in terms of workplace spirituality. In this vein, Ashmos and Duchon (2000, p. 137) discuss the "recognition that employees have an inner life which nourishes and is nourished by meaningful work taking place in the context of a community." For some, work can be a form of prayer, and this can be a way to integrate work and faith (Miller, Ewest, & Neubert, 2019). The religious identification of the entrepreneur is then expressed in their venture and workplace through the practice of faith and religious behaviors and by building a business with some form of workplace spirituality, even though (and perhaps due to the fact that) resources are extremely scarce.

Faith and Decision-Making

The faith-based poverty entrepreneur is apt to pray over major decisions, ponder what God would want him or her to do, and may look for divine guidance in terms of potential courses of action. They may or may not believe God speaks to them, but they look for signs or indicators from the Divine regarding significant actions. As a result, religious values can influence a wide range of major decisions, such as whether or not to take on debt, hire employees and the types of person one is willing to hire, take on a major new account or type of business activity, make a significant purchase, demonstrate more or less proactiveness in marketing, and innovate, among others (Assouad & Parboteeah, 2018; Dana, 2010; Du et al., 2022). Without a clear direction based on their faith, they may be otherwise cautious in taking actions that could, ostensibly, move the business in new directions.

Similarly, religious principles, values, and beliefs frequently provide a framework or code for determining how a variety of business situations are addressed as they arise (Carswell & Rolland, 2007). Such a framework can include the relative importance of (depending on one's faith tradition) humility, truth, generosity, love, fairness, kindness, compassion, individual obligations, and the collective good when engaging in business-related actions. This kind of faith-based framework can guide how the entrepreneur deals with issues encountered in everyday operations, such as with product or service quality, payment of bills, satisfaction of commitments and obligations, problematic employees or customers, and so forth.

In addition, religion and faith help the entrepreneur interpret outcomes and setbacks. People have a need to attach meaning to events and make sense of them. When encountering both favorable and unfavorable developments within or surrounding the business, there may be a greater tendency among those with strong faith to attribute these events to God's will or a part of God's larger plan (Lee et al., 2023; Spilka, Shaver, & Kirkpatrick, 2019). This is especially the case with things that the individual believes are, to a greater or lesser extent, beyond their control. There is an acceptance that things in life are ultimately under the control of a higher power. Such an attribution does not suggest the entrepreneur does not matter or has no responsibility. However, when good things occur, it is a reflection of God's blessing or God watching out for me. When encountering adverse developments, I may not have been deserving, did not pray or work hard enough, did not behave in the way God would have wanted, or did not listen or pay attention to signals God was sending. Religious attribution also tends to be positive, as the person may give God the credit and thanks when good things occur, but does not blame God when bad things occur.

Churches as Sources of Social Capital, Customers, and Other Resources

Religious congregations are fertile environments for building bonding social capital (Wuthnow, 2002), and poverty entrepreneurs can leverage relationships, particularly with people from similar economic circumstances and backgrounds. Churches and worship places are settings for poverty entrepreneurs to get ideas and feedback on their product offerings. Based on the kinds of businesses frequently started by those in poverty conditions, early customers may be reached through strong-tie relationships with fellow church members and other faith-based community members (Putnam, 2000).

Further, religious organizations can serve as a vehicle for developing bridging social capital—that is, social connections with individuals from outside groups. Churches frequently exist at the nexus of different community entities and engage in activities that bring different parties together. The entrepreneur can be exposed to new knowledge and information sources and make connections to resources of which he or she might have otherwise been unaware. It becomes possible to establish weak-tie relationships between individuals or groups with dissimilar characteristics and backgrounds (Putnam, 2000; Scott, 2007). These connections can serve to expand the entrepreneur's opportunity horizon (see Chapter 6). However, churches can also be fairly closed communities, limiting connections and constraining opportunity horizons (Henley, 2017).

Churches can also provide a range of other resources. Examples include serving as a meeting or operating space, information hub, or kitchen, or providing the entrepreneur with training or sponsorship (Shirk & Wadia, 2009; Moore, 2014). Communities get together at worship places and poverty entrepreneurs can use this space to create awareness of their new business, display marketing materials, and spread word of mouth. Beyond this, religious organizations represent a type of social safety net by offering daycare services, meals, help with transportation or running errands, guidance on following the rules, and assistance with filing taxes or applying for government support. Overall, the church is an important source of assistance with material, emotional, social, and spiritual support for individuals in adversity (Sullivan, 2012). Moreover, individuals more rapidly accept and trust in the support supplied by churches because they are embedded in the relationships that affirm their dignity as followers of God (Mooney, 2009). Also, the principles of religion are to receive and to give back, so when individuals in poverty receive support from the institution, they know they also give back with their active participation in the services and activities of the church, which means that the support provided is less perceived as a handout.

Faith as a Factor in the Development of the Entrepreneur

A primary purpose of most religions is to enrich one's life and give it meaning and value (Woodburne, 1932). However, faith can also provide a number of benefits to the poverty entrepreneur attempting to navigate the difficult challenges involved in building a sustainable business. These benefits can contribute to the development of the individual and to their perceived well-being.

Given the volatile and unpredictable nature of the entrepreneurial journey and the many setbacks experienced by the person in poverty conditions, faith can be an important source of comfort and anxiety reduction (Kay et al., 2010). Belief in a higher power, or in the notion that God has a larger plan, or in some sort of divine reward for living a life guided by faith, can provide a calming influence. It can also help the individual process adverse events, contributing to sense-making and meaning-making as they rationalize and accept adverse developments (Morris et al., 2012). In this sense, faith represents a coping mechanism, where the entrepreneur's lack of control is countered by the perception of divine control.

The safety net provided by religion can also be experienced at the spiritual level. Churches are providers of spiritual resources, as they are a sacred space where poverty entrepreneurs can set themselves apart from the worries, burdens, and demands of their daily lives and where they can go to encounter God and experience profound spiritual experiences that help them feel renewed. Poverty entrepreneurs can also find assistance and counseling through pastors, priests, or other congregants who provide emotional support. This type of counseling may contribute to poverty entrepreneurs building a positive reenvisioning of themselves in light of how society sees them, disentangling from the typical perception of a marginalized and stigmatized group.

The venture experience, when influenced by strong religious values, can contribute to the entrepreneur's sense of purpose in life. Most anyone can find purpose in the basic work involved in running a business, such as by producing quality products and services, satisfying customer needs, and addressing diverse operational needs. However, to the extent that the venture serves a higher, faith-inspired purpose, such as contributing to one's community, creating jobs for others from disadvantage, and serving God, then the individual may attribute a deeper sense of purpose and meaning to their own life. The venture becomes what they were meant to do as part of God's plan.

Similarly, strong faith-based convictions can accentuate learning and competency mastery by these entrepreneurs. Particularly where the individual has a stronger sense of purpose, greater learning might be expected from the trial and error involved in venture creation and the many roles the business owner must master (Justina, 2015; Moran, 2019). Enhanced learning and the perception that one is accomplishing the religiously inspired purpose or mission of the venture can positively impact the individual's self-confidence (Ampountolas, Shaw, & James, 2019).

An especially critical personal outcome as the venture experience unfolds is the emergence or enhancement of an identity or self-concept. Here, a religious identity channeled into the business can not only be inforced, but extended to include an entrepreneurial identity. Hoang and Gimeno (2010) note different role dimensions of an entrepreneurial identity, while Morris,

Neumeyer, Jang, and Kuratko (2018) demonstrate how entrepreneurial identities can vary depending on the type of venture being created (i.e., survival, lifestyle, managed growth, aggressive growth) (see Chapter 3). The merging of a religious and an entrepreneurial identity, or at least the interaction between the two, represents an intriguing topic, particularly in terms of how each impacts the other. We would posit that one's religious identity is likely to be the dominant influence. How the individual construes their identity as a job creator, builder of an organization, innovator, or based on some other aspect of their entrepreneurial experience is apt to be construed within the context of the faith-based purpose and principles that underlie the venture.

Finally, as discussed in Chapter One, the venture creation experience has the potential to contribute to the perceived well-being of the entrepreneur. Morris, Soleimanof, and Tucker (2023) have demonstrated how creating a venture that escapes the commodity trap results in a higher sense of well-being. With an individual for whom faith-based beliefs are core to their existence, the ability to build a sustainable enterprise that is predicated on and driven by these beliefs would seem to contribute to this perception of well-being. Such an accomplishment would especially reinforce the spiritual dimension of well-being, and this dimension is likely to be weighted more heavily than other aspects of well-being (e.g., financial, emotional, social aspects).

CONCLUSION

For a variety of reasons, the poor frequently demonstrate a stronger faith-based orientation relative to others in society. The question addressed in this chapter is how such an orientation could impact their experiences with the unpredictable and emergent nature of the entrepreneurial process. The chapter has focused on three potential ways in which faith and religiosity affect the entrepreneurial journeys of low-income and disadvantaged entrepreneurs: (a) providing a sense-making framework for the decision to pursue entrepreneurship and a motive for starting a venture; (b) acting as a source of guidance and direction affecting decision-making as a venture evolves; and (c) serving as a source of support that influences how the entrepreneur is affected by and personally develops based on his or her entrepreneurial experiences. As a result of these influences, faith can play a significant role in determining what gets started, how it develops, and outcomes for the individual and the enterprise.

This discussion has referenced individuals with strong faith-based beliefs and values. However, it is important to recognize that faith traditions vary considerably in their impacts on the entrepreneur and how a venture is approached. They can vary in how much they believe a divine power directly speaks to or them guides the decisions of the entrepreneur, how much faith provides a moral or ethical framework to influence how the entrepreneur approaches running a business, the kinds of repercussions from actions that are not consistent with one's faith, whether poverty conditions are one's own making, the nature of any afterlife, and the extent to which the individual's path and personal outcomes are pre-destined, among other considerations. The relative effects of faith can also be expected to vary depending upon the individual entrepreneur, the extent and manner that they interpret and interact with their faith tradition, and the nature of their entrepreneurial experiences.

A central theme of this book is the potential for venture creation to be a source of integral human development and positively impact individual well-being. As a possible moderator of this impact, faith and religiosity could have both positive and negative impacts on the venture and its founder. While we generally believe the impacts to be more positive and have mostly highlighted such impacts, religious beliefs can also be associated with a collectivist (or anti-individual) orientation, conservative approaches to decision-making, rigid thinking, less growth, reinforcement of gender-based stereotypes, guilt, and depression (Basedau, Gobien, & Prediger, 2018; Koenig, 2013). As a result, the complex ways in which faith and religion interact with an individual in the context of venture creation make it quite difficult to conclude what the net impact is likely to be.

NOTE

1. We use the term "God" inclusively, recognizing the belief in one or more superior beings that is central to the major religions around the world, excepting Buddhism.

REFERENCES

Ampountolas, A., Shaw, G., & James, S. (2019). Active learning to improve self-confidence and decision-making skills through the use of hotel simulation. *Journal of Hospitality & Tourism Education, 31*(3), 125–138.

Ashmos, D. P., & Duchon, D. (2000). Spirituality at work: A conceptualization and measure. *Journal of Management Inquiry, 9*(2), 134–145.

Assouad, A., & Parboteeah, K. P. (2018). Religion and innovation. A country institutional approach. *Journal of Management, Spirituality & Religion, 15*(1), 20–37.

Audretsch, D. B., Bönte, W., & Tamvada, J. P. (2013). Religion, social class, and entrepreneurial choice. *Journal of Business Venturing, 28*(6), 774–789.

Balog, A. M., Baker, L. T., & Walker, A. G. (2014). Religiosity and spirituality in entrepreneurship: A review and research agenda. *Journal of Management, Spirituality & Religion, 11*(2), 159–186.

Bandura, A. (1977). Self-efficacy: Toward a unifying theory of behavioral change. *Psychological Review, 84*(2), 191–215.

Basedau, M., Gobien, S., & Prediger, S. (2018). The multidimensional effects of religion on socioeconomic development: A review of the empirical literature. *Journal of Economic Surveys*, *32*(4), 1106–1133.

Beckford, J. A. (2003). *Social theory and religion*. Cambridge: Cambridge University Press.

Berger, P.L. (2001). Reflections on the sociology of religion today. *Sociology of Religion, 62*(4), 425–429.

Block, J., Fisch, C., & Rehan, F. (2020). Religion and entrepreneurship: A map of the field and a bibliometric analysis. *Management Review Quarterly, 70*, 591–627.

Carswell, P., & Rolland, D. (2007). Religion and entrepreneurship in New Zealand. *Journal of Enterprising Communities: People and Places in the Global Economy*, *1*(2), 162–174.

Corner, P. D., Singh, S., & Pavlovich, K. (2017). Entrepreneurial resilience and venture failure. *International Small Business Journal, 35*(6), 687–708.

Crabtree, S, (2010). Religiosity highest in world's poorest nations. Retrieved from https://news.gallup.com/poll/142727/religiosity-highest-world-poorest-nations .aspx.

Dana, L. P. (2010). Introduction: Religion as an explanatory variable for entrepreneurship. In *Entrepreneurship and religion*, Dana, L. P. (Ed.), p. 1–24. Edward Elgar Publishing.

Dik, B. J., & Duffy, R. D. (2009). Calling and vocation at work: Definitions and prospects for research and practice. *The Counseling Psychologist, 37*(3), 424–450.

Dodd, S. D., & Seaman, P. T. (1998). Religion and enterprise: An introductory exploration. *Entrepreneurship Theory and Practice, 23*(1), 71–86.

Du, X., Zeng, Q., Chang, Y., & Du, Y. (2022). Value of faith: Religious entrepreneurs and corporate longevity. *Journal of Management & Organization, 28(*4), 849–887.

Hackett, C., Grim, B., Stonawski, M., Skirbekk, V., Potančoková, M., & Abel, G. (2012). *The global religious landscape*. Washington, DC: Pew Research Center.

Henley, A. (2017). Does religion influence entrepreneurial behaviour? *International Small Business Journal, 35*(5), 597–617.

Hoang, H., & Gimeno, J. (2010). Becoming a founder: How founder role identity affects entrepreneurial transitions and persistence in founding. *Journal of Business Venturing*, *25*(1), 41–53.

Hofstede, G. (1984). *Culture's consequences: International differences in work-related values*. Newbury Park, CA: Sage.

Hofstede, G., & Usunier, J. C. (2003). Hofstede's dimensions of culture and their influence on international business negotiations. *International Business Negotiation, 60*(3), 137–153.

House, R. J. & Javidan, M. (2004). Overview of the globe research program. In House, R. J., Hanges, P. J., Javidan, M., Dorfman, P. W., & Gupta, V. (Eds.).

Culture, leadership, and organizations: The GLOBE study of 62 societies. London, UK: Sage.

Hoverd, W. J., Bulbulia, J., & Sibley, C. G. (2013). Does poverty predict religion? *Religion, Brain & Behavior*, *3*(3), 185–200.

Justina, R. (2015). Motivational factors that enhance students learning/achievement. *Journal of Teaching and Education*, *4*(02), 323–332.

Kay, A. C., Shepherd, S., Blatz, C. W., Chua, S. N., & Galinsky, A. D. (2010). For God (or) country: The hydraulic relation between government instability and belief in religious sources of control. *Journal of Personality and Social Psychology*, *99*(5), 725.

Keister, L. A. (2003). Religion and wealth: The role of religious affiliation and participation in early adult asset accumulation. *Social Forces, 82*, 173–205.

Keister, L. A. (2005) *Getting rich: America's new rich and how they got that way*. Cambridge: Cambridge University Press.

Keister, L. A. (2008). Conservative Protestants and wealth: How religion perpetuates asset poverty. *American Journal of Sociology, 113*(5), 1237–1271.

Keister, L. A. (2011). *Faith and money: How religion contributes to wealth and poverty.* Cambridge University Press, Cambridge.

Khenfer, J., Roux, E., Tafani, E., & Laurin, K. (2017). When god's (not) needed: Spotlight on how belief in divine control influences goal commitment. *Journal of Experimental Social Psychology*, *70*, 117–123.

Koenig, H. G. (2013). *Is religion good for your health?: The effects of religion on physical and mental health*. Oxfordshire, UK: Routledge.

Lee, H. J., Marin, A. B., Sun, J., & Richert, R. A. (2023). Does god comfort you when you are sad? Religious diversity in children's attribution of positive and negative traits to god. *Religions*, *14*(9), 1181.

Lozano, F. A. (2017). The rise of secularism and its economic consequences. *IZA World of Labor.* https://wol.iza.org/articles/the-rise-of-secularism-and-its-economic-consequences/long

Lybbert, T. J., & Wydick, B. (2018). Poverty, aspirations, and the economics of hope. *Economic Development and Cultural Change, 66*(4), 709–753.

McCullough, M. E., & Willoughby, B. L. B. (2009). Religion, self-regulation, and self-control: Associations, explanations, and implications. *Psychological Bulletin 235*(1), 69–93.

Miller, D. W., Ewest, T., & Neubert, M. J. (2019). Development of the integration profile (TIP) faith and work integration scale. *Journal of Business Ethics, 159*, 455–471.

Mooney, M. (2009). *Faith makes us live: Surviving and thriving in the Haitian diaspora*. Univ of California Press.

Moore, A. J. (2014). *The food fighters: DC Central Kitchen's first twenty-five years on the front lines of hunger and poverty*. Bloomington, IN: IUniverse LLC.

Moran, S. (2019). Is personal life purpose replacing shared worldview as youths increasingly individuate?: Implications for educators. *International Journal of Learning, Teaching and Educational Research, 18*(5), 8–23.

Morris, M. H., Kuratko, D. F., Schindehutte, M., & Spivack, A. J. (2012). Framing the entrepreneurial experience. *Entrepreneurship Theory and Practice*, *36*(1), 11–40.

Morris, M. H., Miyasaki, N. N., Watters, C. E., & Coombes, S. M. (2006). The dilemma of growth: Understanding venture size choices of women entrepreneurs. *Journal of Small Business Management*, *44*(2), 221–244.

Morris, M. H., Neumeyer, X., Jang, Y., & Kuratko, D. F. (2018). Distinguishing types of entrepreneurial ventures: An identity-based perspective. *Journal of Small Business Management*, *56*(3), 453–474.

Morris, M. H., Soleimanof, S., & Tucker, R. (2023). Drivers of fragility in the ventures of poverty entrepreneurs. *Small Bus Econ*, *61*, 305–323. https://doi.org/10.1007/s11187-022-00687-6

Ong, A. D., Edwards, L. M., & Bergeman, C. S. (2006). Hope as a source of resilience in later adulthood. *Personality and Individual Differences*, *41*(7), 1263–1273.

Pargament, K. I. (2001). *The psychology of religion and coping: Theory, research, practice.* Guilford Press.

Pargament, K. I., Magyar-Russell, G. M., & Murray-Swank, N. A. (2005). The sacred and the search for significance: Religion as a unique process. *Journal of Social Issues*, *61*(4), 665–687.

Pew Research Center (2018). *Religious landscape study*. Accessed at https://www.pewresearch.org/religion/religious-landscape-study/income-distribution/

Pratt, M. G., & Ashforth, B. E. (2003). Fostering meaningfulness in working and at work. In Cameron, K., & Dutton, J. E. (Eds.), *Positive organizational scholarship: Foundations of a new discipline*. Berrett-Koehler Publishers, pp. 309–327.

Putnam, R. D. (2000). Bowling alone: America's declining social capital. In *Culture and politics* (pp. 223–234). Springer.

Rosso, B. D., Dekas, K. H., & Wrzesniewski, A. (2010). On the meaning of work: A theoretical integration and review. *Research in Organizational Behavior*, *30*, 91–127.

Rotter, J. B. (1954). *Social learning and clinical psychology*. Englewood Cliffs, NJ: Prentice-Hall.

Schieman, S., Pudrovska, T., Pearlin, L. I., & Ellison, C. G. (2006). The sense of divine control and psychological distress: Variations across race and socioeconomic status. *Journal for the Scientific Study of Religion*, *45*(4), 529–549.

Schieman, S. (2010). Socioeconomic status and beliefs about God's influence in everyday life. *Sociology of Religion*, *71*(1), 25–51.

Schwadel, P. (2009). Neighbors in the pews: Social status diversity in religious congregations. *Interdisciplinary Journal of Research on Religion*, *5*(2), 1–23.

Schwartz, S. H. (2017). The refined theory of basic values. In *Values and behavior* (pp. 51–72). Springer, Cham.

Scott, W. R. (2007). *Institutions and organizations: Ideas and interests*. Sage Publications, Thousand Oaks, CA.

Shirk, M., & Wadia, A. S. (2009). *Kitchen table entrepreneurs: How eleven women escaped poverty and became their own bosses*. Basic Books.

Smith, B. R., Conger, M. J., McMullen, J. S., & Neubert, M. J. (2019). Why believe? The promise of research on the role of religion in entrepreneurial action. *Journal of Business Venturing Insights, 11*, e00119.

Smith, B. R., McMullen, J. S., & Cardon, M. S. (2021). Toward a theological turn in entrepreneurship: How religion could enable transformative research in our field. *Journal of Business Venturing, 36*(5), 106139.

Spilka, B., Shaver, P. R., & Kirkpatrick, L. A. (2019). A general attribution theory for the psychology of religion. In *The psychology of religion* (pp. 153–170). Routledge.

Stark, R. (1972). The economics of piety: Religious commitment and social class. In Thielbar, G. W. & Feldman, S. D. (Eds.), *Issues in social inequality* (pp. 483–503). Boston: Little, Brown.

Stasna, H. (2015, March 15). The more wealthy a nation, the less religious it is except for America. Deseret News. https://coastalcourier.com/coastal-living/faith/the-more-wealthy-a-nation-the-less-religious-it-is-except-for-america/

Sullivan, S. C. (2012). *Living faith: Everyday religion and mothers in poverty*. Chicago: University of Chicago Press.

Tracey, P. (2012). Religion and organization: A critical review of current trends and future directions. *Academy of Management Annals, 6*(1), 87–134.

Trevino, K., Pargament, K., Cotton, S., Leonard, A., Hahn, J., Caprini-Faigin, C., & Tsevat, J. (2010). Religious coping and physiological, psychological, social, and spiritual outcomes in patients with HIV/AIDS: Cross-sectional and longitudinal findings. *AIDS and Behavior*, *14*, 379–389.

Walker, A. G. (2013). The relationship between the integration of faith and work with life and job outcomes. *Journal of Business Ethics, 112*, 453–461.

Wilson, B. R. (2016). *Religion in secular society: Fifty years on*. Oxford, UK: Oxford University Press.

Woodburne, A. S. (1932). The goal of religion. *The Journal of Religion*, *12*(2), 214–229.

Wuthnow, R. (2002). Religious involvement and status-bridging social capital. *Journal for the Scientific Study of Religion, 41*(4), 669–684.

PART IV

Fostering an Entrepreneurial Revolution

Chapter Eleven

Interventions, Contraventions, and the Pathway to Sustainability

Given the unique challenges that poverty entrepreneurs must overcome, as well as the significant diversity among these entrepreneurs, how can their ventures best be supported? While our interest includes increasing the number of low-income individuals who start ventures, the primary concern is how these ventures can become sustainable, generating enough profit to improve the economic circumstances of the entrepreneur. Our final three chapters address this question by first proposing a general approach to fostering new ventures created by those in poverty circumstances, and then, in the next two chapters, exploring the roles of the institutional environment, local ecosystems, and public policy in supporting these ventures.

Filling an unmet gap, the current chapter introduces the SPODER model of poverty entrepreneurship. As a general rule, entrepreneurship by the poor has been approached in the same manner as entrepreneurship in general. Yet, as we have seen in earlier chapters, conventional perspectives tend to produce ventures that are problematic and do not move people out of poverty. The SPODER model addresses the unique experiences of these entrepreneurs and adopts a process perspective. It is built around six critical shortcomings or challenges confronted by those in poverty when attempting to launch a business.

We argue that the challenges to be addressed in each stage of the SPODER model cannot be adequately dealt with using the more prominent approaches to entrepreneurship training and development relied upon today. The chapter raises concerns about two popular approaches, the first of which centers on so-called "business plan logic" and the second employing what might be termed "lean start-up logic." We review each of these approaches and why they are not especially effective when working with poverty entrepreneurs. As a more viable alternative for tapping their immense entrepreneurial potential, we introduce a step-wise logic, one that breaks the entrepreneurial journey into steps and measures progress toward a sustainable business one step at a time.

Lastly, building upon the SPODER model and our stepwise logic, we turn to the question of what an effective community-based intervention program looks like. Based on our years of working with low-income and disadvantaged entrepreneurs around the world, the chapter provides an example of a dynamic intervention approach built on seven core principles and includes six key components. While generic, the program design lends itself to modification and replication in different contexts.

It is the combination of the overall model, our general logic for how poverty entrepreneurs might approach venture creation, and a sample intervention program that together produce our integrative framework for fostering sustainable venture creation. Such a framework is intended as a guide for government officials as they formulate policies to empower the poor through entrepreneurship and for those organizations and individuals at the local entrepreneurial ecosystem level assisting these entrepreneurs in building sustainable enterprises.

A GENERAL MODEL FOR ENHANCING ENTREPRENEURSHIP AMONG THE POOR

While the evidence is mixed as to whether those in poverty circumstances have a higher or lower new venture start-up rate than those with higher incomes, entrepreneurial activity is very common among the poor. Whether it is a full-time effort or a side hustle, or whether the business is formally registered or operates informally, hundreds of millions of low-income individuals are engaged in some form of entrepreneurship at any point in time. Yet, for most of these entrepreneurs, the venture they are operating may provide some level of income, but does not move them out of poverty.

Those in sustained poverty conditions represent a heterogeneous group. They are diverse in terms of gender, age, race, ethnicity, education, work experiences, family circumstances, and a host of other variables. They differ in the degree of poverty they experience and its impact on their personal development, life experiences, and sense of well-being (see Chapter 2). Yet their common thread is a set of unique challenges when it comes to starting and developing a business. We have labeled these challenges as the four liabilities of poorness (see Chapter 5). The severity of each challenge varies across individuals, but they exist in some combination for virtually all poverty entrepreneurs. The result is often significant compromises to the kinds of capabilities that can produce a venture that enhances their overall well-being.

The existing societal mechanisms relied upon to facilitate entrepreneurial activity generally fail to serve the needs of those in poverty circumstances (Neumeyer, Santos, & Morris, 2019; Shakiba, Delangizan, & Mohamadifar, 2022). Different approaches are needed to develop and deliver the kinds of support these entrepreneurs require. The ability to do this in a systematic manner requires an integrative model that captures the major challenges and needs confronted by a low-income individual when attempting to create a sustainable business. Further, such a model should reflect the process nature of entrepreneurship. To fill this gap, we propose the SPODER model (see Figure 11.1). The name is an acronym capturing the six major elements that comprise the model. Let us further explore each of these elements.

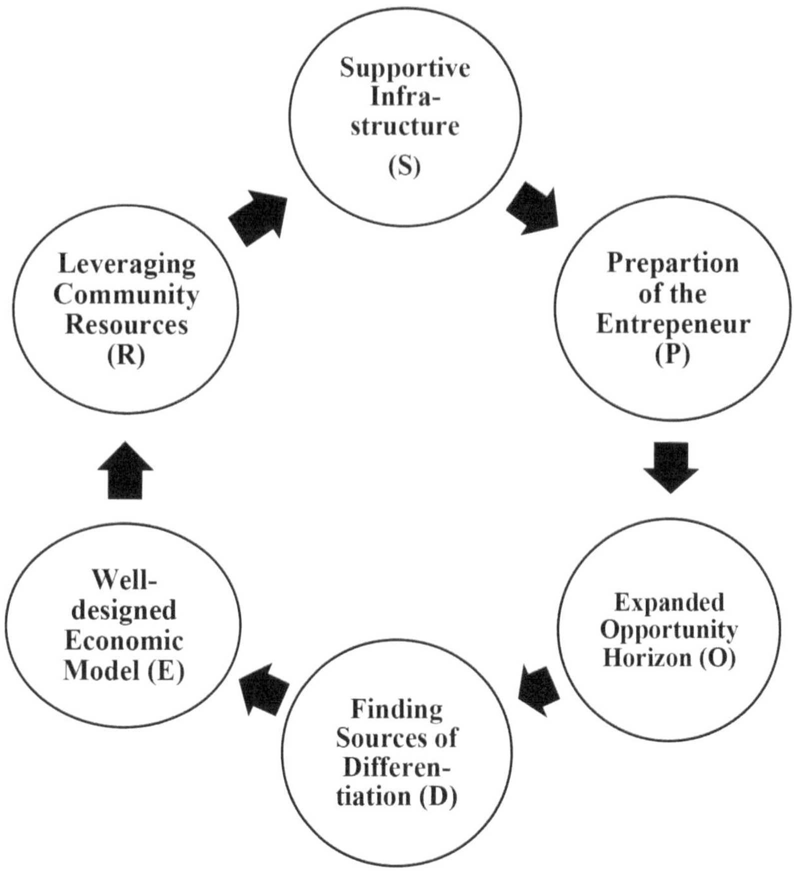

Figure 11.1. The SPODER Model for Fostering Low-income Entrepreneurship.
Created by Authors

Development of Supportive Infrastructure (S)

If we consider a low-income person attempting to start a business, they must meet both survival needs and needs related to their nascent venture. At the community level, they are constrained by severely underdeveloped infrastructure, which can be further broken down into general and entrepreneurial infrastructure (also referred to as entrepreneurial ecosystems). General infrastructure includes housing, schools, utilities, transportation, police and fire protection, healthcare, and access to affordable food. The entrepreneurial ecosystem includes training mechanisms, financial resources, co-working spaces and incubators/accelerators, a supportive business community, vehicles for social networking, small business support organizations and service providers, and entrepreneurial role models and mentors, among others.

These two elements of infrastructure are related. Entrepreneurs who are about to be evicted from their homes or cannot feed their families will struggle to focus on (or get assistance with) proper inventory management or market differentiation approaches for their business. Similarly, lack of adequate healthcare resources (including health insurance), affordable daycare services, or dependable transportation are tied to general infrastructure, but can undermine the ability to access elements of the ecosystem. The implication is not simply that basic infrastructure is the first priority, but that some of these needs can be addressed in tandem.

In terms of entrepreneurial priorities, education and training programs are at the forefront of many initiatives directed at the poor, but they typically do not focus on how to build a business or adequately fill key literacy gaps (Sutter, Bruton, & Chen, 2019). Additionally, the financial infrastructure must be reinvented in ways that provide poverty entrepreneurs with affordable financing options, freeing them from a reliance on expensive credit cards, costly payday and subprime loans, and other forms of high-interest debt (Bruton, Nuhu, & Qian, 2021; Tirado, 2015). Further, access to information and communication technology in most low-income communities is weak or unaffordable, with public libraries or internet cafes often serving as IT hubs (Urquhart, Liyanage, & Kah, 2008). Access to space to operate a business is another obstacle, with churches or other non-profit organizations providing facilities and operating venues to help people jumpstart their ventures (Walker & Bantebya-Kyomuhendo, 2014). Overall, community ecosystem resources are undeveloped and not tailored to the poor. As we shall discuss in Chapters 12 and 13, filling these gaps will require novel forms of collaboration among government, corporate, and community entities.

Preparation for Entrepreneurship (P)

The most important resource in a venture is the entrepreneur. Ventures succeed based on the passion, optimism, creativity, learning, adaptation, tenacity, and resilience of the founder (Morris et al., 2012). When someone has a deficient pool of emotional, spiritual, mental, and/or physical resources, they can struggle to learn from the negative and positive events encountered as a venture unfolds and make appropriate adjustments to the business model. For those who do start something, resource constraints often force them to create poorly performing ventures. As their opportunity costs and required rates of return can be quite low, the poor can often stretch resources and keep a marginal venture going for a prolonged period.

The ability to create ventures that enhance well-being is tied to capabilities (see Chapter 2). When those in poverty complete fewer years of education compared to the general population and attend lower-quality schools, capabilities can be compromised (Duncan & Magnuson, 2005; Hoff, 2003). This is reflected in under-developed functional, financial, technology-related, economic, and business literacies (Chapter 5). These literacies interact with one another when addressing tasks surrounding a new venture.

Capabilities are also tied to the development of two categories of venture-related competencies. The first of these is general business competencies, which include the ability to plan, organize, hire, supervise, sell, manage cash flow, keep financial records, and oversee inventory and logistics. The second category is entrepreneurial competencies such as opportunity recognition and assessment, risk mitigation, resource leveraging, creative problem-solving, and guerrilla skills. Those in poverty conditions encounter relatively few opportunities to develop such competencies, so they are forced to develop them as their new venture unfolds.

Expansion of the Opportunity Horizon (O)

The challenge for many low-income entrepreneurs is that they start with an idea for a business with little clear sense of the underlying opportunity. Yet, they often create ventures in highly competitive, low growth markets. As we explored in Chapter 6, less alertness to opportunity and limited opportunity horizons lead the poor to pursue ventures with lower revenue potential. Moreover, they are less able to adapt the business model over time as new opportunities emerge.

Aspects of poverty (e.g., hunger, illness, emotional strain, violence, fatigue) can make an individual less alert to entrepreneurial opportunities. Further, he or she may develop fairly fixed interpretation frameworks in a struggle to address basic survival (Yu, 2001). The possibilities are often limited to what the poor observe in their immediate environments (Berkman, 2015).

Finding ways to systematically expand opportunity horizons becomes a critical priority for building sustainable enterprises. This means creating new types of educational opportunities, mechanisms for growing personal networks, easier access to new information sources, exposure to idea-sharing forums, and new types of internships and exchange programs, among other possibilities.

Finding Sources of Differentiation (D)

In Chapter 8, we introduced the concept of the commodity trap, where the entrepreneur struggles with a business having a fairly generic offering and experiences low volumes and margins. Overcoming this trap requires sustainable sources of differentiation, which, in turn, can enable low-income entrepreneurs to charge more, better target their marketing, and establish greater loyalty among their clientele. Creating sustainable differentiation means offering something unique that creates perceived value for enough customers or specializing in a narrow market niche. It represents a unique challenge for someone who is poor.

Identifying and evaluating potential sources of differentiation can require an in-depth understanding of market segments, competitors, supplier capabilities, and available technologies. Poverty entrepreneurs need help with this critical aspect of the venture. They must be able to identify differences that are tied to things they can control and afford. Examples might include customizing products/services, selling things that reflect particular needs of local market niches, designing unique customer experiences, providing superior and more personalized customer service or after-sale support, creating convenience, and providing offerings perceived to be more genuine.

Development of a Viable Economic Model (E)

The logic of profit can challenge many low-income individuals attempting to start ventures. The firm's economic model concerns the combination of profit margins, volumes, cost structure, and how revenue is captured. All four of these elements often work against poverty entrepreneurs. They experience extremely low margins, small volumes, high relative unit costs (but a corresponding lack of key equipment, personnel, and technology), and limited revenue sources. This combination often produces losses or small and inconsistent profits. It places the venture in a highly vulnerable position where any major disruption can lead to failure.

The entrepreneur needs assistance in changing this scenario. It begins with pricing. For a variety of reasons, poor entrepreneurs tend to underprice. As discussed above, the business may not be well-differentiated, with intense competition keeping prices low. Further, the entrepreneur may view low prices as a source of advantage when it is usually a source of disadvantage. Pricing tends to be cost-based and not value-based. With costing, operations tend to be lean yet relatively inefficient. The entrepreneur needs support acquiring critical equipment and incorporating basic technologies that reduce unit costs. He or she must find ways to expand capacity and purchase inputs in larger volumes at wholesale prices. Innovative low-cost marketing tactics are needed to grow sales and reach higher potential market segments. Finally, with revenue drivers, creativity is needed to identify the different things the entrepreneur can charge for and alternative approaches to how and when revenue is captured.

Leveraging the Resources of Others (R)

If we consider the mix of physical, relational, organizational, human, intellectual, and financial resources needed to build a successful venture, and then compare them to the shortfalls in the resources of the poor, one can appreciate the intimidating position of disadvantage from which the low-income entrepreneur operates. At the same time, there are ways to bridge this gap. It begins by recognizing that entrepreneurship is not about owning resources but simply finding creative ways to access them. The key to doing so lies in the concepts of bootstrapping, resource leveraging, and guerrilla behavior.

Bootstrapping involves making creative use of the resources that one has at hand. Where possible, the entrepreneur does the bookkeeping and builds the website. He or she relies on unpaid family members as employees, pays bills as late as possible while collecting from customers as early as possible, sells on consignment, and uses supplier credit. *Leveraging* is about using other people's resources to accomplish tasks. It can include obtaining resources through borrowing, sharing, renting, bartering, collaborating, and giving up equity, as well as using one resource to obtain another. The entrepreneur tries to see things as resources that others may not. Guerrilla behavior finds the entrepreneur employing a set of tactics to generate sales that rely on time, energy, surprise, and imagination rather than money. The efforts are novel and unconventional and consumers are targeted in unexpected places and ways.

While one wants to accomplish as much as possible without spending much, accessing sources of money clearly matters. The poor face serious difficulties obtaining venture financing, which is why they put less money into the venture at startup compared to other entrepreneurs (Blank & Barr, 2009). They lack savings and do not have collateral or the credit history to qualify for conventional debt (Fafchamps, 2013). Moreover, traditional sources of debt financing do not cater to the needs of the poor, and, in some cases, actually discriminate against or create barriers for low-income entrepreneurs (Servon, 1999, 2006). In terms of equity, the poor lack access to angel investors and traditional venture capitalists and generally do not have the kinds of scalable business models that would appeal to these sources of capital. Finally, they have limited retained earnings to reinvest in the business.

To address this funding gap, there is a need for regulatory reforms, new policy initiatives, and community actions that facilitate a significant expansion of microcredit, crowdfunding, social investing, grants, and peer-to-peer lending, among other vehicles. We will revisit these issues in the final two chapters of this volume.

The SPODER model in Figure 11.1 is presented as a circle. This shape reflects the idea that a cycle is involved, one that is ongoing. Hence, as a venture is launched and the initial cycle is completed, another cycle begins. The venture now interfaces with the infrastructure to gain new inputs, the entrepreneur continues to learn and improve, new market opportunities are discovered, enhanced sources of differentiation are identified, the economic model is refined, and additional resources are leveraged to enable venture growth.

THE NEED FOR A STEPWISE LOGIC

One of the most common responses when someone asks for help when starting a business is "do you have a business plan?" The business plan document has become a centerpiece of how entrepreneurial education and assistance programs are organized (Wheadon & Duval-Couetil, 2014). The entrepreneur is expected to carefully work through sections of the plan (e.g., industry, market, operations, design and development, marketing, financial statements, etc.) and then implement things according to what is written in the plan. While they impose a certain logic and discipline on the venture creation process, writing business plans tends to be a fairly problematic exercise for those in poverty circumstances. The combination of literacy gaps, a short-term scarcity mindset, lack of access to sources of industry and market data (and the knowledge on how to use them), and lack of time, among other factors, makes it difficult to map out a detailed business plan that projects how things are going to emerge over the next three to five years. We find that low-income entrepreneurs are often better able to create a business plan once they have the business up and running.

Yet another logic for helping people start businesses can be found in the popular lean start-up methodology (Bortolini et al., 2021). It is a hypothesis-driven logic that encourages the entrepreneur to develop a "minimum viable product" or rough version of their offering that is not yet finalized. Through an iterative process of experimentation and obtaining customer feedback, making rapid changes, getting more customer feedback, and so on, the entrepreneur develops a viable business model. This build-measure-learn feedback loop keeps the entrepreneur from wasting resources on product designs and features the market does not want. It is a method developed for novel, scalable, technology-based products, but it does not work especially well with the kinds of products and services launched by poverty entrepreneurs.

Given the inadequacies of both the business plan and lean startup logics, we need an alternative logic for guiding the entrepreneurial journeys of the poor. An especially promising approach, and one that helps overcome the liabilities of poorness, is what might be termed "stepwise logic." Here, the journey to a sustainable enterprise is broken down into activity steps, and the entrepreneur is encouraged to take a few steps at a time. It imposes a more flexible type of discipline, but one that centers on action. The individual is not overwhelmed with all the complexities of starting a business; instead, they move sequentially through a logical progression of steps. Importantly, progress in properly completing a given step can have a motivating impact while enhancing the learning that is taking place. As a result, progress tends to beget progress, particularly as steps build upon one another, and completion of a given step facilitates the accomplishment of subsequent ones.

As an illustration, we have identified 80 activity steps in the journey to sustainability, itemized in Table 11.1. Note that these steps have to be adapted to reflect a given developed or developing country context. The steps are broken down into three stages: the planning or pre-launch stage (27 steps), the launch and early operations stage (31 steps), and the stabilization stage (22 steps). Some of the steps are relatively simple (e.g., selecting a name for the business), while others are more complex (e.g., creating a website). The steps are also labeled in terms of their general area of focus (self-development, marketing, financial management, operations, bookkeeping/administration, and planning/strategizing—see key at the bottom of Table 11.1).

Writing a business plan is important but should not be a roadblock to starting a business. The stepwise approach is more action-oriented in nature. The entrepreneur is learning by doing and adapting as he or she progresses. One can simply focus on the number of steps they want to accomplish in the next thirty days. Then, based on the progress made, they determine the steps to be taken in the following thirty days. For those in poverty conditions, this can represent a more viable pathway to sustainability.

Table 11.1. Eighty Steps to a Sustainable Venture

Planning Phase

1. Attend an entrepreneurial training program or course **(S)**
2. Assess your personal strengths and weaknesses when it comes to running a business, identify methods for addressing weaknesses **(S)**
3. Get an entrepreneurial mentor (a successful entrepreneur) **(S)**
4. Interview at least thirty potential customers and write up findings **(P)**
5. Visit four competitor businesses and identify what they do well **(P)**
6. Research best practices and the latest trends in your industry **(P)**
7. Determine if this will be full-time or part-time initially, whether you will keep an existing job while starting the business, and hours per week you can commit **(S)**
8. Determine whether you want to start a survival, lifestyle, managed growth, or aggressive growth business and how this affects commitment and resource needs **(P)**
9. Formulate a unique value proposition **(P)**
10. Establish a business or brand name **(M)**
11. Apply for a patent, copyright, or trademark **(P)**
12. Determine how many revenue drivers you will initially have & which will generate the most revenue **(P)**
13. Estimate your first year start-up, fixed and variable costs **(F)**
14. Determine your pricing strategy and price points **(M)**
15. Determine your profit margin per unit and your breakeven sales level **(F)**
16. Understand your volume (hi, med, lo) and margin (hi, med, lo) relationship **(P)**
17. Determine how much money you need to actually start the business and get to a positive cash flow **(F)**
18. Determine how much income you need from the business, if any, to survive **(S)**
19. Segment the market and identify priority target audiences **(M)**
20. Determine whether to initially work from home or have premises—if premises, prioritize locations **(O)**
21. Determine if you will make online sales, sell in person, sell through retailers or middlemen, or sell through your own store (and % of sales through each) **(M)**
22. Systematically identify and list resources you have or that you can leverage from your community **(P)**
23. Identify sources of differentiation **(M)**
24. Design operating model (step-by-step chart of how you make your product or deliver your service) **(O)**
25. Put formal business model on paper **(P)**
26. Completion of business plan **(P)**
27. Make pitch for money to family, friends, banks, potential investors, or conduct crowdfunding campaign **(F)**

Launch Phase

28. Register the business **(O)**
29. Create an operating agreement **(A)**
30. Obtain any required or relevant licenses or permits **(A)**
31. Obtain business insurance **(A)**
32. Establish a board of advisors **(A)**
33. Get an Employer Identification Number (EIN) **(A)**
34. Open business bank account **(A)**

35. Create invoices and receipts **(A)**
36. Establish system to collect and pay sales and other taxes **(A)**
37. Establish system for accepting credit card and electronic payments **(F)**
38. Sign lease or rental agreement if you are not working from home **(O)**
39. Purchase, lease, or leverage key equipment, tools, furnishings **(O)**
40. Obtain signage **(O)**
41. Prepare facility or site for operations **(O)**
42. Create system to monitor daily management of cash payments **(A)**
43. Create system to track revenues and expenses (including labor time) **(A)**
44. Set up payroll system to pay yourself and any employees **(A)**
45. Implement full bookkeeping system **(A)**
46. Get business cards, letterhead **(M)**
47. Create logo **(M)**
48. Create and launch website **(M)**
49. Create social media presence **(M)**
50. Become active in community organizations and events **(M)**
51. Develop and implement guerrilla marketing tactics **(M)**
52. Identify sources of supply and acquire (and manage) inventory or needed materials **(O)**
53. Do trial production or operating run and determine approach for ensuring quality & consistency **(O)**
54. Establish system for delivery/shipping, decide whether customer is charged **(O)**
55. Determine any family members or friends that will initially work in business, how much they will be paid, and their hours per week **(O)**
56. Create job descriptions, employment contract, and hire first employee **(O)**
57. Have grand opening **(M)**
58. Make first sale by developing your sales pitch **(M)**

Stabilization Phase

59. Establish standard operating procedures **(O)**
60. Set monthly sales targets **(P)**
61. Create customer database for use in marketing/explore CRM options **(M)**
62. Determine where you have cash flow shortages, explore options for filling cash flow gaps **(F)**
63. Assess patterns in expenses and costs, identify where costs can be reduced **(O)**
64. Determine patterns in sales and profits by customer and product category **(M)**
65. Establish and implement survey or system for getting customer feedback **(M)**
66. Refine customer segmentation and targeting approach **(M)**
67. Establish loyalty program for repeat customers **(M)**
68. Adjust product/service mix and inventory levels **(O)**
69. Add new products or services **(M & O)**
70. Assess adequacy of sources of supply, identify additional vendors, improve purchasing efficiencies **(O)**
71. Hire additional employees **(O)**
72. Learn from the customers you have attracted so far, adjust marketing accordingly **(M)**
73. Continue to employ guerrilla marketing tactics but implement formal advertising media efforts **(M)**
74. Adjust prices **(M)**

(continued)

Table 11.1. ***(continued)***

75.	Integration or improvement of better accounting software to track numbers, generate financial statements **(A)**
76.	Create human resource management guidelines and procedures **(O)**
77.	Create system for evaluating employees and providing feedback **(O)**
78.	Obtain woman-owned, minority-owned, or veteran-owned certification **(M)**
79.	Apply for business credit card **(F)**
80.	Apply for bank financing to support enhanced operations **(F)**

Key (type of activity):

F = financing and financial management activity

O = operations, production, logistics, or procurement activity

M = marketing activity

A = administrative, record keeping, and accounting activity

P = planning and strategizing activity

S = self-development activity

A SAMPLE INTERVENTION APPROACH

Using the general SPODER model together with the stepwise logic, what might a community-level intervention approach intended to assist low-income entrepreneurs look like? To be effective, such a program would have to be designed around a core set of principles. These include:

- *Tailored to reflect the liabilities of poorness:* Teaching and interaction approaches must explicitly address the challenges of literacy gaps, a scarcity mindset, non-business distractions, and lack of any safety net.
- *Cohort- and community-based:* These entrepreneurs need to recognize they are not isolated or alone. Toward this end, going through a program as a cohort with others from disadvantaged circumstances is both motivating and reassuring while allowing for sharing and collaboration. Further, programming should be delivered in the neighborhoods or areas where these entrepreneurs reside, meeting people where they are.
- *Multi-staged and integrated:* Intervention approaches are more effective when they integrate multiple components over a prolonged period, as opposed to discrete training or mentoring initiatives;
- *High quality and high touch:* Online learning activities are generally less effective than in-person efforts when attempting to advance the businesses of low-income entrepreneurs, as the personal interaction is better able to fully engage them.
- *Communicated in understandable language:* The language of finance, economics and general business is often foreign to low-income

entrepreneurs. Concepts and tools must be communicated in simple, straightforward terms and illustrated using examples and stories that reflect the world in which these entrepreneurs live.
- *Respectful of the ideas of those being served:* The field of entrepreneurship can be dominated by an "idea killing" mindset, finding reasons why a given business idea will not work. This kind of "pick the winners" approach is less effective with the poor. The ideas that these entrepreneurs have in mind must be respected. The goal is to work with these ideas to help the individual make as much money as they can and then incrementally adapt the idea over time in directions that can be more profitable. Similarly, it is a mistake to impose alternative venture ideas on the poor (ideas that are not their own).
- *Evidence-based:* Programs must be based on evidence regarding what works with those from poverty circumstances. Ongoing adaptations in program content, examples, and delivery approaches must be made based on continual learning regarding the entrepreneurs who do and those who do not make meaningful progress in advancing their ventures.

Building on these principles, a sample program design is illustrated in Figure 11.2. It unfolds over eleven months and includes six inter-related components: training, mentoring, consulting, community connections, a pathway to microcredit, and database tracking. The program is based on the successful Urban Poverty and Business Initiative (UPBI) coordinated by the University of Notre Dame in the USA and operating in forty cities around the world. In each city, it is led by a local university or nonprofit organization and involves several community partners. The cohort size ranges from 25 to 70 delegates, depending upon the city. The delegates tend to be equally divided between those at the idea stage, those with a product or service they are selling but no business, and those with an established business struggling to get traction. The goal is for each entrepreneur to complete at least twenty-five activity steps (beyond those already completed when they enter the program) over the course of the intervention.

The training component includes classes held once a week for six weeks. It consists of content presentations, interviews of successful entrepreneurs who overcame adversity, and subject matter experts. Delegates are expected to advance their journeys by applying learnings to the venture concept they are pursuing. Content delivery is accomplished through lectures, stories, and examples with which delegates can identify. Modules cover the nature of the entrepreneurial journey, what one needs to know about the numbers, how to think and operate strategically, resource leveraging and finance, penetrating markets, and managing operations. Sessions reinforce one another, helping delegates appreciate how decisions impact one another.

Mentoring is done over four months in a coordinated fashion by successful entrepreneurs. This period can be extended if the mentor and delegate agree. Mentors are first introduced to the context of these ventures and coached on areas of focus, which includes the development of the entrepreneur, the business model, and functional areas within the business. Mentors and delegates are matched systematically based on input from both parties. The meetings are conducted on a one-on-one basis, and progress is regularly assessed.

The consulting phase involves students from a nearby university or college working on problem-solving (e,g., creating bookkeeping systems, websites, social media campaigns, registering businesses, etc.) over a four-month period. A process consulting methodology is employed. The consultants first meet with the mentor who has been working with the entrepreneur. Small student teams initially capture the entrepreneur's business model and then set priorities with the entrepreneurs for deliverables to be produced. The engagements are structured and closely supervised.

Community connection events are held to expand the entrepreneurs' networks and generate community support for these businesses. Two connection events are organized per year, with differing formats. The entrepreneurs may pitch their ventures, sell their wares, or participate in open discussions about their needs and opportunities. A priority at these events is to get local businesses to engage with the entrepreneurs in creative ways and share their established connections.

A subset of any given cohort may be ready to take on debt. Here, assistance is provided with a business plan, projected financial statements, improving credit scores, and preparing loan applications. The program, which has

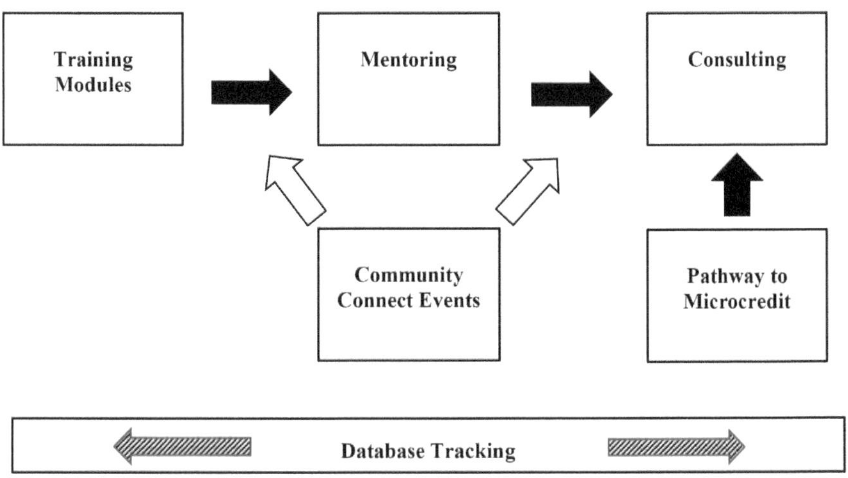

Figure 11.2. A Sample Approach to Interventions with Low-Income Entrepreneurs.
Created by Authors

effectively done due diligence on the ventures based on the other program components, works with a network of microcredit funds, community banks, and other financial institutions.

The final component involves tracking these ventures on a large number of metrics, including satisfactory accomplishment of any of the eighty steps, for three years. Data is collected when the entrepreneur enters the program and at six-month intervals. The tracking efforts enable the identification of best practices and general patterns and allow for ongoing modifications and improvements to the overall program.

The interactive nature of the six components is critical, such that the stages reinforce one another. Program adaptations are made based on developed or developing country contexts. For example, group mentoring is utilized in rural areas where entrepreneurial mentors may be harder to find. The success of the initiative is tied to leveraging community resources, a topic we will further explore in Chapter 12.

CONCLUSION

There is a rich reservoir of business ideas and entrepreneurial dreams among those living in poverty conditions. Yet, while they bring energy, creativity, and tenacity to new venture creation, the poor frequently lack key capabilities. This chapter has presented an integrative approach for intervening with low-income entrepreneurs—one that reflects their unique needs and requirements. The problem is not simply getting something started, but instead, building a business that can be sustainable. The corresponding solution is not simply making more money available to these entrepreneurs but systematically addressing the liability of poorness factors and overcoming the tendency to fall into the commodity trap. It is about thinking about resources differently and pursuing the entrepreneurial journey one step at a time.

Our fundamental message in this chapter is that entrepreneurship has to be approached differently if it is to serve as a pathway out of poverty. Different concepts and tools are required. Our integrative framework, stepwise logic, and sample intervention program are a starting point, but much more work is needed here. As we move forward, the central theme must be one of using the venture creation process as a platform for developing capabilities, not just generating profits. We now turn to the parallel roles of communities and governments in facilitating the developmental journeys of low-income entrepreneurs.

REFERENCES

Berkman, E. (2015, September 22). It's not a lack of self-control that keeps people poor. *The Conversation*. https://theconversation.com/its-not-a-lack-of-self-control-that-keeps-people-poor-47734

Blank, R. M., & Barr, M. S. (2009). *Insufficient funds: Savings, assets, credit, and banking among low-income households*. New York: Russell Sage Foundation.

Bortolini, R. F., Nogueira Cortimiglia, M., Danilevicz, A. D. M. F., & Ghezzi, A. (2021). Lean Startup: A comprehensive historical review. *Management Decision*, *59*(8), 1765–1783.

Bruton, G. D., Nuhu, N., & Qian, J. J. (2021). Informal finance in settings of poverty: Establishing an agenda for future entrepreneurship research. *Journal of Developmental Entrepreneurship*, *26*(2), 2150011.

Duncan, G. J., & Magnuson, K. (2005). Can family socioeconomic resources account for racial and ethnic test score gaps? *The Future of Children*, *15*(1), 35–54.

Fafchamps, M. (2013). Credit constraints, collateral, and lending to the poor, *Revue d'Économie du Développement*, *21*(2), 79–100.

Hoff, E. (2003). The specificity of environmental influence: Socioeconomic status affects early vocabulary development via maternal speech. *Child Development*, *74*(5), 1368–1378.

Morris, M. H., Kuratko, D. F., Schindehutte, M., & Spivack, A. (2012). Framing the entrepreneurial experience, *Entrepreneurship Theory and Practice*, *36*(1), 11–40

Neumeyer, X., Santos, S. C., & Morris, M. H. (2019). Who is left out: Exploring social boundaries in entrepreneurial ecosystems. *The Journal of Technology Transfer*, *44*, 462–484.

Servon, L. (1999). *Microenterprises and the American poor*. Washington, DC: Brookings Institution.

Servon, L. (2006). Microenterprise development in the United States: Current challenges and new directions, *Economic Development Quarterly*, *20*(4), 351–367.

Shakiba, H., Delangizan, S., & Mohamadifar, Y. (2022). Inclusive urban entrepreneurial ecosystem policies: An application of the meta-synthesis approach. *Poverty & Public Policy*, *14*(4), 342–380.

Sutter, C., Bruton, G. D., & Chen, J. (2019). Entrepreneurship as a solution to extreme poverty: A review and future research directions. *Journal of Business Venturing*, *34*(1), 197–214.

Tirado, L. (2015). *Hand to mouth: Living in bootstrap America*, New York: Penguin.

Urquhart, C., Liyanage, S., & Kah, M. M. (2008). ICTs and poverty reduction: A social capital and knowledge perspective. *Journal of Information Technology*, *23*(3), 203–213.

Walker, R., & Bantebya-Kyomuhendo, G. (2014). *The shame of poverty*. Oxford University Press, Oxford, UK.

Wheadon, J. D., & Duval-Couetil, N. (2014). Business plan development activities as a pedagogical tool in entrepreneurship education. *The Journal of Engineering Entrepreneurship*, *5*(1), 31–48.

Yu, T. (2001). Entrepreneurial alertness and discovery. *The Review of Austrian Economics, 14*(1) (2001), pp. 47–63.

Chapter Twelve

Institutional Voids and the Role of Community

While entrepreneurship can be a critical vehicle for developing the capabilities of those in poverty, enabling them to build sustainable ventures and improve their overall well-being (see Chapter 2), it all depends on context. By this we mean contextual variables play a major role in determining whether entrepreneurship can provide a pathway out of poverty for many or just a few. One of the most critical contextual variables is the kind of support system available to these entrepreneurs. The institutional environment plays a central role in determining the nature of this support system (Baumol & Blinder, 2008).

Dominant views of institutions within economies emphasize their role in establishing the "rules of the game" of how resources should be allocated to provide for societal needs (North, 1990). Other definitions of institutions highlight cultural-cognitive, normative, and regulative elements that provide stability and meaning to social life (Scott, 2001). Chowdhury, Audretsch, and Belitski (2019) emphasize the norms, rules, incentives, and constraints that operate as tools of governance for exchanges among individuals. For the purposes of this discussion, we adopt Webb's (2021) system-level view of institutions to understand how institutions influence entrepreneurship in the context of poverty. Here, institutions are "*systems comprised of rules that establish social expectations, the entities that establish, monitor and enforce these rules, and the frameworks and tangible manifestations constructed to facilitate, incentivize and sanction other economic actors with the intent of meeting societal needs*" (Webb, 2021, p. 4). Institutions are, therefore, multi-faceted (i.e., comprising such facets as laws and policies, regulatory agencies, governing bodies, religions, cultures, infrastructure, etc.) and are defined as multi-tiered systems (i.e., existing at local, regional, state, federal, national levels) (Webb, 2021; Ostrom, 2005).

In this chapter, we explore the important role of the institutional environment in general, and especially the importance of general infrastructure, entrepreneurial ecosystems, and local community support, in facilitating (and sometimes hindering) the entrepreneurial journeys of the poor. The related role of government and public policy will be addressed in the following chapter. Building on the notion of conversion factors from capabilities theory (Sen, 2000; Robeyns, 2005), we provide a comprehensive framework to account for how the institutional environment can influence the entrepreneurial efforts of those in disadvantaged circumstances. In doing so, we address the manner in which, when the environment is more conducive, these enterprises can contribute to the overall well-being of entrepreneurs.

INSTITUTIONAL ENVIRONMENTS, VOIDS, AND THE POVERTY ENTREPRENEUR

Rates of entrepreneurship vary from country to country, and the institutional environment helps explain why. As Sen puts it using the lens of capabilities theory, "*individuals live and operate in a world of institutions. Our opportunities and prospects depend crucially on what institutions exist and how they function*" (Sen, 2000, p. 142). A host of institutional characteristics can facilitate entrepreneurial activity. Examples include environments that have secure property rights, a strong court system and rule of law, protection for personal bankruptcy, limits to personal liability for actions resulting from one's business, less corruption, cultures that are compatible with individualism and self-achievement, religious beliefs that support hard work and material accomplishment, strong resource endowments, accessible sources of business finance, and entrepreneurial expertise, among other characteristics (Estrin, Korosteleva, & Mickiewicz, 2013; Lee et al. 2022; Sine & David, 2010; Stenholm et al. 2013). The presence of these kinds of institutional elements is likely to vary based on the level of economic development in a society. Stated differently, entrepreneurs can encounter significant institutional voids or inadequacies in institutions when it comes to supporting efficient and effective market transactions.

In a key study, Chowdhury, Audretsch, and Belitski (2019) provide empirical evidence of the effects of different institutional variables on the quantity and quality of entrepreneurial activity across seventy countries. To the extent that those in poverty conditions often create survival and lifestyle ventures that perform marginally, these are considered by some to be a lower quality of entrepreneurship (see Chapter 3). It appears that the quantity of entrepreneurship is associated with the availability of domestic credit and equity financing, knowledge and skills related to entrepreneurship, entrepreneurial opportunities, lower tax rates, labor market protections, bankruptcy protections, corruption, and government support. Alternatively, the quality of entrepreneurship is associated with the availability of domestic credit and venture capital finance (with a stronger effect in developing countries and a stronger effect for equity finance), knowledge and skills related to entrepreneurship, and available entrepreneurial opportunities (with a stronger impact in developing countries), lower tax rates, bankruptcy protections (with a bigger impact in developing countries), lower corruption, and government support.

While there is little in the way of comparative data about rates of poverty entrepreneurship across nations, the institutional environment may play an even more critical role here than it does for entrepreneurship in general. In fact, institutional arrangements that support entrepreneurship in general might actually work to the detriment of the entrepreneur in poverty conditions. To the extent that institutions prioritize scalable, growth-oriented ventures over survival and lifestyle ventures, the poverty entrepreneurs are left behind. The multi-dimensional nature of poverty (Chapter 2), and the four liabilities of poorness (Chapter 5), suggest that the pursuit of entrepreneurship may require different support from institutions (when compared to those who are better off) in order to achieve the same beings and doings (Sen, 2000).

THE IMPORTANCE OF CONVERSION FACTORS

Institutions directly and indirectly affect the ability of the poverty entrepreneur to develop the capabilities that enable them to create sustainable ventures (Robeyns, 2005). Capability development is concerned with how an individual can convert resources (means) into the successful performance of activities (ends), such as the ability to plan, produce quality products, sell those products, manage cash flow, or hire and supervise employees. The disadvantaged entrepreneur struggles not only with obtaining resources but with their conversion into outcomes. Sen (2009) discusses three categories of conversion factors: personal, social, and environmental. Figure 12.1 illustrates the role of these conversion factors in transforming resources into the poverty entrepreneur's capability set, affecting the real opportunities and choices available to them.

Personal Conversion Factors. These refer to individual-level characteristics which influence how a person converts resources into capabilities. They can include such factors as age, gender, health conditions, educational background, and skills acquired. Similarly, conversion can be affected by characteristics such as a person's metabolism rhythms, physical or mental handicaps, psychological disorders, levels of anxiety, or height and weight. In an entrepreneurial context, they impact whether a business is started, the kind

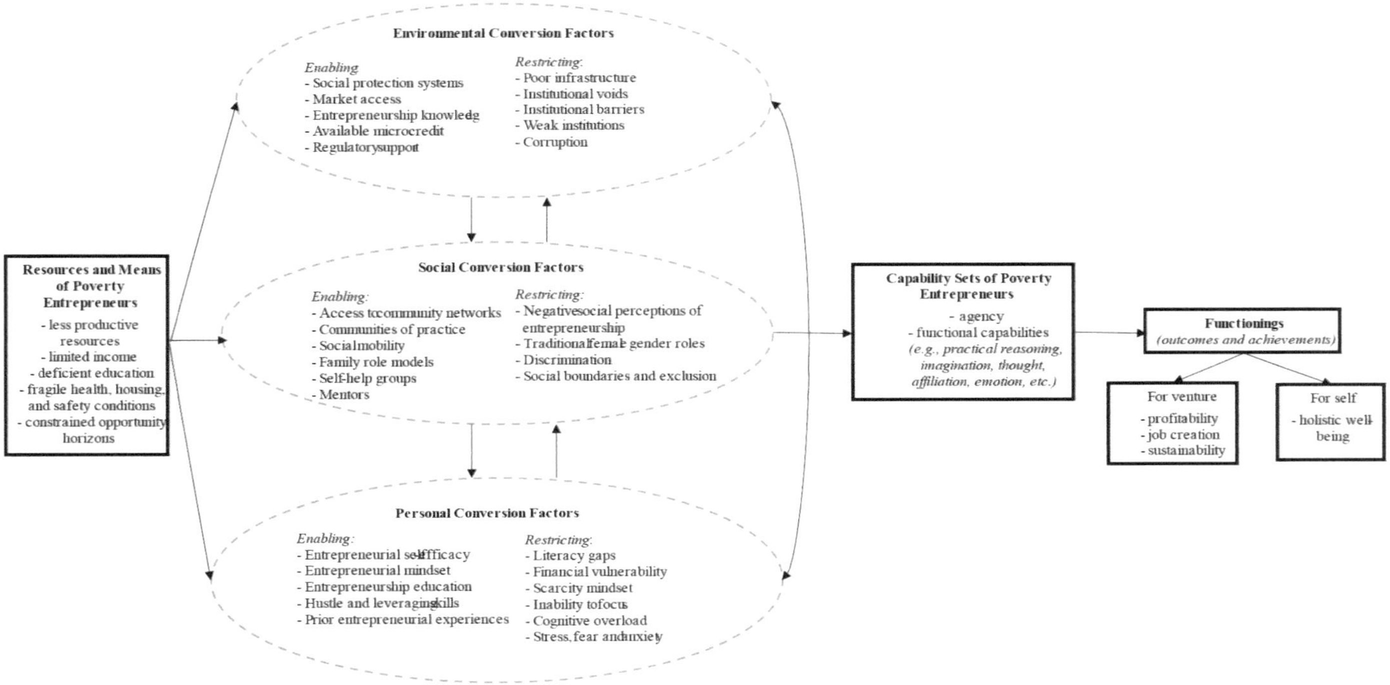

Figure 12.1. Conversion factors and the transformation of resources into capabilities and functionings.
Created by Authors

of business created, the time and effort devoted to the business, and how decisions are made. For entrepreneurs in poverty contexts, specific examples of enabling personal conversion factors would be entrepreneurial self-efficacy, creative thinking, guerilla skills, and prior experience in running a business. Examples of restricting personal conversion factors include limited schooling, fragile health conditions, the cognitive overload imposed by the demands of the context of poverty, and even fear of failure and success.

Social Conversion Factors. Social conversion factors reflect the influence of societal and contextual elements on an individual's ability to convert resources into capabilities and functionings. Social norms, cultural practices, discrimination, gender roles, access to key individuals through social networks, availability of social services, power relationships, family support, and the overall socio-economic environment can impact how effectively individuals can use resources to enhance their capabilities. For individuals trying to start a business, social conversion factors may include both positive and negative perceptions toward entrepreneurship and self-employment from relevant others (parents, family members, peers, friends, community members, mentors). Subjective norms towards entrepreneurial activities impact self-efficacy beliefs, shape outcome expectations, and influence the likelihood of engaging in entrepreneurship (Kautonen, van Gelderen, & Fink, 2015; Santos & Liguori, 2020). For example, women can be deterred from pursuing entrepreneurship because this is not congruent with their social gender role. Such norms may inhibit women from converting their resources and means into desirable outcomes. In the context of poverty, Hussain et al. (2019) demonstrate how gender discrimination and conservative religious values adversely impact women's access to microcredit. As other examples, social stigmas against people in poverty, severely limited social networks, and limited understanding of social conventions (and often even the way to communicate) can undermine conversion abilities. However, social conversion factors can also be enablers of the pursuit of entrepreneurship when in poverty. This can be accomplished, for example, through the participation of the entrepreneur in community networks, communities of practice, and self-help groups, and the existence of family and community role models.

Environmental Conversion Factors. These factors concern elements and circumstances in an individual's larger environment that affect their ability to convert resources into capabilities and functionings (Robeyns, 2005). Examples of environmental aspects include one's geographic location, the economic climate, the availability of infrastructure, and natural resources that can significantly shape a person's capabilities. These types of factors highlight the importance of the characteristics of the place where the individual resides. For example, operating in farm households in rural Kenya represents a place-specific set of environmental parameters, which can lead to different expectations regarding entrepreneurial possibilities and outcomes (Kimmitt et al., 2020). Poor infrastructure (water, roads, transportation systems, housing, sanitation systems, schools, healthcare facilities, criminal justice resources, broadband access) in a neighborhood, region, or country hinders trading, commerce, and the distribution of goods, thus discouraging individuals from pursuing entrepreneurship. Institutional voids and poor performance of formal institutions, as is predominant in base of the pyramid markets, undermine efficient market transactions and operations (Webb et al., 2010). For poverty entrepreneurs trying to access and utilize resources, weak institutions restrict conversion factors. On the other side of the coin, social protection systems (free or low-cost health insurance, affordable housing, subsidized childcare and transportation services), accessible financial institutions, and entrepreneurship training and development programs are examples of enabling environmental factors that are critical for the conversion of resources for poverty entrepreneurs.

Institutions are the underlying thread that connects and drives these conversion factors (Hodgson, 2006). They define what resources are available to whom, how those resources can be deployed, the returns that can be generated, and how they are distributed.

It is also important to stress the relevance of the cognitive processes through which situations are perceived and responses are made (Mantzavinos, 2001). This includes the cognitive processing by both the entrepreneur and other parties. Poverty can impose certain preconceptions, biases, and beliefs that impact how an entrepreneur interacts with a potential resource or resource provider. Similarly, these outside parties process their interactions with the entrepreneur through a cognitive lens that includes assumptions, perceptions, norms, and expectations related to poverty. Consider a disadvantaged woman with difficulty obtaining credit for her business because of gender bias and lack of credit history and collateral. In this case, the response of traditional banking and financial institutions is the outcome of established rules and judgments embedded in individual thinking. How the person is treated can be based on (mis)perceptions regarding the entrepreneur's financial and business literacies, stereotypical assumptions about the person's likelihood of success, and fixed approaches that financial institutions use by default when a woman from poverty asks for credit. A micro-credit institution, non-governmental organization, or a specialized program to foster entrepreneurship in poverty contexts that wants to reverse this situation would have to overcome the social constraints around gender bias and perceptions of risk in granting credit to aspiring women entrepreneurs.

THE LACK OF INSTITUTIONAL SUPPORT FOR POVERTY ENTREPRENEURS

Institutionalized rules, norms, and shared understandings are interpreted, disseminated, and reinforced by a wide range of organizations and systems that govern society and human life. Most notable here are governmental, religious, educational, financial, healthcare, cultural and arts, media, social, and family entities. For a low-income individual attempting to start and grow a business, such entities are often sources of obstacles, but can also serve as important facilitators.

The beginning point in affecting change involves changes in how societies think about poverty and entrepreneurship. Rather than denigratinng or ignoring the ventures of the poor, treating them as non-contributors, or assuming they have no desire to be entrepreneurs and instead start ventures only out of pure necessity, institutions must celebrate this kind of entrepreneurial activity (in both the informal and formal sectors). They should appreciate the nobility and dignity associated with building a successful business. There is a need to recognize the meaningful contribution these entrepreneurs make to overall gross domestic product, the millions of low-income people employed because they started a business, the market niches these ventures serve, and the ways in which they can stabilize neighborhoods and communities. More critically, we must recognize that institutions often represent impediments to capability development by these entrepreneurs, and undermine the potential of these ventures to contribute to overall human well-being. In some instances, this occurs without those behind the institutions realizing the impact they are having.

Many potential ways exist for institutions to better support poverty entrepreneurs. However, five areas are particularly critical. The first of these concerns *regulatory support*. This includes simplifying the process of registering and licensing a business, removing bureaucratic hurdles to operating when and where the entrepreneur desires, reducing associated costs, and not penalizing unregistered businesses. Bureaucratic red tape can put poverty entrepreneurs at a significant disadvantage when trying to access formal institutions for any purpose (Kaufmann et al., 2018). Arguably, the costs to society of such red tape outweigh the potential benefits from its elimination. Similarly, relief from compliance with a host of business regulations for the first three years of operation for these entrepreneurs, or until they achieve a certain level of revenue, can be instrumental in their ability to stabilize business operations.

A second role for institutions involves *access to capital*. Quite simply, the financial needs of poverty entrepreneurs at the early stages of business development are largely ignored by conventional sources of finance. Using traditional metrics, loans to these entrepreneurs are not especially profitable given the amounts being borrowed and the associated transaction costs. Equity finance is unavailable for most of these ventures due to their lack of significant growth prospects. As a result, there is a need to re-think the incentives made available to sources of capital who support the ventures of the poor while also finding creative ways to lessen the costs to these sources. Similarly, it is important to allow financial institutions to work collaboratively in establishing alternative loan approval criteria, collateral requirements, and interest rates for some percentage of their loans that support the ventures of the poor in their early stages of development. The microfinance revolution has been a reaction to the institutional voids created by the mainstream financial sector, providing billions of dollars in relatively small loans to borrowers who otherwise would not qualify for a traditional loan (Brown, 2010). Yet, it has come with its own drawbacks, which can include high interest rates, money provided to people who do not need it or were unprepared for it, and providing loans that are not coupled to training, incubation, mentoring, and other forms of entrepreneurial support (Hudon & Sandberg, 2013; Morris, Santos, & Neumeyer, 2018). Ultimately, a more holistic approach is needed, one that considers the needs of individual poverty entrepreneurs at different stages of enterprise development. Such an approach could include alternative forms of loans, as well as grants, subsidies, peer-to-peer lending, rotating savings and credit groups, impact equity investments, vouchers, public-private partnerships, and crowdfunding.

The third priority concerns institutions that affect *access to markets* by poverty entrepreneurs. These entrepreneurs struggle to sell to customers outside their immediate networks and neighborhoods. They confront severe limitations in their abilities to access data on markets, properly define market boundaries, understand how to segment and target different customer groups, and find ways to differentiate the business. Further, they may be unable to access key sales venues and channels of distribution, or transaction processing mechanisms. Beyond this challenge, market access is constrained by the limited production capacity and logistical capabilities of these ventures. Rather than reinforce these difficulties, institutions need to find ways to facilitate market access. The most obvious vehicle for doing so is where certain institutions buy from these entrepreneurs. An example is government and private sector set-aside programs where a percentage of their purchases are are directed at low-income and disadvantaged entrepreneurs (VanSandt & Sud, 2012). Yet, even here, such procurement programs can involve considerable bureaucracy while placing unrealistic demands on the entrepreneur.

Our fourth priority centers on *entrepreneurial training and development*. Here, we prioritize the development of the person over the development of the venture. Those in poverty generally have little to no exposure to the entrepreneurial mindset (Chapter 7). This way of thinking and acting is not part of their early life experiences and not integrated into whatever educational opportunities they are exposed to. They generally do not have exposure to the operations of successful ventures, nor do they have entrepreneurial role models. While it is a common refrain that the key to poverty alleviation is education, it can also be argued that the key to entrepreneurship as a poverty alleviation tool is entrepreneurship education. Yet, it is not a norm in school systems, vocational training, or general job programs—particularly, the education and training activities to which low-income people are exposed. Where it exists, entrepreneurship education is not targeted or tailored to address the circumstances and needs of those in poverty conditions. Further, the quality and quantity of education available tend to produce gaps in terms of functional, financial, technological, economic, and business literacies (Morris et al., 2018). Insufficient access to quality education and other opportunities for skill development hamper one's ability to learn and develop new capabilities, which can have negative implications for starting and growing a sustainable business.

Finally, the *technical assistance and support* provided by institutions is frequently limited in terms of its availability, quality, and ability to reflect the unique needs of the poor. Technical support is concerned with the development of the venture. As was explored in Chapter 11, the journey to a sustainable enterprise can be broken down into eighty steps. The development of support systems that serve entrepreneurial ventures in general must be adapted to reflect how these steps can be navigated by someone who may be a single parent, underemployed, suffering literacy gaps, dealing with a mix of daily threats (i.e., housing, crime, food, family health problems), with limited social networks, undependable transportation, and no social safety net. Further, such assistance must reflect the struggles of survival and informal sector businesses and ventures confronting the difficulties of the commodity trap (see Chapter 8).

Absent attention to these five basic issues, the institutional environment serves to heighten the levels of uncertainty and ambiguity surrounding poverty entrepreneurship. The result for many in poverty, when considering or actually launching a business, can be less sense of control together with heightened levels of stress, anxiety, feelings of helplessness, and loss of hope.

THE PROBLEM WITH LOCAL ENTREPRENEURIAL ECOSYSTEMS

A critical instrument when it comes to improving the environment for entrepreneurship is the notion of an entrepreneurial ecosystem, particularly at a local level. Entrepreneurial ecosystems are an agglomeration of interrelated individuals, institutions, organizations, and regulatory entities in a particular geographic area that act upon and promote entrepreneurial initiatives and actions (Isenberg, 2010; Malecki, 2011). In practice, they frequently do not operate as a coordinated system, and are in different stages of development depending on the location. Nonetheless, in recent years the concept of ecosystems has become relevant both in advanced and emerging economies, serving as an important resource allocation mechanism (Shi & Shi, 2022).

An entrepreneurial ecosystem can include financial institutions, private investors, colleges and universities, research parks, chambers of commerce, established entrepreneurs and businesses, professional service providers (e.g., lawyers, accountants), economic development officials, governmental units, nonprofit organizations, and others. Each player brings some sort of expertise or resource that can support the launch and development of new enterprises. Individually or in collaboration with others, these players may provide training programs, entrepreneurship conferences and symposia, incubators and accelerators, investor forums, seed investment and microcredit programs, business plan and pitch competitions, voucher programs, pro bono entrepreneurial assistance, prototyping labs and makerspaces, mentoring and internship programs, coaching and consulting initiatives, technical assistance, and social networking events. Collectively, they can constitute a complex reality (Roundy et al., 2018).

While there are certainly exceptions, in many parts of the world, the poor have been left out of (or are underserved by) entrepreneurial ecosystems (Cao & Shi, 2021; Neumeyer, Santos, & Morris, 2019). There are a number of possible reasons for this exclusion. Most notably, these ecosystems are inherently predicated on market logics and the ability to create an economic return that owners can appropriate (Pache & Santos, 2013). For their part, assisting the poor is more associated with social welfare logics. Hence, those in poverty are often not part of the conversation when discussing entrepreneurial ecosystems. Yet, social welfare logic can have a positive influence on the economy when it coexists with market logic (Zhao & Lounsbury, 2016).

A major issue for their neglect concerns the types of ventures most frequently created by low-income individuals (i.e., survival and lifestyle ventures, which are perceived to have very limited economic potential). As a result, the services and support available from the ecosystem are tailored to a different kind of entrepreneur and venture. The ventures of the poor do not qualify for most incubators or accelerators, are uninteresting to investors and angel networks, have little chance of winning most business plan or pitch competitions, and cannot afford the services of specialized law firms or tax consultants (Huang et al., 2022).

In addition, the social networks of the poor are often not connected to key individuals within ecosystems, while transportation challenges and long working hours make it difficult for individuals in poverty to access opportunities in the ecosystem when they are available. Further, ecosystems typically consist of a disparate set of players whose activities often overlap and are not coordinated (Alvedalen & Boschma, 2017). Individual components can act in isolation or as silos and communication among the players can be limited (Isenberg, 2010). This reality makes it all the more difficult for those in poverty to identify and interact with the parts of the ecosystem most relevant to their needs. When they are able to access the components of mainstream entrepreneurial ecosystems, they can have problems understanding who to communicate with for a particular need, what to ask for, and how to convince people to help them. Here, literacy shortcomings and a lack of awareness of hidden rules regarding communications and behaviors can affect interactions with members of the ecosystem and make the poverty entrepreneur feel excluded and segregated.

RETHINKING ECOSYSTEMS: THE ROLE OF COMMUNITY ENGAGEMENT

The question becomes how entrepreneurial ecosystems can play a more pronounced role in serving those in poverty. Addressing this question requires that we take a broader view of an ecosystem. Specifically, we propose the concept of a "community-driven entrepreneurial ecosystem" which is deeply embedded within the community and its social fabric, reflecting the unique historical, cultural, political, and demographic characteristics and associated needs of these communities. This differs from approaching the ecosystem as a set of disparate entities that directly support entrepreneurs. In essence, the community becomes a key driver and participant in an inclusive ecosystem (Morris & Tucker, 2021). Such an approach can better ensure that the available resources, functions, and support systems are serving those from poverty and disadvantaged circumstances. Figure 12.2 illustrates this revised concept of entrepreneurial ecosystems, and below, we expand on its key components.

A community-centric approach begins with the *existing entrepreneurial infrastructure within the community*, although even here we adopt a broader view. Hence, existing incubators and accelerators, competitions, training programs, lending and investment programs, and so forth are identified, together with ways in which these existing initiatives can be adapted to serve low-income entrepreneurs. Importantly, entities not normally considered part of the entrepreneurial ecosystem now receive attention. Examples include public libraries, which can provide low-income entrepreneurs with literacy training (functional, financial, technological), as well as free computer and internet access, and librarians who can help them conduct industry and market research while also introducing them to key online databases, free or low-cost

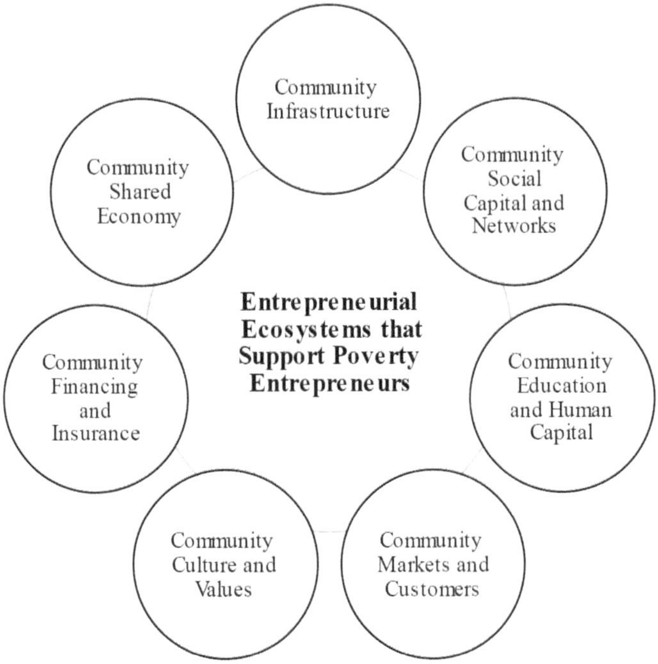

Figure 12.2. The components of entrepreneurial ecosystems in poverty.
Created by Authors

software (e.g., for accounting, scheduling, design of marketing materials) that can be downloaded, and free or low-cost online service providers (e.g., for logos, legal assistance, assistance with the use of social media). Community gathering centers also represent venues for meetings and broadband access.

An alternative approach to the existing community infrastructure concerns creative approaches to leveraging the resources of established organizations to support poverty entrepreneurs. For instance, unused space in buildings owned by businesses, nonprofits, or local government might be used as incubators or co-working spaces for these entrepreneurs. Companies could have their staff provide so many hours of free marketing or accounting assistance, or back office support, to these businesses. They could engage in collaborative procurement arrangements so poverty entrepreneurs can benefit from wholesale prices available from large volume purchases.

A major opportunity lies in *leveraging and further developing the shared economy* at the community level. The shared economy, made popular through the wild successes of businesses such as Uber and Airbnb, has significant potential to address social needs and causes (Ritter & Schanz, 2019). Community resource sharing can take many forms. Networks of community members and organizations can be created to share tools, computer and office equipment, software, vehicles, marketing resources, and a host of other products and services needed by poverty entrepreneurs. Communities can also come together to organize shared child and family care services, or shared delivery services. Different models are possible here, including pay-it-forward and barter-based approaches.

Yet another pathway involves new ways for the poor to tap into *community-based social capital and local networks*. Arguably, network connections are even more critical than financial capital injections in helping early-stage poverty ventures get traction (Hertel, Bacq, & Belz, 2019). Networking and gathering events within the community become critical. Such events serve as places for connections that open doors to opportunity and access to resources. Community social forums are valuable places to expand the entrepreneur's visibility and create awareness of their business. Critical discussion forums expose the entrepreneur to new ideas, new ways of accomplishing a given task, and feedback on their products and services. Strong relationships developed within the community help build the pool of existing social capital and bridge connections with stakeholders outside the immediate area (Ansari et al., 2012). Organizing such forums, creating a speaker series (particularly those that feature entrepreneurs who have overcome adversity), and venues where the ventures of poverty entrepreneurs can be connected to the larger business community are examples of such community-driven possibilities. Through such mechanisms, social capital and networking can become a means for capability expansion (Ansari et al., 2012).

In addition, opportunity lies in innovative approaches to *education and human capital development*. It begins with entrepreneurship education in schools attended by low-income individuals starting in the primary grades where experiential learning opportunities are integrated into the curriculum (Baxter et al., 2014). As community colleges and universities are pushed to become more relevant for the communities where they are based, training by faculty and consulting by students that are focused on the poor and disadvantaged become a priority. Integrating entrepreneurship into local job training programs is yet another area of focus. Local businesses and nonprofits can support these efforts through expertise, internships, apprenticeships, and job shadowing initiatives. Local entrepreneurs can serve as mentors. The key is to coordinate such efforts around a mix of offerings that include (a) learning opportunities that address both personal and venture development, (b) training that addresses the five literacies and other liability of poorness factors (see Chapter 5), as well as a range of entrepreneurship-related topics, and c) educational programming that reflects needs based on different demographics (e.g., age, gender) and forms of disadvantage (e.g., formerly incarcerated, refugees, those from shelters or with disabilities), and d) support for entrepreneurs at different stages in the entrepreneurial process (e.g., idea stage, launch stage, growth stage).

This expanded concept of local ecosystems also includes a proactive approach to *community-based markets and customers*. Here, we focus on the role of community members in conveying product and service needs to, and buying from, these entrepreneurs while also serving as word-of-mouth ambassadors. Formal or informally-driven community marketing can help expand awareness and market reach for poverty entrepreneurs (Thakur, 2015). The creation of co-marketing websites that feature the businesses of low-income entrepreneurs is an example. Marketing support can also come from chambers of commerce and community service organizations. Another fruitful avenue is a concerted effort on the part of local businesses, non-profit organizations, and governmental units to purposefully redirect more of their procurement spending to the ventures of the poor.

The failure of financial institutions to adequately support the entrepreneurial pursuits of low-income individuals suggests a need for creative approaches to *community financing and insurance*. For example, community-based microcredit schemes can find companies, local government units, financial institutions, and community members contributing to funds that award small grants and low-interest microloans to poverty entrepreneurs. A variation here is to build such funds to serve as guarantees to loans for these entrepreneurs provided through conventional bank lending. Community banks are especially important here, as they are embedded in the local environment and may be in a position to offer more flexible terms and conditions for loans, while having lower transaction costs when compared to mainstream financial institutions. A number of models exist to guide such efforts (Srinivas, 2015). More focus should also be placed on rotating saving and credit associations and peer-to-peer lending schemes that can help facilitate access to local pools of capital for low-income entrepreneurs.

Alternatively, with the growth of impact investing (Brest & Born, 2013; Clarkin & Cangioni, 2016), more equity investors appear willing to direct investment toward social causes. Addressing poverty through entrepreneurship is one such cause that could be addressed through the creation of local angel investor networks. Other community members working with poverty entrepreneurs could nominate them to pitch to these investor groups.

Community-based crowdfunding initiatives represent yet another alternative funding source for vulnerable communities (Figueroa-Armijos & Berns, 2022). Using these platforms, poverty entrepreneurs can access a network of potential backers, people that are willing to contribute to their ventures and who otherwise would be very difficult to reach. Specifically, reward-based crowdfunding reduces the financial risks associated with traditional financing because investors do not expect to be paid back. In addition to providing access to financial resources, crowdfunding is also a good opportunity to generatecomments and suggestions from the public to fine-tune projects, services, or products, and can serve as a community-building activity.

When formal institutions fail to provide adequate insurance coverage for poverty entrepreneurs, an option can be informal forms of insurance (Kazianga & Udry, 2006). With community-based insurance, individuals come together to create a mutual support and risk-sharing system to help manage unexpected financial burdens (Banerjee & Duflo, 2011). Such insurance is more affordable, tailored to the economic capacity and specific needs of the community, and rooted in community support and trust. Community members contribute to a shared fund, and when an entrepreneur in the community faces a crisis, they have a place to turn.

Finally, at a more basic level, there is a need to focus on building *community culture and values*. Culture, values, and community identity are important components of the entrepreneurial ecosystem. A culture that values and celebrates the contributions of low-income and disadvantaged entrepreneurs must be cultivated and reinforced, highlighting examples of entrepreneurs who came from disadvantaged circumstances, built successful enterprises, hired others from the community, and were able to give back, can contribute to elevating social norms regarding entrepreneurship and diversity. The strong culture and values of the community are also important in providing a sense of belonging and a safety backup support system for entrepreneurs who face failures or setbacks. Building such a culture can be driven by community leaders and a wide mix of public and private organizations, including those playing roles in the efforts described above.

A STAGED APPROACH TO ECOSYSTEM ENGAGEMENT

The needs of poverty entrepreneurs vary by stage of venture development. Let us consider three general stages: pre-startup, launch-stabilization, and growth. When it comes to the poor, problematic aspects of each of these stages should guide community ecosystem support (see Figure 12.3).

At the pre-startup stage, one is trying to provide individuals with an understanding of entrepreneurship as an option and prepare them for the entrepreneurial journey. The concern becomes educational programs to develop key literacies, expand the nascent entrepreneur's opportunity horizon (see Chapter 6), and provide entrepreneurship-related training that focuses on planning and research skills together with basic entrepreneurial competencies. In terms of community action, examples include locally based multi-literacy programs, small business apprenticeships and internships, entrepreneurial

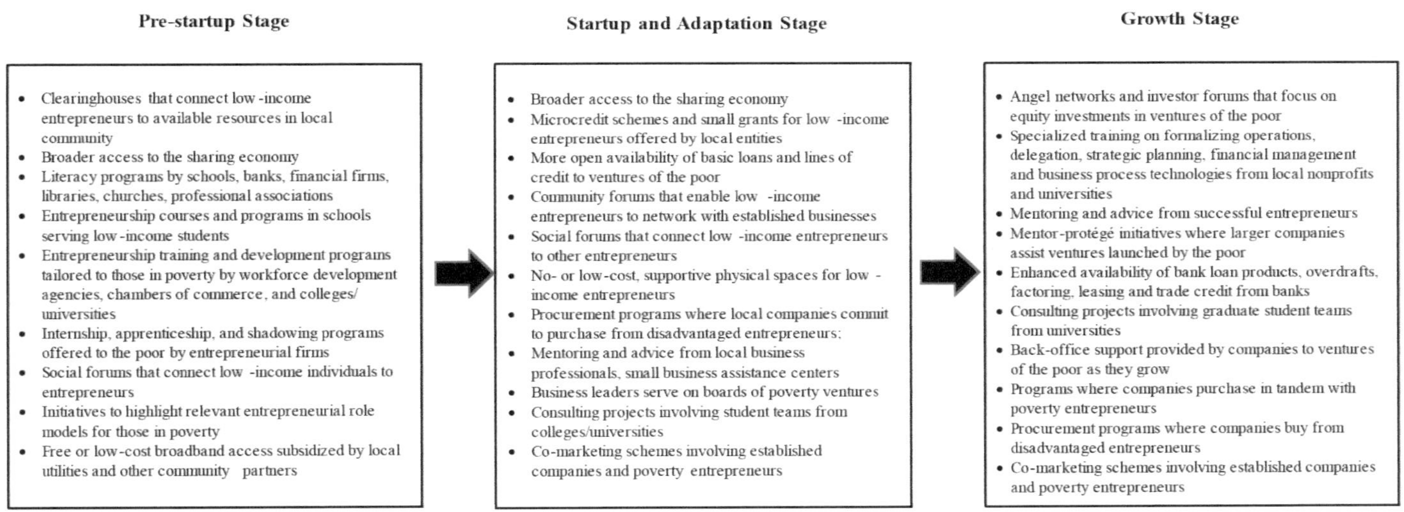

Figure 12.3. Linking Community Initiatives to Stages of Development in Ventures of the Poor.
Created by Authors

role models and coaches, networking forums, access for the poor to business plan competitions and pitches, lending circles, and portals that connect low-income individuals to a range of local resources that could help them start ventures. It can include encouragement of entrepreneurship-related programs in public schools, subsidies to support free broadband access, access to knowledge resources, and the creation of co-working spaces.

In the launch and stabilization stage, the priorities for the poor include ways to enhance value propositions, lower transaction costs, improve efficiencies (reduce the reliance on the entrepreneur to do everything), and overcome severe resource constraints as a business takes form and adapts to its competitive context. Overcoming the commodity trap is a core requirement (see Chapter 8). Examples of key community actions include enhanced access to the local sharing or collaborative economy, availability of coaches and mentors with expertise in resource leveraging and addressing the specific challenges of commodity-like ventures, launch of microcredit funds and business grant programs, and training on the use of low-cost technologies that improve efficiencies. Also important are vouchers to use with professional service providers or to pay for premises and the awarding of procurement contracts by local organizations to ventures of the poor.

Finally, for the low-income entrepreneur, navigating the growth stage can be especially problematic. This can be traced to the complex demands growth poses in terms of advanced financial, technological, and business literacies, the detrimental effects of a short-term orientation, fear of growth once one has a successful enterprise, an inhospitable investment climate, and a tendency to suffer from lingering elements of the commodity trap. At the community level, growth can be fostered through investor forums that concentrate on growing ventures of the poor, low-cost accelerator space, and specialized university outreach programs that teach advanced financial management skills and provide student consulting teams. Especially important are mentor-protégé programs that partner high growth entrepreneurs with low-income business owners and the creation of expertise pools that assist with the fundamental changes that growth necessitates in terms of management skills and styles, the resource pool, organizational systems and structures, and culture.

CONCLUSION

The institutional environment can have a significant impact on the development of key capabilities by poverty entrepreneurs. In addition to providing resources to these entrepreneurs, it is important to address their abilities to convert resources into functionings or outcomes. Included here are personal, social, and environmental conversion factors, each of which can be both constrained and enhanced based on the institutional environment. As such, they are a key to determining whether the empowering potential of entrepreneurship is realized when it comes to the poor.

In this chapter, we have highlighted the central role of institutions of all types in determining whether people in poverty start ventures, the kinds of ventures they launch, and the ability of those ventures to improve the entrepreneur's economic status and overall well-being. At the root of this influence is the effect of the institutional environment on the individual's ability to access capital and markets, overcome regulatory and social constraints, develop their personal knowledge and competencies, and receive technical assistance for their ventures.

As a core part of the institutional environment, entrepreneurial ecosystems have generally not evolved in a manner that adequately serves those in poverty circumstances. When it comes to the poor, ecosystems are often not inclusive, fail to understand the needs of the poor, and inadequately address those needs. As a result, we need to rethink entrepreneurial ecosystems and design them around a more holistic and community-centric model. Such a model considers the role of the community in helping to leverage existing infrastructure, tap into the shared economy, develop novel approaches to training and development, provide alternative sources of finance and insurance, build social capital, and access local markets. Driving all of this must be intentional efforts to build community cultures that respect and prize entrepreneurial activities by those in disadvantaged circumstances.

REFERENCES

Ahmed, M. (2011). Defining and measuring literacy: Facing the reality. *International Review of Education, 57*(1), 179–195.

Alvedalen, J., & Boschma, R. (2017). A critical review of entrepreneurial ecosystems research: Towards a future research agenda. *European Planning Studies, 25*(6), 887–903.

Ansari, S., Munir, K., & Gregg, T. (2012). Impact at the "bottom of the pyramid": The role of social capital in capability development and community empowerment. *Journal of Management Studies, 49*(4), 813–842.

Banerjee, A. V., & Duflo, E. (2011). *Poor economics: A radical rethinking of the way to fight global poverty*. Public Affairs.

Baumol, W. J., & Blinder, A. (2008). *Macroeconomics: Principles and policy*. Cincinnati, OH: South-Western College Publishing.

Baxter, A., Chapman, D. W., DeJaeghere, J., Pekol, A. R., & Weiss, T. (2014). Youth entrepreneurship education and training for poverty alleviation: A review of international literature and local experiences. In *International educational innovation*

and public sector entrepreneurship (International perspectives on education and society, Vol. 23), Emerald Group Publishing Limited, Bingley, pp. 33–58.
Brest, P., & Born, K. (2013). When can impact investing create real impact. *Stanford Social Innovation Review, 11*(4), 22–31.
Brown, G. (2010). When small is big: Microcredit and economic development. *The Open Source Business Resource,* 14–20. Available from: https://timreview.ca/article/392
Cao, Z., & Shi, X. (2021). A systematic literature review of entrepreneurial ecosystems in advanced and emerging economies. *Small Business Economics, 57*, 75–110.
Chowdhury, F., Audretsch, D. B., & Belitski, M. (2019). Institutions and entrepreneurship quality. *Entrepreneurship Theory and Practice*, *43*(1), 51–81.
Clarkin, J. E., & Cangioni, C. L. (2016). Impact investing: A primer and review of the literature. *Entrepreneurship Research Journal*, *6*(2), 135–173.
Estrin, S., Korosteleva, J., & Mickiewicz, T. (2013). Which institutions encourage entrepreneurial growth aspirations? *Journal of Business Venturing*, *28*(4), 564–580.
Figueroa-Armijos, M., & Berns, J. P. (2022). Vulnerable populations and individual social responsibility in prosocial crowdfunding: Does the framing matter for female and rural entrepreneurs? *Journal of Business Ethics, 177*, 377–394.
Hertel, C., Bacq, S., & Belz, F. M. (2019). It takes a village to sustain a village: A social identity perspective on successful community-based enterprise creation. *Academy of Management Discoveries*, *5*(4), 438–464.
Hodgson, G. (2006). What are institutions? *Journal of Economic Issues, 40*, 1–25.
Huang, S., Pickernell, D., Battisti, M., Dann, Z., & Ekinsmyth, C. (2022). Disadvantaged entrepreneurship and the entrepreneurial ecosystem: A critical literature review and introduction. In Pickernell, D. G., Battisti, M., Dann, Z., & Ekinsmyth, C. (Eds.) *Disadvantaged entrepreneurship and the entrepreneurial ecosystem (Contemporary issues in entrepreneurship research, Vol. 14),* Emerald Publishing Limited, Bingley, pp. 1–8.
Hudon, M., & Sandberg, J. (2013). The ethical crisis in microfinance: Issues, findings, and implications. *Business Ethics Quarterly*, *23*(4), 561–589.
Hussain, J., Mahmood, S., & Scott, J. (2019). Gender, microcredit and poverty alleviation in a developing country: The case of women entrepreneurs in Pakistan. *Journal of International Development, 31*(3), 247–270.
Isenberg, D. J. (2010). How to start an entrepreneurial revolution. *Harvard Business Review, 88*(6), 40–50.
Kaufmann, W., Hooghiemstra, R., & Feeney, M. K. (2018). Formal institutions, informal institutions, and red tape: A comparative study. *Public Administration, 96*(2), 386–403.
Kautonen, T., van Gelderen, M., & Fink, M. (2015). Robustness of the theory of planned behavior in predicting entrepreneurial intentions and actions. *Entrepreneurship Theory and Practice*, *39*(3), 655–674.
Kazianga, H., & Udry, C. (2006). Consumption smoothing? Livestock, insurance and drought in rural Burkina Faso. *Journal of Development Economics, 79*(2), 413–446.

Kimmitt, J., Muñoz, P., & Newbery, R. (2020). Poverty and the varieties of entrepreneurship in the pursuit of prosperity. *Journal of Business Venturing, 35*(4), 105939.

Lee, C. K., Wiklund, J., Amezcua, A., Bae, T. J., & Palubinskas, A. (2022). Business failure and institutions in entrepreneurship: A systematic review and research agenda. *Small Business Economics*, *58*(4), 1997–2023.

Malecki, E. J. (2011). Connecting local entrepreneurial ecosystems to global innovation networks: Open innovation, double networks and knowledge integration. *International Journal of Entrepreneurship and Innovation Management, 14*(1), 36–59.

Mantzavinos, C. (2001). *Individuals, institutions, and markets (Political economy of institutions and decisions).* Cambridge: Cambridge University Press.

Morris, M. H., & Tucker, R. (2021). Poverty and entrepreneurship in developed economies: Re-assessing the roles of policy and community action. *Journal of Poverty, 25*(2), 97–118.

Morris, M. H., Santos, S. C., & Neumeyer, X. (2018). *Poverty and entrepreneurship in developed economies.* Edward Elgar Publishing.

Neumeyer, X., Santos, S. C., & Morris, M. H. (2019). Who is left out: Exploring social boundaries in entrepreneurial ecosystems. *Journal of Technology Transfer, 44*(2), 462–484. https://doi.org/10.1007/s10961-018-9694-0

North, D. C. (1990). *Institutions, institutional change and economic performance.* Cambridge University Press.

Ostrom, E (2005). *Understanding institutional diversity.* Princeton, NJ: Princeton University Press.

Pache, A. C., & Santos, F. (2013). Inside the hybrid organization: Selective coupling as a response to competing institutional logics. *Academy of Management Journal, 56*(4), 972–1001.

Ritter, M., & Schanz, H. (2019). The sharing economy: A comprehensive business model framework. *Journal of Cleaner Production, 213*, 320–331.

Robeyns, I. (2005). The capability approach: A theoretical survey. *Journal of Human Development, 6*(1), 93–117.

Roundy, P. T., Bradshaw, M., & Brockman, B. K. (2018). The emergence of entrepreneurial ecosystems: A complex adaptive systems approach. *Journal of Business Research*, *86*, 1–10.

Santos, S. C., & Liguori, E. W. (2020). Entrepreneurial self-efficacy and intentions: Outcome expectations as mediator and subjective norms as moderator. *International Journal of Entrepreneurial Behavior & Research, 26*(3), 400–415.

Scott, W. R. (2001). *Institutions and organizations,* 2nd ed. Thousand Oaks, CA: Sage.

Sen, A. K. (2000). *Development as freedom*. Oxford University Press.

Sen, A. K. (2009). *Capitalism beyond the crisis.* New York Review of Books.

Shi, X., & Shi, Y. (2022). Unpacking the process of resource allocation within an entrepreneurial ecosystem. *Research Policy*, *51*(9), 104378.

Sine, W. D., & David, R. J. (2010). Institutions and entrepreneurship. In *Institutions and Entrepreneurship* (Vol. 21, pp. 1–26). Emerald Group Publishing Limited.

Srinivas, H. (2015). *Microfinance—credit lending models*. GDRC Continuing Research Series E0059.

Stenholm, P., Acs, Z. J., & Wuebker, R. (2013). Exploring country-level institutional arrangements on the rate and type of entrepreneurial activity. *Journal of Business Venturing*, *28*(1), 176–193.

Thakur, R. (2015). Community marketing: Serving the base of the economic pyramid sustainably. *Journal of Business Strategy*, *36*(4), 40–47.

VanSandt, C. V., & Sud, M. (2012). Poverty alleviation through partnerships: A road less travelled for business, governments, and entrepreneurs. *Journal of Business Ethics*, *110*, 321–332.

Webb, J. W. (2021). A system-level view of institutions: Considerations for entrepreneurship and poverty. *Journal of Developmental Entrepreneurship, 26*(2), 2150010.

Webb, J. W., Kistruck, G. M., Ireland, R. D., & Ketchen, D. J. (2010). The entrepreneurship process in base-of-the-pyramid markets: The case of multinational enterprise/nongovernment organization alliances. *Entrepreneurship Theory and Practice, 34*, 555–81.

Zhao, E. Y., & Lounsbury, M. (2016). An institutional logics approach to social entrepreneurship: Market logic, religious diversity, and resource acquisition by microfinance organizations. *Journal of Business Venturing, 31*(6), 643–662.

Chapter Thirteen

A New Policy Paradigm

Fostering Capabilities and Well-being

This book has explored the promise of entrepreneurship as a potential tool for addressing global poverty, arguing that context is critical in determining the extent to which this promise is realized. While the potential of entrepreneurship has been stressed by many (e.g., Bruton et al., 2013; Webb et al., 2013), specifying the relevant contextual variables and how they can facilitate the poverty entrepreneur are subjects for ongoing investigation (Naminse et al., 2019; Dzingirai, 2021). In Chapter 12, we stressed the importance of the institutional environment, discussing a range of institutional influences, and highlighting the importance of community entrepreneurial ecosystems. In this closing chapter, we expound upon the role of another institutional player, the public sector, and how government policies can influence the entrepreneurial journeys of those in poverty circumstances.

As we have seen, most of the ventures started by low-income individuals do not move them out of poverty (see Chapters 2 and 8). This is a function, at least in part, of a lack of resources. More critically, however, it often reflects deficient capabilities in converting resources into positive venture outcomes. For its part, public policy can be a vital factor in determining the relative attractiveness of entrepreneurship to the poor, the resources available for its pursuit, and the preparation of low-income individuals for the entrepreneurial journey. Where evidence has been produced that shows significant improvements in economic well-being by the poor when they launch ventures (e.g., Amorós et al., 2021; Santos et al., 2022), it is due to factors that government policies and programs can directly or indirectly influence.

Across the globe, governments spend trillions of dollars annually on poverty programs. Much of this spending centers on basic needs such as food, housing, and healthcare (Anderson et al., 2018; Celikay & Gumus, 2017). Hence, the spending represents a lifeline that helps the impoverished survive. When it comes to actually moving people out of poverty, the effectiveness of governments is less apparent (see Chapter 1). This criticism is especially the case when it comes to venture creation as a poverty solution. Entrepreneurship is generally not well-understood by policymakers, particularly when it is pursued by those in poverty conditions. As a result, government efforts to date have largely been piecemeal and disjointed, failing to reflect the needs of the person in poverty and the particular challenges faced by the types of ventures the poor tend to create.

This chapter argues that there is much the government can do. We continue to build on our argument for a person-centered approach based on the principles of capability theory. As Sen (1999) has asserted, policy has been preoccupied with economic growth as the key objective, where its main purpose should be to improve human lives and promote well-being. Accordingly, we bring the focus of policy back to people and agency, focusing on the intrinsic (rather than instrumental) value of policies that promote the development of capabilities related to successful venture creation. Such a capability approach has been important in driving normative thinking regarding policies promulgated by the United Nations that target poverty, hunger, child and maternal health, control of global diseases, and the fostering of environmental sustainability (Fukuda-Parr, 2011; United Nations, 2015; Weiss, Jolly, & Emerij, 2009). In this chapter, we advocate for a novel policy focus that supports and complements local entrepreneurial ecosystems, while fostering the kinds of ventures that can enhance human well-being.

RULES OF THE GAME AND NEW VENTURE CREATION

Government policies establish the rules of the game for those in business. At a basic level, they allow for private property ownership, the earning of profits and interest, and protection of intellectual property. They encourage risk-taking by limiting the liability of business owners and providing bankruptcy protections. They help create more stable environments for conducting business by enforcing contracts and penalizing theft and corruption. Beyond this, governments attempt to limit unfair business practices such as price fixing and collusion, or the making of fraudulent claims about one's products or services. They pass laws to ensure worker safety, require the payment of a minimum wage, limit discrimination in hiring and compensation, and stop the use of child labor. They impose payroll taxes on companies to support workers who are laid off or fired, or contribute to pension funds for the retirees. Some go further, with laws to protect consumer rights or to penalize companies for polluting the environment.

These and other public policies do not affect all businesses equally. The burden of regulatory red tape and associated costs tend to disproportionately impact new and small businesses. At the same time, governments increasingly recognize how new businesses add dynamism to an economy by introducing new products and processes and creating new jobs. As a result, governments craft distinct policies aimed at the entrepreneurial sector. These efforts have included a diverse mix of tax incentives, investment funds, loan guarantees, regulatory relief, support for special visa programs, creation of innovation hubs and technology clusters, research and development grants, and technical assistance, among others.

While these kinds of policy efforts have merits, they also raise concerns (Audretsch et al., 2007; Shane, 2009). In general, government policies addressing entrepreneurship are often isolated efforts that are not especially well-targeted, and involve little accountability for outcomes. Some of the criticisms put forward include:

- Policymakers are generally ill-equipped (lack the research evidence) to understand the role of policy in entrepreneurship (Smallbone, 2016).
- Responsibility for entrepreneurship policy falls across a range of agencies and ministries, with no coordinating entity (Audretsch & Thurik, 2004).
- Entrepreneurship policy-making is complex and messy (Lundstrom & Stevenson, 2005).
- The process involved in formulating entrepreneurship policies is dominated by powerful actors who influence outcomes in ways that serve their own interests (Arshed, Carter, & Mason, 2014).
- Policies aimed at fostering entrepreneurship fail to resolve market failures, are wasteful, and do not increase the pool of entrepreneurs (Acs et al., 2016).
- Regulation that is favorable toward entrepreneurship in general can have unintended negative consequences for certain types of ventures (Spencer & Gómez, 2004).
- Direct financial and other firm-specific support for knowledge intensive startups is less productive than efforts to facilitate ecosystem development (Hefferan & Fern, 2018).
- Policy efforts that remove impediments to start-up activity have a greater impact than those providing direct support to entrepreneurs (Dennis, 2011).

The implication is that nations struggle with an integrated legal and regulatory framework for fostering entrepreneurial activity. Instead, what often emerges is a hodgepodge of laws, regulations, and programs, some emphasizing existing small- and medium-sized enterprises (SMEs), others prioritizing particular types of new startups (e.g., high-tech businesses, aggressive growth ventures), and still others focusing on spurring entrepreneurial activity in general (Patzelt & Shepherd, 2009). More critically, there is little consensus among those formulating public policies regarding what entrepreneurship is, the forms it takes, and the priority needs of entrepreneurs at different stages of venture development (Dennis, 2011).

GOVERNMENT POLICY AND THE POVERTY ENTREPRENEUR

When it comes to the ventures of the poor, the policy environment is even more problematic. To be effective, policies directed at poverty alleviation must consider its holistic nature and the context in which it is being experienced. Banerjee and Duflo (2011) talk of assuming the "view from below." While nations create programs to address fundamental needs such as housing, child nutrition, job training, energy, and healthcare, these efforts do not generally reflect a targeted, cohesive, or comprehensive approach towards poverty. These efforts often appear to be a patchwork of attempts to address obvious gaps, and function as mere band-aids rather than working on the root of the issue or cause of the problem. They neglect the agency of the poor and their role in guiding the design and implementation of policy (Piven & Minnite, 2016). As a result, one could question the extent to which these programs only serve to help people survive, as opposed to empowering them to escape the cycle of poverty and enhance their well-being. Additionally, the poor often face significant challenges when it comes to learning about, understanding, applying for, and qualifying for specific government programs, as well as satisfying the associated administrative requirements.

As a generalization, governments (at all levels) lack a strategy for poverty and entrepreneurship. Many policies and initiatives are created without the poor in mind, but contain elements that apply to low-income entrepreneurs. Some targeted (to the poor) programs can be found in particular countries, but they tend to be disjointed initiatives with little evidence regarding effectiveness. For instance, governments have invested in microcredit programs, loan guarantees, and grants targeting the disadvantaged. Some provide funding to community-based small business assistance centers. Others have attempted to insert mandatory entrepreneurship education into schools, or expanded job training programs to include basic courses on starting a business (Martinez et al., 2010; O'Connor, 2013). In many countries, disadvantaged businesses are given preferential access to government procurement opportunities. Others have experimented with income subsidies for low-income people trying to start businesses or voucher programs to help poverty entrepreneurs pay for business services.

To create a more equal playing field and actually make a dent in poverty, a more strategic, integrated, and holistic approach must be adopted. As a starting point, we propose a three-level policy pathway, with policies developed first to (a) ensure basic survival while attacking poverty's adverse impacts on personal development; and then to (b) build an entrepreneurial foundation; and finally to (c) promote entrepreneurial action (see Figure 13.1). With each of these levels, policy is driven by different goals and objectives.

We begin with policies to address basic survival needs, where the priority is the infrastructure shortcomings discussed in Chapter 12. To ensure the basic physical, cognitive, and emotional well-being of the individual at a systemic-level, coordinated programs must address fundamental housing, energy, education, safety, health, nutrition, and transportation needs, as well as access to legal protections and social safety nets (Goel & Rishi, 2012). Here, the underlying causes of the liabilities of poorness (see Chapter 5) are intentionally addressed. Unless basic literacy gaps, the constancy of poverty-induced crises, the inability to plan for tomorrow, and the vulnerability caused by a complete lack of any safety net are dealt with, the burden placed on the individual can be overwhelming. Poverty conditions represent more

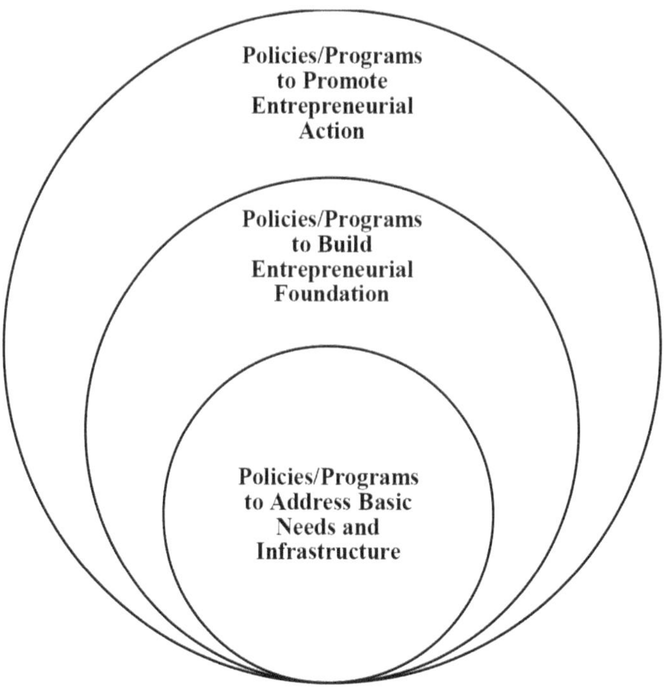

Figure 13.1. Three-level policy pathway for entrepreneurship in poverty.
Created by Authors

than a set of temporary setbacks, as the potential damage to capability development can be lifelong. Aspirations can be restricted, with boundaries placed on available opportunities, access closed off to resources of all types, and the ability to realize one's potential severely compromised.

Without this attention to basic infrastructure, efforts to foster entrepreneurship are likely to be in vain. However, when constructed on top of core infrastructure, government policies and programs are better able to establish a foundation for entrepreneurship. This is our second level in the policy pathway. It centers on helping people see themselves and the poverty context through an entrepreneurial lens. Entrepreneurship is approached as a means of empowerment, vehicle for change, source of identity, and mechanism for contributing to one's community. This pathway becomes more relevant when those in poverty can recognize their innate entrepreneurial potential, while also understanding the different ways in which entrepreneurship can manifest itself in their lives. Initiatives are needed that expose those in poverty circumstances to what it means to think and act in entrepreneurial ways (see Chapter 7), while helping them develop key entrepreneurial competencies (see Chapter 11). Part of this effort involves extending basic literacy development (e.g., financial and technological literacies) to reflect the requirements of the new venture context. Policies are needed that infuse entrepreneurship education in schools, make entrepreneurial training and mentorships accessible, highlight entrepreneurial role models, pay for internships, and subsidize participation in experiential learning programs. The policy goals should be to reduce the perceived costs of venture creation while simultaneously enhancing the perceived benefits.

The third policy level relates to initiatives and programs that facilitate entrepreneurial action. Efforts here center on fostering the launch of ventures by the poor, enabling them to stabilize these businesses, and helping them to grow. A particular focus must be avoidance of the commodity trap (Chapter 8). Examples from among the many possibilities for government action could include regulatory relief for these ventures, financial support for microcredit and grant programs, offering loan guarantees for banks providing credit to these entrepreneurs, provision of space in incubators and accelerators, awarding of government procurement contracts to poverty entrepreneurs, tax incentives or subsidies to purchase equipment, and vouchers to use for training and professional service providers, as well as child care and transportation support.

The effectiveness of this three-level policy pathway is based upon several underlying properties. The first of these is *level-dependency*, meaning that each level is dependent upon the one below it. Second, *level-reciprocity*, means that initiatives and activities at one level can influence and reinforce the other levels. Third, the *dynamic nature* of this framework means that policies and initiatives should not be developed in isolation, but approached as interacting, co-occurring, and changing over time. In sum, we believe this kind of multi-level, nested approach can better facilitate development of the types of capabilities that can produce sustainable enterprises (Moore, 1995; Wu, Ramesh, & Howlett, 2015).

A POLICY TOOLKIT FOR STIMULATING POVERTY ENTREPRENEURSHIP

For the purposes of this book, the challenges in Levels Two and Three in our three-level framework warrant particular attention. To actually support the ventures of the poor, we need a simple framework to capture the range of tools available to government officials (Morris & Tucker, 2021). Table 13.1 presents a set of eight policy levers that national or local governments can utilize. Let us briefly explore each of these levers and how they might be tailored to assist poverty entrepreneurs.

Our policy toolkit begins with tax policies, which can be used to encourage (or discourage) certain behaviors. Tools included here are tax deductions, tax credits, preferential tax rates, deferrals of tax payments, or exclusion of income from taxation. They can be used to encourage certain types of people to start businesses, prioritize particular types of businesses, or locate or keep businesses in designaed areas. They can help entrepreneurs purchase equipment, hire employees, improve facilities, develop innovations, and save for retirement. Tax incentives can also be offered to people and organizations that put money into microlending programs, or invest money, equipment, or other resources into the ventures of the poor.

A second lever is income subsidy programs, where the government provides direct payments to the poor to augment their income (OECD/European Union, 2016). With low-income or unemployed individuals, income subsidies could involve payments tied to launching a business and keeping it going for the first few years of operations. This income could also be tied to achieving certain milestones in terms of business performance. A variation of this tool was used in some countries during the COVID-19 epidemic where companies who retained employees received payments.

Loan guarantees represent another policy tool. Here, a loan is usually made to a low-income entrepreneur by a commercial bank or other financial institution, and the government guarantees all or most of the loan should the borrower default. This enables the lending institution to loan money to those who otherwise might not qualify, and or to provide loans at more attractive interest rates. The loans can also target particular groups, such as females, ethnic or racial minorities, or people in rural areas. The loan program can also

Table 13.1. A Sample Public Policy Toolkit to Support Poverty Entrepreneurship

Income subsidies	– monthly subsidy paid to low-income individuals as they make progress during venture's first two years – payments to cover health insurance, retirement funds, and other social benefits for low-income entrepreneurs
Taxation policies	– tax waivers or lower tax rates on the income of the business for some initial time period, or on profits below some threshold – tax credits for particular actions, such as hiring employees, buying equipment, improving facilities, locating business in particular areas – tax credits for individuals or entities that make equity investments in ventures of the poor
Lending-related support	– government guarantees for bank loans provided to low-income entrepreneurs – capital access programs where lenders and small businesses contribute a percentage of loan amounts into reserve fund that insures loans in case of a default, supporting entrepreneurs who do not qualify for conventional loans – honor loans from government to low-income entrepreneurs that do not require collateral or other forms of guarantee – government investments of capital into microlending schemes
Procurement set-asides	– government agencies buying a certain percentage of their purchases of goods and services from low-income entrepreneurs
Voucher programs	– low-income entrepreneurs are awarded certificates they can use to pay for critical business-related services, such as business registration, legal assistance, attending training programs, website development, bookkeeping, marketing materials, training, or tax preparation, where the government reimburses the service provider
Grants	– cash grants to help low-income entrepreneurs start businesses – grants awarded to low-income entrepreneurs that achieve certain targets in their businesses, such as sales growth or jobs created
Regulatory policies and relief	– liberal bankruptcy laws – contract enforcement – making it easy for entrepreneur to obtain limited liability protection – streamlining regulations to make it easier to start a business – waiver of fees for licenses and permits – providing exemptions where low-income entrepreneurs do not have to comply with particular regulations until business achieves a certain size – regulations that make it easier to create and administer microcredit funds –legal frameworks for peer-to-peer lending and community-based group lending initiatives
Business assistance	– government-run or government-subsidized agencies that provide training – counseling, mentoring, incubation space, and other forms of support to low-income entrepreneurs

be tied to other forms of support, such that the borrower must also receive mentoring, business counseling, training, or assistance with bidding for government contracts. A variant of the loan guarantee is a program where banks make loans to entrepreneurs who are higher risk borrowers, but a percentage of each loan goes into a reserve fund that insures the loan in case of a default. Yet another option is for governments to provide their own loan programs at low or no interest, such as the honor loans given by some European countries to fight unemployment or encourage informal sector businesses to formalize (OECD/European Union, 2016).

Our fourth lever takes advantage of the large amounts of spending done by the government. With this lever, the government might mandate that a certain percentage of spending must go to small or earlier-stage businesses. So-called set-asides enable small firms to get contracts without competing with larger companies. Preferential procurement is given priority in vendor selection to firms that meet certain criteria, such as being in poverty, minority-owned, woman-owned, based in economically deprived areas, or under a defined size.

Another policy lever available to combat poverty involves voucher programs (Colin, 2005). Vouchers are government subsidies that people use to pay for food, housing, or other items. A voucher document is provided by the recipient to a vendor, who is then reimbursed by the government. If we consider venture creation, vouchers could be used by a low-income entrepreneur to pay for assistance with registering a business, bookkeeping, development of logos and marketing materials, creation of websites, writing a business plan, attending training courses, and paying rent in an incubator, among other business services.

A sixth policy lever is the potential of governments to provide grants to entrepreneurs (Beam & Conlan, 2002). Grants are effectively free money, although they often come with conditions. They can either be made directly to the beneficiary, or to intermediate organizations that then administer smaller grants to beneficiaries, thereby allowing for more flexibility and tailoring of allocations to reflect local circumstances and needs. With regard to entrepreneurship, grants could be used to help entrepreneurs develop products or services, upgrade a facility, locate in particular areas, incorporate technology into operations, or hire an employee. Separately, larger grants can play an important role in seeding microcredit loan funds administered by independent organizations.

The seventh policy lever involves regulatory relief. Early-stage businesses are often disproportionately affected by laws or regulations. The costs of compliance are a higher portion of their available resources, and a disproportionate amount of time and money are required to figure out how to comply with a given regulation. Beyond making regulations easier to understand and follow, or hiring government staff to assist small businesses with compliance, regulations can be designed in ways that exempt businesses that are newer and/or smaller, especially those that are run by low-income or disadvantaged entrepreneurs. Similarly, where fees must be paid for a license, permit, variance, or government exemption, these can be waived for those in poverty. The government also regulates the financial system, and there is room to liberalize regulations affecting venture financing. For example, making it easier to create and administer microcredit, peer-to-peer lending, and community-based group lending initiatives could open up large pools of capital to low-income entrepreneurs.

Our final lever involves the creation and financial support of government-affiliated organizations that provide services directly to the poor. Public health clinics, homeless shelters, community food banks, and housing assistance agencies would be examples. For low-income entrepreneurs, governments can fund centers offering training, mentoring, business advice, networking opportunities, and hands-on assistance (e.g., with business plans, bookkeeping, marketing). These centers could also assist the entrepreneurs in accessing some of our other levers, such as government procurement contracts, income subsidies, or grants. In addition, governments often support workforce development programs that target the impoverished and unemployed, and these programs can be expanded to include training and incentives for entrepreneurship as a career option. Many other possibilities exist, such as using the postal service to provide low-cost credit to the poor, or using government office space for community incubators for early stage businesses (Baradaran, 2016).

The question then becomes how to creatively design a mix of policies from this toolkit that reflect the needs of disadvantaged entrepreneurs in particular contexts and at different stages in the entrepreneurial process. While this is an ambitious objective, it is one that might be possible if public policy efforts are combined with the efforts of community-based entrepreneurial ecosystems.

CONNECTING THE POLICY TOOLKIT TO LOCAL ECOSYSTEM DEVELOPMENT

Careful consideration of our levels of policy development suggests that, by itself, policy is likely to have a fairly nominal impact on poverty entrepreneurship. This is probably true at all three levels, but particularly at levels two and three. This is not to suggest that government support is useless, but rather that the role of government must be reconsidered.

In Chapter 12, we discussed the central importance of entrepreneurial ecosystems in facilitating entrepreneurship by the poor. It is in this vein that a critical question arises when it comes to the effectiveness of public policy.

To what extent should policy efforts focus on providing various forms of support directly to low-income entrepreneurs, or instead, on support for local ecosystems that can, in turn, assist these entrepreneurs and their ventures? We believe both are needed, but the primary focus should be on ecosystem support.

Chapter 12 presented an alternative view of ecosystems, one that was much more community-driven than has historically been the case. We argue that it is the interface between public policy and community ecosystems that offers the most potential for reducing poverty through entrepreneurship. Trein and Tosen (2019, p. 3) have demonstrated how the involvement of private actors (e.g., local entrepreneurs, nonprofits, financial players, and the business community) is likely to result in better policy design and implementation and increase the legitimacy of the policies being implemented (see also Stam, 2015).

To better understand the interplay between government and actors at the community level, we must first clarify the shortcomings of market mechanisms in the context of poverty and entrepreneurship, particularly at the community level. Mair and Marti (2009) argue that traditional market mechanisms are insufficient for encouraging entrepreneurship among the poor. Although some of the community-based activities that assist poverty entrepreneurs have market-based roots, such as local banks that make loans to disadvantaged entrepreneurs, the creation of buying cooperatives, and establishment of "buy local" campaigns in low-income neighborhoods, such efforts are generally driven by social objectives. Hence, even when an inner city incubator charges rent, or a micro-credit fund expects principal and interest payments, the purpose is tied to social outcomes, not profit. While the market is ultimately a source of incentive to any entrepreneur, the poverty context creates barriers to the realization of marketplace benefits (i.e., adequate financial returns). These barriers, combined with the social nature of the objectives, suggest a need for public policies that help level the playing field. Toward this end, Hall et al. (2012) found that entrepreneurship policies addressing both economic and social perspectives foster more productive entrepreneurial outcomes, although at a more constrained pace of economic development. This suggests that the outcomes of entrepreneurship policy in poverty contexts are not immediate, but instead take time to emerge (Santos et al., 2022; Bruton et al., 2013).

To accomplish this mix of objectives, we emphasize the interface between the design and administration of government policies/programs and community-driven entrepreneurial ecosystems. The relationship must be interactive, where policy serves as a catalyst for a range of local initiatives that empower the poor to launch sustainable ventures, while the needs of (and inputs from) local entrepreneurial ecosystems drive the formulation of public policies

(Rinkinen & Harmaakorpi, 2019). To appreciate this relationship, the various options in our policy toolkit can be further distinguished based on the extent to which they directly target low-income entrepreneurs, or work through an intermediary (see Figure 13.2). Examples of policies where the government deals directly with the entrepreneur include tax credits, regulatory relief, preferential contracting, and income subsidies. Among the initiatives involving intermediaries are government guaranteed loans offered through banks, funding of small business development centers, and policies that support local microcredit institutions. These intermediaries are typically community-based organizations and should be embraced as part of local entrepreneurial ecosystems.

With policies directly targeting the low-income entrepreneur, individuals and organizations in the community can be instrumental in making business owners aware of and helping them qualify for various programs. Thus, a mentor or small business service provider might help a low-income entrepreneur take advantage of tax incentives or government procurement opportunities. Alternatively, where policies target or explicitly involve intermediaries, the intermediary is the conduit for delivery of the government initiative, such as banks offering government-backed loans or a local small business assistance center providing mentoring.

At the same time, as we saw in Chapter 12, there are a host of ways the community can facilitate low-income entrepreneurs who are independent of public policy. These activities can serve to complement or augment policy-driven efforts. A training program or consulting initiative provided to low-income entrepreneurs by a local university, or an inner city incubator funded by local businesses are cases in point. Communities have an array of untapped, under-utilized, or unrecognized resources for entrepreneurship, and these can be leveraged to support the poor. Especially critical is the need for creativity in recognizing the diverse mix of available resources, encouraging novel collaborations and partnerships between individuals and organizations, and promoting highly visible communication efforts that create awareness and connections among stakeholders.

CONNECTING THE POLICY TOOLKIT TO STAGES OF VENTURE DEVELOPMENT

Another key consideration, particularly at level three of our policy development framework, concerns the need for policy approaches that reflect the needs of poverty entrepreneurs at different stages in the entrepreneurial process (Servon, 1999). As low-income entrepreneurs progress through this process, their needs for skill development, equipment, technology, mentoring, financing, and other resources change in fundamental ways.

As summarized in Table 13.2, the initiatives captured in our policy toolkit can play different roles in the pre-startup, launch and stabilization, and growth stages of a venture. At the pre-startup stage, this could mean encouragement of entrepreneurship-related programs in public schools, subsidies to support free broadband access, access to knowledge resources, creation of co-working spaces and hatcheries in government facilities, and assistance with licensing and permitting, among other possibilities. It could include planning grants and vouchers that help address limitations in skills and fill resource gaps in terms of childcare, transportation, training, and related needs.

In the launch and stabilization stage, income subsidies and tax incentives tied to achieving particular milestones on the path to a sustainable business model become relevant. Further, there is a need for regulation that supports creation and funding of microcredit programs and liberalizing restrictions on the credit policies of banks. Also important are vouchers to pay for professional service providers or premises; the awarding of procurement contracts to ventures of the poor; and exclusion or relief from regulations and associated reporting requirements that drive up transaction costs and keep the low-income entrepreneur from gaining traction in the marketplace. Government subsidized health insurance for poverty entrepreneurs can keep them focused on developing their businesses.

Finally, as we have seen in earlier chapters, navigating the growth stage may represent the most overwhelming challenge for the low-income entrepreneur. Examples of policy initiatives that could be effective at this stage

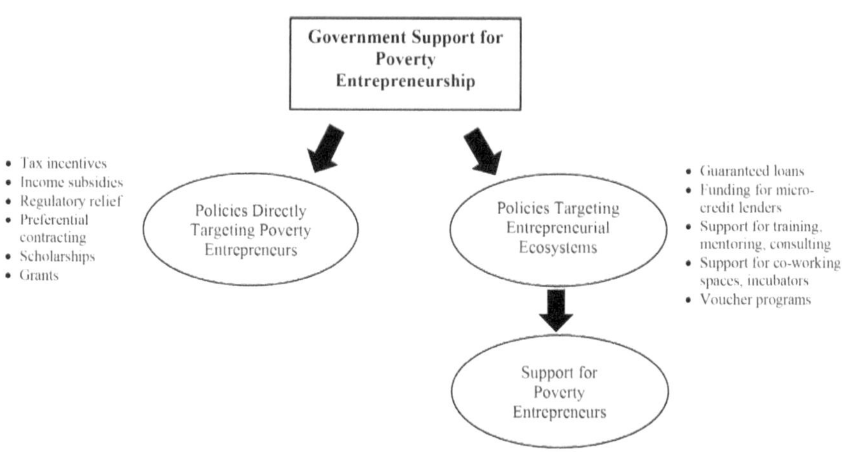

Figure 13.2. One- and Two-tiered Policy Approaches for Supporting Poverty Entrepreneurs.
Created by Authors

include tax incentives for accredited investors who support growth activities of low-income entrepreneurs, and income subsidies tied to their achievement of specific growth targets. Other relevant initiatives include low-interest loans and tax credits for purchases of equipment, technology, and facility expansion. Also valuable are programs to support export sales and award larger government procurement contracts based on firm growth rates.

MECHANISMS FOR COORDINATING GOVERNMENT POLICY AND LOCAL ECOSYSTEMS

The different players at the government and ecosystem levels are driven by differing motives. This raises the question of how the various efforts to alleviate poverty through entrepreneurship can be coordinated at the government, the community, and the interface levels. Given the plethora of government agencies dealing with aspects of poverty, and other agencies responsible for policies related to economic development, establishing an organized approach to poverty and entrepreneurship is an elusive undertaking. Although Metcalfe's (1994) notion of very close policy integration is unlikely, some level of strategic coordination would seem possible. Of the various mechanisms available for policy coordination, the networking and collaboration approaches proposed by Peters (2018) may represent a more viable solution. As the policies involved encompass taxation, regulation, income transfers, procurement, and programmatic spending, and some are part of programs that serve other stakeholders beyond the poor, establishing some type of hierarchical structure or poverty czar may not be feasible. Instead, a single government agency might be designated as a central clearinghouse for information and links to all public sector programs that could help the poor start ventures. Trein and Tosun (2019) provide an example of such a coordinating unit in discussing policies to address youth unemployment in European countries. Further, this kind of agency would be in a position to build a network of individuals from different government units having interests or responsibilities related to poverty and business activity. It can conduct research, identify gaps or problem areas, and provide feedback to decision-makers when it comes to entrepreneurship as a pathway out of poverty.

At the community level, social entrepreneurs are needed to create and lead some of the intermediary organizations, but also to connect the elements within the ecosystem that can serve the poor. Activist leaders from among the participating parties (businesses, universities, non-profits, local government offices) or the larger community can help identify and bring together local resources and tie them to the stages in the venture creation process. Priorities for these social entrepreneurs include establishing an accessible portal linking

Table 13.2. Using Public Policy to Support Poverty Entrepreneurs Across Venture Stages

Pre-startup	*Launch and Stabilization*	*Entrepreneurial Growth*
– Prioritization in public schools and libraries of curricula and programming that develop functional, financial, technological, business and economic literacies – Entrepreneurship tracks and exchange programs in schools – Programs to facilitate access to entrepreneurship-related books, manuals, software, databases, websites, hardware, machinery – Supplemental income assistance tied to progress in preparing for creation of a venture – Vouchers for transportation, childcare, training, and attendance of conferences, trade shows, fairs, workshops – Support for small business assistance centers that help the poor with startup training and planning – Creation of co-working spaces in government facilities for use by low income nascent entrepreneurs – Subsidies to support broadband, internet & telecommunications access for the poor – Tax incentives for private investors to invest in low-income communities and community development entities	– Income subsidies and tax credits for low income individuals who launch ventures – Vouchers to use local providers of business services – Government loan guarantees to start ups of the poor – Legislation making microcredit & peer-to-peer lending programs easier to create & administer – Grants to fund microcredit programs – Regulatory relief & simplified compliance for poverty entrepreneurs – Fiscal incentives for investors & platforms to promote participation in peer-to-peer lending to poor entrepreneurs – Tax incentives for others who share facilities, equipment and technologies with low income entrepreneurs – Vouchers to pay for branding, marketing, bookkeeping, and intellectual property development – Gov't procurement contracts directed at ventures of the poor – Funding of incubation spaces for low income entrepreneurs – Economic development grants to cities tied to start-up rates by the poor – Support for small business assistance centers that help the poor with business launches – Government subsidized health insurance for poverty entrepreneurs and their families	– Liberalizing rules on accredited investors and crowdfunding programs supporting ventures of the poor – Tax incentives for private investors/angels to invest in ventures of the poor – Negative income tax or tax credits for poverty entrepreneurs tied to achieving growth targets, facility expansion, investments in capital equipment and R&D – Larger government procurement contracts directed at growth ventures of the poor – Subsidized rent programs for inclusion of ventures of the poor in business accelerators – Government-backed bank loans for venture expansion – Tax credits for job creation by low income entrepreneurs who hire the poor – Liberal carry-forward loss provisions in tax code – Programs to facilitate export sales by low income entrepreneurs – Enhancing ability of low income entrepreneurs to use contract labor – Exemptions to regulatory compliance for growing ventures launched by the poor – Programs to give low income entrepreneurs enhanced access to government-owned technologies – Increasing incentives for operating growing businesses in economically disadvantaged areas – Government subsidized health insurance for poverty entrepreneurs and their families

the available local resources for assisting low-income entrepreneurs, forming a steering committee to guide these efforts going forward, fostering communication among role players including the poor, encouraging joint programming, and synchronizing support efforts to the pathway from pre-startup to launch to stabilization and then growth.

The final linkage concerns the interface between government programs and stakeholders at the community or ecosystem level. Individual linkages certainly exist between government agencies and particular local organizations, such as with reporting requirements for a government-supported microcredit fund or entrepreneurial support organization.. They also exist between government agencies and individual entrepreneurs, such as in the awarding of government procurement contracts. But real change requires a more strategic approach, where the role of the public sector is to support the capacity of local ecosystems to serve the poor (Rinkinen & Harmaakorpi, 2019). The goal should be to nurture a connection between a central agency serving the coordinating role for government initiatives and those involved in steering community efforts to foster low-income entrepreneurship at the community level. A two-way relationship is critically important. Community efforts are pursued in tandem with, and in ways that capitalize upon, policy efforts. For their part, policy efforts can be designed to encourage the creation of new community entities and initiatives, while also supporting existing programs. The coordinating government agency would share the portfolio of policy initiatives available, provide linkages to other agencies, and otherwise help facilitate access to government programs. It would share best practices based upon evidence-based practice, suggesting a role for community leaders in terms of data collection and tracking of local efforts in working with the poor. Community-based leaders would help interpret, synthesize, and apply government initiatives in ways that best serve low-income residents. In addition, these local points of contact can provide critical inputs regarding policy gaps and conflicts.

THE NEED FOR EVIDENCED-BASED POLICY FORMULATION

One of the biggest barriers to using public policy to facilitate poverty entrepreneurship is a significant lack of data. National, regional, and local statistics on the ventures of the poor are surprisingly lacking. As a result, relatively little is known in a given geographic area regarding the number of poor people who launch businesses, their demographics, the kinds of ventures they launch, success and failure rates, and the extent to which they take advantage of government and community-driven programs. The result is a picture that is both scant in terms of details and filled with mixed and sometimes conflicting findings (De Vos & Zaidi, 1997; Morris & Tucker, 2021). These shortcomings have significant implications when formulating government policies.

Policy-relevant evidence requires credible data, rigorous research, and findings that are actionable and communicated in an effective way. Researchers and policymakers need to establish robust connections with the community, listen to local inputs, and develop relationships of trust (Court & Maxwell, 2005). Moreover, evidence-based policy requires a concern for praxis and more effective connections between theory and practice, that is, between the supply and demand sides of policymaking. On the supply side, researchers need to be more focused on tangible, real issues faced by those trying to start a business when in poverty, and also on seeing the transformation of their research into practical actions that produce sustainable ventures that improve well-being. A diverse range of people and perspectives must be captured, and adequate frameworks, tools, analytical methods, and processes have to be developed to ensure the provision of relevant and effective policies (Washington, 2023). On the demand side, it is important not only that policy makers rely on evidence, but that they are inventive in translating such evidence into creative government initiatives that build ecosystems and reflect the needs of poverty entrepreneurs at different stages of the entrepreneurial process (Court & Maxwell, 2005).

We started this chapter by emphasizing the importance of contextual variables in determining the extent to which entrepreneurship is a pathway out of poverty. The proper role of government institutions in influencing the context of the poverty entrepreneur is certainly open to debate. While we have advocated for a fairly robust role, and one tied to the development of community ecosystems, much in the way of new insights are needed to clarify what works and what does not. We leave the reader with four overarching questions in this regard:

- When it comes to poverty entrepreneurs, should the role of government center on staying out of the way and removing obstacles, or proactively facilitating the development of sustainable ventures?
- To what extent should governments prioritize direct support for the ventures of the poor versus the development of community-level entrepreneurial ecosystems that can support poverty entrepreneurs?
- How do these government policies impact the quantity versus quality of the ventures created by the poor, and what are the implications for changes in the overall well-being of the poverty entrepreneur?

and

- Under what conditions are the various tools in the policy toolkit more effective in helping develop the critical capabilities that enable those in poverty conditions to build ventures that are sustainable?

CONCLUSION

In this closing chapter we have reflected on the role of governments in fostering entrepreneurial activities in poverty conditions. We found that, where they exist, initiatives that support poverty entrepreneurs are not usually part of an integrated, holistic approach, and instead tend to be established on a more piecemeal basis. Further, they often are not tailored to reflect the complex nature of poverty and what we have labeled the liabilities of poorness, while also not addressing the heterogeneous nature of those in poverty. Instead, they rely upon approaches generic to anyone considering starting a business (Fairlie & Robb, 2007).

As an alternative, we have proposed a three-level policy pathway that emphasizes the nexus of public policy and community action to achieve capability development within the context of venture creation. This framework includes policies to address basic survival, build an entrepreneurial foundation, and promote entrepreneurial action, where actions at each level are dependent upon making progress at the preceding level. Key policy levers were identified and these are distinguished based on whether they directly target poverty entrepreneurs, or instead, foster the development of community entrepreneurial ecosystems in ways that support these entrepreneurs. Further, we demonstrate why and how the design of these levers must be tied to changes in the needs of the poverty entrepreneur across the stages of venture evolution.

To date, the most effective approach to poverty alleviation has tended to emphasize public policies that support general economic growth (see Chapter 1). Meanwhile, the ventures of the poor have not generally been viewed as an especially important economic contributor, nor as a vehicle for poverty alleviation. These perceptions are rooted in a preoccupation with conventional metrics when it comes to evaluating venture performance. A new paradigm is needed, one that is focused on the "view from below" and that recognizes entrepreneurship as vehicle for capability development, enhanced human functioning, and improved human well-being. In this paradigm, public policy can help create the contexts for the poor to create their own pathways out of poverty.

REFERENCES

Acs, Z., Åstebro, T., Audretsch, D., & Robinson, D. T. (2016). Public policy to promote entrepreneurship: A call to arms. *Small Business Economics, 47*(1), 35–51. https://doi.org/10.1007/s11187-016-9712-2

Amorós, J. E., Ramírez, L. M., Rodríguez-Aceves, L., & Ruiz, L. E. (2021). Revisiting poverty and entrepreneurship in developing countries. *Journal of Developmental Entrepreneurship, 26*(02), 2150008.

Anderson, E., d'Orey, M. A. J., Duvendack, M., & Esposito, L. (2018). Does government spending affect income poverty? A meta-regression analysis. *World Development, 103*, 60–71.

Arshed, N., Carter, S., & Mason, C. (2014). The ineffectiveness of entrepreneurship policy: Is policy formulation to blame? *Small Business Economics, 43*, 639–659.

Audretsch, D. B., & Thurik, A. R. (2004). A model of the entrepreneurial economy (No. 1204). *Papers on Entrepreneurship, Growth and Public Policy.*

Audretsch, D. B., Grilo, I., & Thurik, A. R. (2007). Explaining entrepreneurship and the role of policy: A framework. In D. B. Audretsch, I. Grilo, & A. R. Thurik, *The handbook of research in entrepreneurship policy*. Northhampton: Edward Elgar, pp. 1–17.

Banerjee, A. & Duflo, E. (2011). *Poor economics: A radical rethinking of the way to flight global poverty.* New York: Public Affairs.

Baradaran, M. (2016), *How the other half banks: Exclusion, exploitation, and the threat to democracy*. Cambridge, MA: Harvard University Press.

Beam, D.R. & Conlan, T. (2002), Grants. In L. Salamon (ed.), *The tools of government: A guide to the new governance*. New York: Oxford University Press.

Bruton, G. D., Ketchen Jr., D. J., & Ireland, R. D. (2013). Entrepreneurship as a solution to poverty. *Journal of Business Venturing, 28*(6), 683–689.

Celikay, F., & Gumus, E. (2017). The effect of social spending on reducing poverty. *International Journal of Social Economics, 44*(5), 620–632.

Colin, F. (2005), "Public service vouchers," *International Review of Administrative Sciences, 71*(1), 19–34.

Court, J., & Maxwell, S. (2005). Policy entrepreneurship for poverty reduction: Bridging research and policy in international development. *Journal of International Development: The Journal of the Development Studies Association, 17*(6), 713–725.

De Vos, K., & Zaidi, M. A. (1997). Equivalence scale sensitivity of poverty statistics for the member states of the European community. *Review Of Income and Wealth, 43*(3), 319–333. doi:10.1111/roiw.1997.43.issue-3

Dennis, W. J., Jr. (2011). Entrepreneurship, small business and public policy levers. *Journal of Small Business Management, 49*(1), 92–106. https://doi.org/10.1111/j.1540-627X.2010.00316.x

Dzingirai, M. (2021). The role of entrepreneurship in reducing poverty in agricultural communities. *Journal of Enterprising Communities: People and Places in the Global Economy, 15*(5), 665–683.

Fairlie, R. W., & Robb, A. M. (2007). Why are black-owned businesses less successful than white-owned businesses? *Journal of Labor Economics, 25*(2), 289–323. https://doi.org/10.1086/510763

Fukuda-Parr, S. (2011). Theory and policy in international development: Human development and capability approach and the millennium development goals. *International Studies Review, 13*(1), 122–132.

Goel, G., & Rishi, M. (2012). Promoting entrepreneurship to alleviate poverty in India: An overview of government schemes, private-sector programs, and initiatives in the citizens' sector. *Thunderbird International Business Review, 54*(1), 45–57.

Goetz, S. J., Partridge, M. D., Deller, S. C., & Fleming, D. A. (2010). Evaluating US rural entrepreneurship policy. *Journal of Regional Analysis and Policy, 40*(1), 20–33.

Hall, J., Matos, S., Sheehan, L., & Silvestre, B. (2012). Entrepreneurship and innovation at the base of the pyramid: A recipe for inclusive growth or social exclusion? *Journal of Management Studies, 49*(4), 785–812.

Hefferan, M., & Fern, A. (2018). Questioning the value of government support for start-up, knowledge-intensive companies. *Australasian Journal of Regional Studies, 24*(1), 78–95.

Lundstrom, A., & Stevenson, L. (2005). *Entrepreneurship policy: Theory and practices*. New York: Springer

Mair, J., & Marti, I. (2009). Entrepreneurship in and around institutional voids: A case study from Bangladesh. *Journal of Business Venturing, 24*(5), 419–435.

Martinez, A. C., Levie, J., Kelley, D. J., Sæmundsson, R. J., & Schøtt, T., (2010). *Global Entrepreneurship Monitor Special Report: A Global Perspective on Entrepreneurship Education and Training*. Available at: https://www.gemconsortium.org/report

Metcalfe, L. (1994). International policy co-ordination and public management reform. *International review of administrative sciences*, *60*(2), 271–290.

Moore, M. H. (1995). *Creating public value: Strategic management in government*. Cambridge: Harvard University Press.

Morris, M. H., & Tucker, R. (2021). Poverty and entrepreneurship in developed economies: Re-assessing the roles of policy and community action. *Journal of Poverty, 25*(2), 97–118.

Naminse, E. Y., Zhuang, J., and Zhu, F. (2019). The relation between entrepreneurship and rural poverty alleviation in China. *Management Decision,* 57(9), 2593–2611.

O'Connor, A. (2013). A conceptual framework for entrepreneurship education policy: Meeting government and economic purposes. *Journal of Business Venturing, 28*(4), 546–563.

OECD/European Union (2016). *Inclusive business creation: Good practice compendium*, Paris: OECD Publishing. http://dx.doi.org/10.1787/9789264251496-en

Partridge, M. D., Olfert, M. R., & Ali, K. (2009). Lessons from the evaluation of Canadian and US Rural Development Policy. *Journal of Regional Analysis and Policy, 39*(2), 109–125.

Patzelt, H., & Shepherd, D. (2009). Strategic entrepreneurship at universities: Academic entrepreneurs and policy programs. *Entrepreneurship Theory & Practice, 33*(1), 319–340. https://doi.org/10.1111/j.1540-6520.2008.00291.x

Peters, B. G. (2018). The challenge of policy coordination. *Policy Design & Practice, 1*(1), 1–11.

Piven, F. F., & Minnite, L. C. (2016). Poor People's Politics, in David Brady, and Linda M. Burton (eds), The Oxford Handbook of the Social Science of Poverty, Oxford Handbooks (2016; online edn, Oxford Academic, 5 Apr. 2017), https://doi.org/10.1093/oxfordhb/9780199914050.013.34

Rinkinen, S., & Harmaakorpi, V. (2019). Business and innovation ecosystems: Innovation policy implications. *International Journal of Public Policy, 15*(3–4), 248–265.

Santos, S. C., Costa, S., & Morris, M. H. (2022). Entrepreneurship as a pathway into and out of poverty: A configuration perspective, *Entrepreneurship & Regional Development, 34*(1–2), 82–109. https://doi.org/10.1080/08985626.2022.2030413

Sen, A. (1999). *Development as freedom*. New York: Random House.

Servon, L. (1999). *Microenterprises & the American poor*. Brookings Institution.

Shane, S. (2009). Why encouraging more people to become entrepreneurs is bad public policy. *Small Business Economics, 33*(2), 141–149.

Smallbone, D. (2016). Entrepreneurship policy: Issues and challenges. *Small Enterprise Research, 23*(3), 201–218.

Spencer, J. W., & Gómez, C. (2004). The relationship among national institutional structures, economic factors, and domestic entrepreneurial activity: A multicountry study. *Journal of Business Research, 57*(10), 1098–1107. https://doi.org/10.1016/S0148-2963(03)00040-7

Stam, E. (2015). Entrepreneurial ecosystems and regional policy: A sympathetic critique. *European Planning Studies, 23*(9), 1759–1769

Trein, P., & Tosun, J. (2019). Varieties of public–private policy coordination: How the political economy affects multi-actor implementation. *Public Policy Administration*, 0952076719889099.

U.S. Department of Labor (2019). *Adult training programs, Washington: U.S. Department of Labor*. https://www.dol.gov/general/topic/training

United Nations (2015). *Transforming our world: The 2030 agenda for sustainable development.* https://sdgs.un.org/sites/default/files/publications/21252030%20Agenda%20for%20Sustainable%20Development%20web.pdf.

Washington, S. (2023). An infrastructure for building policy capability—lessons from practice. *Policy Design and Practice, 6*(3), 283–298, DOI: 10.1080/25741292.2022.2139952

Webb, J. W., Bruton, G. D., Tihanyi, L., & Ireland, R. D. (2013). Research on entrepreneurship in the informal economy: Framing a research agenda. *Journal of Business Venturing, 28*(5), 598–614.

Weiss, T. G., Jolly, R., & Emerij, L. (2009). *UN ideas that changed the world.* Bloomington and Indiannapolis: Indiana University Press.

Wu, X., Ramesh, M., & Howlett, M., (2015). Policy capacity: A conceptual framework for understanding policy competencies and capabilities. *Policy and Society, 34*(3–4), 165–171.

Index

(Page references for figures and tables are italicized)

About the Authors

Michael H. Morris is Professor of Entrepreneurship & Social Innovation at the University of Notre Dame's Keough School of Global Development. The entrepreneurship programs he has built at three universities have received global recognition for excellence. His work is focused on the empowering potential of entrepreneurship, and his outreach efforts have facilitated the development of thousands of ventures. He currently directs the *Urban Poverty and Business Initiative*, the *Global Partnership for Poverty and Entrepreneurship*, and *Entrepreneurship Empowerment in South Africa*. Professor Morris has authored sixteen books and published over 150 scholarly journal articles. He is a Past President of the United States Association for Small Business and Entrepreneurship. He has been awarded the Academy of Management's Dedication to Entrepreneurship Award, the Leavey Award from the Freedoms Foundation for impacting private enterprise education, the Oberwager Prize for affecting students beyond the classroom, and the Legacy Award from the Global Consortium of Entrepreneurship Centers.

Susana C. Santos is an Associate Professor of Entrepreneurship in the Jim Moran College of Entrepreneurship at Florida State University in Tallahassee, Florida. She received her Ph.D. from ISCTE-IUL Business School, Instituto Universitário de Lisboa, Portugal. Dr. Santos has published more than 50 peer-reviewed papers. Her primary research interests focus on the intersection of entrepreneurship and adversity, in particular under conditions of poverty. She co-authored the book *Poverty and Entrepreneurship in Developed Economies*, and co-edited *Annals of Entrepreneurship Education and Pedagogy* (volumes 5 and 6) and *The Emergence of Entrepreneurial Behavior: Intention, Education and Orientation*. Other research interests include social entrepreneurship, gender, entrepreneurship education, and individual and team processes in entrepreneurship.

www.ingramcontent.com/pod-product-compliance
Ingram Content Group UK Ltd.
Pitfield, Milton Keynes, MK11 3LW, UK
UKHW041834031026
15587UKWH00002B/764

9 781666 933802